THE Church Supper COOKBOOK

A SPECIAL COLLECTION OF

OVER 400 POTLUCK RECIPES

FROM FAMILIES AND CHURCHES ACROSS THE COUNTRY

EDITED BY DAVID JOACHIM

RODALE

Printed in the United States of America
Rodale Inc. makes every effort to use acid-free ∞, recycled paper ♻.
Cover Design by Christina Gaugler
Interior Design by Christopher Rhoads
Interior Photography by Mitch Mandel

Library of Congress Cataloging-in-Publication Data

The church supper cookbook : a special collection of over 400 potluck recipes from families
and churches across the country / edited by David Joachim.
   p.   cm.
Includes index.
ISBN-13 978–1–59486–202–1 hardcover
ISBN-10 1–59486–202–8 hardcover
   1. Cookery, American.   2. Church dinners.   I. Joachim, David.
TX715.C5648   2005
641.5973—dc22   2005004411

      8   10 9   7   hardcover

*In all Rodale cookbooks, our mission is to provide
delicious and nutritious recipes. Our recipes also
meet the standards of the Rodale Test Kitchen for
dependability, ease, practicality, and, most of all, great
taste. To give us your comments, call (800) 848-4735.*

We inspire and enable people to improve their lives and the world around them
For more of our products visit **rodalestore.com** or call 800-848-4735

Thank you to all the wonderful cooks and recipe testers who contributed their recipes and expertise to The Church Supper Cookbook, *and to the churches and their members who made this book possible.*

Contents

A Word about the Recipes

The idea for *The Church Supper Cookbook* sprang from a conversation among food editors many years ago. One editor brought up the notion that some of the best food in any community was to be found at a local church supper or potluck, to which the best cooks in the area are asked to bring "your lasagna," or "that marvelous lemon pie," or whatever their specialty. Another remarked that rarely could one go home and duplicate such a local favorite from a recipe out of a standard cookbook. The only way to get such a recipe is to ask the cook.

The Church Supper Cookbook has done just that. We contacted churches across the country and asked them for favorite recipes from parish members. The response was staggering—hundreds and hundreds of recipes poured in. The best ones were hand-picked on the basis of taste, originality, and accuracy. Then, we tested the best recipes and only the ones that taste-tested "delicious" made it into the book—over 400 in all. Here, you'll find recipes for all kinds of casseroles, including beef, pork, lamb, chicken, turkey, eggs and cheese, fish and seafood, and vegetables; plus all the fixin's like salads, breads, rolls, biscuits, doughnuts, cookies, cakes, pies, puddings, and other desserts. These dishes are perfect to take along to a potluck dinner or serve to family or friends. Most of the casseroles yield 6 to 8 generous servings and freeze well so that you can make them ahead of time. There is also a special section of "Recipes to Feed a Big Crowd" of anywhere from 15 to 100 in case you need to prepare food for a wedding or other large gathering.

While slick television cooking shows and high-profile celebrity cookbooks are the norm in today's high-tech world, *The Church Supper Cookbook* harks back to a more community-oriented time in America's history. These are family recipes that have been passed down from generation to generation, evolving over decades and picking up the unique touch of every home cook or baker who has made them. Most recipes include a personal note from the cook as well as the cook's name and church. Every recipe uses easy-to-find, supermarket ingredients and simple cooking methods. Best of all, these recipes have been proven over time at countless family gatherings, church functions, and community get-togethers.

The original edition of *The Church Supper Cookbook* was published in 1980. This revised edition has been carefully updated for the contemporary home cook. The recipes have been edited for greater clarity, and a fresh design gives them a streamlined look so that they are easier to follow, while the original voice and ingenuity of each recipe remains intact.

Conventions and Equivalents

Butter—Wherever butter is called for in a recipe, either butter *or* margarine can be used with equal success. Butter is expensive, margarine more reasonable; there is a slight taste difference—no question, butter *is* better. But if you are used to margarine, use it by all means.

Flour—Unless otherwise specified in the recipe, flour means all-purpose white flour.

Herbs—These are dried unless fresh are specifically required.

Oil, cooking or salad—In all recipes except those for salads, cooking oil means liquid corn, safflower, or other vegetable oil, but *not* olive oil. Salad oil means your favorite kind—including olive oil.

Shortening—When a recipe calls for *shortening*, solid vegetable shortening such as Crisco is meant. Do not use cooking oil, lard, or bacon fat. In a pinch, margarine can be used since it is also solid vegetable shortening, but it is salted and does have a slightly different taste.

Sour cream—Where this is called for, the commercial product is meant, not cream soured in your refrigerator.

Soured milk—You can make your own by putting 2 tablespoons of lemon juice, vinegar, or other acidic liquid into a liquid measuring cup and adding milk to equal 1 cup. The thick texture is similar to buttermilk. You can also substitute buttermilk in recipes calling for soured milk.

Spices—These are ground unless whole cloves, crystalline ginger, or stick cinnamon is specified.

Sugar—Sugar is always white granulated sugar; confectioners' sugar and brown sugar are so specified. Brown sugar measurements are for packed amounts.

Whipped salad dressing—A Miracle Whip–type product.

Baking, beating, or blending times—These may vary slightly with different ovens, beaters, or blenders.

Can sizes—Sizes vary slightly with different brands, but similar size cans usually are similar in content. All can sizes given are based on popular brands with distribution.

Oven heat—Best results are always achieved by preheating the oven to the temperature required in the recipe. Please read recipe through before you begin to mix ingredients and *preheat oven* to specified temperature.

Equivalents

Pinch or dash	less than ⅛ teaspoon
3 teaspoons	1 tablespoon
2 tablespoons	1 liquid ounce
4 tablespoons	¼ cup
8 tablespoons	½ cup
16 tablespoons	1 cup
1 cup	1 gill
2 cups	1 pint
2 pints	1 quart
4 quarts	1 gallon
2 cups liquid	1 pound
2 cups butter	1 pound
2 cups granulated sugar	1 pound
4 cups flour	1 pound
4 cups grated cheese	1 pound
Chocolate, 1 square unsweetened	1 ounce
8 egg whites	1 cup (approximately)
16 egg yolks	1 cup (approximately)
Juice of 1 lemon	2–3 tablespoons
1 cup raw macaroni	2 cups cooked
1 cup raw rice	3–4 cups cooked
1 cup heavy cream	2–2½ cups whipped cream

Beef

In this chapter, you'll find all sorts of new and exciting ways to serve beef, from steaks and roasts to meat loaves and meatballs (with a wide range of savory sauces). When it comes to ground beef, the sky's the limit. Included here are ground beef pies and casseroles, a few different pasta dishes with meat sauce, and several superb beef stews.

Roast "Lion"

The flavors of the two kinds of meat intermingle to create a delicious new taste.
Said to be Amish in origin.

Use equal portions of beef and pork roasts, any cut; total weight depends on crowd size. Allow at least ¼ pound per serving, consisting of a slice of each meat. Choose, for example, a beef rump roast and a pork shoulder of approximately the same weight. Place both meats in one roasting pan, cover the pan, and roast as for pork (35 minutes per pound; 45 minutes for rolled, boned pork roast) at 325°F until done. The beef will be well-done but not dry. Make gravy from the pan juice—the gravy is a most important part of Roast Lion—and serve with noodles or mashed potatoes.

Gayle Flickinger, St. Mark's Episcopal Church, Canton, Ohio

Beef Stroganoff

Onion soup mix adds American ingenuity to this Russian classic.

2 pounds sirloin beef steak, cut into shoestring strips ½" wide × 3" long and rolled in flour
2 tablespoons butter

1 can (4 ounces) mushrooms
3 tablespoons flour
1 envelope onion soup mix
2½ cups water
½ cup sour cream

Brown beef strips in butter. Remove from skillet. Drain mushrooms, reserving liquid, and sauté in drippings in skillet. Remove from skillet. Into drippings stir flour and soup mix. Gradually add water and reserved mushroom liquid, blending well and stirring until thickened. Return meat and mushrooms to skillet, cover, and simmer, stirring from time to time, for about 20 minutes, or until meat is tender. Blend in sour cream and serve over hot egg noodles or boiled potatoes. **Serves 6.**

Mrs. Carlos Castro, Harwinton Congregational Church, Harwinton, Connecticut

Old-Fashioned Boiled Dinner

A classic dish known outside of New England as corned beef and cabbage.
Quantities as you like it; schedule given for dinner to be ready at noon.

7:00 A.M.   Rinse 4-pound piece of corned beef in water and place in bottom of large kettle. Cover completely with cold water. Add 2 tablespoons sugar, 1 teaspoon pickling spice, and 2 bay leaves. Bring to boiling point and boil 5 minutes. Skim scum off top, turn down heat, and simmer, covered, until tender.

9:30 A.M.   Scrub fresh beets within an inch of their lives and add to kettle, leaving skin and a good 4" of stem on each beet to prevent bleeding.

10:00 A.M.   Add peeled turnips, cut coarsely.

11:00 A.M.   Add peeled carrots and onions and a fair-sized cabbage cut into quarters. Add water as necessary to keep liquid level up.

11:30 A.M.   Add peeled, cut-up potatoes.

12:00 noon   All should be cooked by now. Peel beets and arrange dinner on one large platter. Serve with hot cornbread or johnnycake, egg gravy (a regular white sauce with 1–2 chopped hard-boiled eggs added), horseradish, and a cruet of vinegar. Apple pie is the perfect dessert.

P. Grimes, First Congregational Church of Pembroke, Pembroke, New Hampshire

Red Flannel Hash

If there is any Old-Fashioned Boiled Dinner left over, make this the next day.

Into a skilled put some bacon drippings (use bacon bits, too, if desired). Add all the Old-Fashioned Boiled Dinner leftovers to this skillet, chop, and mix together. Heat through and serve.

P. Grimes, First Congregational Church of Pembroke, Pembroke, New Hampshire

Asian-Style Beef Strips

Similar to Chinese Pepper Steak (page 5) but does not need a pressure cooker.

2 pounds round steak,
  ¾" thick
2 tablespoons cooking oil or
  butter
2 cans (8 ounces each) sliced
  mushrooms, liquid reserved
4 tablespoons soy sauce

2 cloves garlic, minced,
  or ¼ teaspoon garlic powder
2 cups diced celery
4 tablespoons cornstarch
½ cup cold water
½ cup water chestnuts, sliced
  Green pepper strips

Cut meat into strips ¼" wide and 3"–4" long. In large heavy saucepan, brown meat on all sides in oil or butter and drain. Add enough water to reserved mushroom liquid to equal 2 cups. Add mushroom liquid, soy sauce, and garlic. Cover and simmer 45 minutes over low heat. Add celery and mushrooms, replace cover, and continue cooking for 15–20 minutes longer. Combine cornstarch and cold water, stirring until well-blended. Gradually add to meat mixture, stirring constantly until liquid boils and thickens. Remove from heat and stir in water chestnuts. Top with pepper strips. Serve over hot rice. *Serves 6–8.*

Ethel Innes, The Unitarian Church, Franklin, New Hampshire

Beefsteak Pie

A good sturdy version of an old favorite.

3 pounds lean beefsteak, cut into
  1" cubes
¼ cup butter
¼ cup olive oil
3 tablespoons flour
1 can (10½ ounces) beef
  consommé
1 cup dry Burgundy
2 medium onions, thinly sliced

1 pound fresh mushrooms, sliced
1 cup chopped celery and leaves
1½ teaspoons dillweed
1 bay leaf
1 tablespoon Worcestershire
  sauce
  Salt and pepper
1 unbaked 9" pie shell
1 tablespoon melted butter

Brown beef in butter and olive oil in large skillet. Sprinkle with flour. Stir in consommé, Burgundy, onions, mushrooms, celery, dillweed, bay leaf, and Worcestershire sauce. Add salt and pepper to taste. Cover and simmer for 45 minutes. Remove and discard bay leaf. Put the mixture into 2-quart casserole and cover with pie shell. Seal edges with fork, brush with melted butter, and bake at 350°F for 30 minutes, or until crust is golden brown. *Serves 6–8.*

Rhoda Miller, The Unitarian Church, Franklin, New Hampshire

Chinese Pepper Steak

If you have a pressure cooker, your church will benefit.

2 pounds boneless beef chuck	2 beef bouillon cubes, dissolved in 1 cup hot water
2 tablespoons fat	
2 large onions, chopped	6 large green bell peppers, cut into eighths
1½ cups sliced celery	
2 cloves garlic, minced	2 tablespoons cornstarch
1 teaspoon salt	¼ cup cold water
⅛ teaspoon pepper	1 tablespoon soy sauce

Trim fat from beef. Cut into thin strips about 1" × 2". Melt fat in pressure cooker. Add meat; cook over direct heat until browned, stirring frequently. Add onions, celery, garlic, salt, pepper, and bouillon. Close cooker, bring to 15 pounds pressure, and process for 3 minutes. Cool (letting pressure go down by itself). Add peppers. Simmer for 5 minutes. Add cornstarch blended with cold water. Cook until thickened. Add soy sauce. Serve with hot cooked rice or canned chow mein noodles. *Serves 6–8.*

Edie Blackstone, Concord Unitarian Church, Concord, New Hampshire

Glorified Hash

This versatile dish is good served for breakfast (with hot rolls and fruit),
lunch (with a salad), or supper (with a vegetable). We didn't think one can of hash
could provide 6 servings. In this recipe, it does!

1 can (15 ounces) corned beef
  hash
1 cup shredded cheese
1 tablespoon flour
¼ teaspoon salt

¼ teaspoon pepper
  Pinch of nutmeg
  Pinch of dry mustard
2 eggs, beaten
1¼ cups milk

Crumble hash in casserole or 9" × 9" pan and sprinkle with cheese. Combine flour, salt, pepper, nutmeg, mustard, eggs, and milk. Pour over corned beef mixture. Bake at 350°F for 35 minutes, or until custard is set. Partially cool. *Serves 6.*

Mildred T. Melvin, Concord Unitarian Church, Concord, New Hampshire

Beef/Ham Loaf with Mustard Sauce

A meat loaf with a brand-new taste destined to become an old favorite.

6 slices dry bread or toast
1 pound ground beef
½ of 10¾-ounce can tomato soup
⅓ cup milk

1 egg
1 medium onion, finely chopped
1 pound cooked ham, ground

Make bread into crumbs. Combine crumbs with beef. Beat together soup, milk, egg, and onion. Combine with beef mixture. Add ham, mix well, and pack into 9" × 5" loaf pan. Bake at 350°F for 1 hour and 15 minutes. Let meat loaf stand 10 minutes after removing from oven. Serve with hot Mustard Sauce. *Serves 8–10.*

Mustard Sauce

½ of 10¾-ounce can tomato soup
1 egg
1 tablespoon sugar

2 tablespoons prepared mustard
1 tablespoon vinegar
1 tablespoon butter

When loaf is almost done, beat soup, egg, sugar, mustard, vinegar, and butter with mixer. Mix well. Pour into saucepan and cook over medium heat, stirring constantly until mixture thickens. Keep warm in double boiler until meat loaf is done.

Jeannette Perron, The Unitarian Church, Peterborough, New Hampshire

Apple Meat Loaf

An excellent loaf with a hint of apple-pie taste built right in.

1 large onion, finely chopped
2 tablespoons butter
2½ pounds ground beef
1½ cups fresh bread crumbs
2 cups finely chopped peeled and
  cored apples
3 eggs, beaten

1 tablespoon chopped parsley
½ teaspoon pepper
2 teaspoons salt
¼ teaspoon allspice
1 tablespoon prepared mustard
  or ¼ teaspoon dry mustard
¼ cup ketchup

Sauté onion in butter until soft. In a large bowl, combine onion, beef, bread crumbs, apples, eggs, parsley, pepper, salt, allspice, mustard, and ketchup. Form into loaf and place in 10" × 14" baking pan or pack into large greased loaf pan. Bake at 350°F for 1 hour. Remove from oven and let sit for 15 minutes before serving. ***Serves 8–10.***

Evelyn I. Johnson, Our Savior Lutheran Church, Hanover, New Hampshire

Barbecue Meat Loaf

The sauce makes the big difference here.

1 onion, minced	1 egg
1½ tablespoons butter	½ cup tomato sauce
1½ pounds ground beef	1½ teaspoons salt
½ cup fresh bread crumbs	¼ teaspoon pepper

Sauté onion in butter until soft. Combine with beef, bread crumbs, egg, tomato sauce, salt, and pepper. Mix well. Form into loaf and place in 10" × 14" baking pan. Pour ½ cup Barbecue Sauce (see below) over loaf. Bake at 350°F for 1 hour, basting from time to time with remaining sauce. *Serves 6.*

Barbecue Sauce

1½ cups tomato sauce	3 tablespoons brown sugar
½ cup water	2 tablespoons prepared mustard
2 tablespoons vinegar	2 teaspoons Worcestershire sauce

Combine tomato sauce, water, vinegar, brown sugar, mustard, and Worcestershire sauce in saucepan, and heat until well-blended, stirring. Use as detailed above to baste meat loaf.

Mona Winn, First Congregational Church, Littleton, New Hampshire

Cheesy Meat Loaf

Needs no gravy; good hot or cold.

½ cup chopped onion
¼ cup chopped green pepper
1 tablespoon butter
2 pounds ground beef
1 can (8 ounces) tomato sauce
2 eggs, beaten

4 ounces Cheddar or American cheese, grated
1 cup soft bread crumbs
¼ teaspoon thyme
1 teaspoon salt
½ teaspoon pepper

Sauté onion and green pepper in butter until onion is soft. Remove from heat and mix with beef, tomato sauce, eggs, cheese, bread crumbs, thyme, salt, and pepper. Blend well. Shape into loaf and place in 10" × 14" baking pan, or pack into large greased loaf pan. Bake at 350°F for 1 hour. *Serves 8–10.*

Terry Lafiosca, The Unitarian Church, Franklin, New Hampshire

Boeuf Abdullah (Lebanese Meatballs)

With its distinctively tart yogurt sauce, this is particularly good served with wheat pilaf.

½ cup chopped onion
3 tablespoons butter
1 pound ground beef
1 egg, beaten
2 slices bread soaked in ½ cup milk

1 teaspoon salt
⅛ teaspoon pepper
1 cup dry bread crumbs
2 cups plain yogurt

Sauté onion in 1 tablespoon butter until transparent. Cool slightly. Mix with beef, egg, bread, salt, and pepper. Shape into 1¼" meatballs and roll them in dry bread crumbs. Brown slowly in remaining 2 tablespoons butter. Drain off all but 2 tablespoons fat. Gently spoon yogurt over and around meatballs. Simmer for 20 minutes. Serve hot with rice or bulgur wheat pilaf. For extra flavor, dissolve a bouillon cube in the water used to cook the rice. *Serves 6–8.*

First Congregational Church, Littleton, New Hampshire

Meatballs and Green Noodles

Green noodles add their own colorful touch, but this is just as good with plain egg noodles. Meatballs and sauce can be made the day before and refrigerated, but allow 5–10 minutes longer for baking time. The recipe is easily multiplied to serve 12 or 24.

1½ cups soft bread crumbs	1 cup milk
½ cup tomato sauce	½ cup grated Parmesan cheese
¾ cup chopped onion	2 tablespoons tomato paste
4½ tablespoons shortening	⅛ teaspoon garlic powder
1¼ teaspoons salt	4 ounces fresh mushrooms,
Pinch of pepper	sliced and sautéed in butter, or
1 pound ground beef	1 can (6 ounces), drained
¼ cup flour	8 ounces green (or egg)
2 cans (15 ounces each) consommé	noodles

Mix bread crumbs with tomato sauce. Sauté onion in 1½ tablespoons shortening. Combine with 1 teaspoon salt, pepper, and beef. Mix well. Shape into 2 dozen meatballs 1¼" in diameter. Sauté in remaining 3 tablespoons shortening in skillet until brown on all sides. Remove from skillet while making sauce.

Measure shortening left in skillet and add or pour off until you have ¼ cup in pan. Blend in flour smoothly over low heat. Add consommé and milk, stirring constantly until thickened. Add cheese, tomato paste, garlic powder, remaining ¼ teaspoon salt, and mushrooms.

Cook noodles according to package directions. In 3-quart greased casserole dish, place half the noodles, all the meatballs, and ⅓ of the sauce. Then put in rest of the noodles and pour remaining sauce over all. Bake at 350°F for about 20 minutes, or until bubbling. Serve with additional Parmesan cheese if you like. *Serves 6.*

Flossie H. Ukena, Sherman Congregational Church, Sherman, Connecticut

Magnificent Meatballs

Good-sized meatballs wrapped in crisp bacon with a distinctive sour cream and tomato sauce. They may be made ahead and reheated without danger of drying out. The recipe is easily doubled or tripled for large groups.

4 pounds ground beef	1½ teaspoons ground black pepper
4 cups canned tomatoes (with juice)	1 teaspoon oregano
2 cups fine bread crumbs	1 tablespoon finely chopped onion
2 eggs	24 slices bacon
3½ teaspoons salt	1½ cups sour cream

Mix together beef, 2 cups tomatoes, bread crumbs, eggs, salt, pepper, oregano, and onion. Form into 24 good-sized (about 3" diameter) meatballs. Wrap each with bacon slice, overlapping bacon carefully. Place meatballs in large flat baking dish (roasting pan is handy) so that overlapped bacon is on bottom. Bake at 400°F for 45 minutes, or until bacon is crisp. Remove from oven and pour off bacon fat. Combine sour cream and remaining 2 cups tomatoes, pour over meatballs, and return to oven. Turn off heat. Serve with rice when sauce is hot. (To reheat from refrigerated state, put in 275°F oven for 30–40 minutes.) *Serves 12.*

Elizabeth F. Bauhan, All Saints Church, Peterborough, New Hampshire

Classic Meatballs

This excellent recipe covers just about any need you'll ever have for meatballs!

1½ cups bread crumbs, soaked in
   ¾ cup milk or tomato juice, or
   1½ cups dry stuffing mix,
   soaked in 3 cups liquid
2 eggs, beaten
1 large onion, chopped and
   sautéed in 2 tablespoons butter
2 pounds ground beef, or 1
   pound beef, ½ pound ground
   pork, and ½ pound ground veal
2 teaspoons salt

¼ teaspoon pepper
   Optional additions (use only
   1 per batch): 4 tablespoons
   grated Parmesan cheese with
   1 tablespoon mixed Italian
   seasoning; 1 cup applesauce
   with ½ teaspoon nutmeg, mace,
   or allspice; 2 tablespoons steak
   sauce or Worcestershire sauce
¼ cup butter

Mix soaked bread crumbs or stuffing mix, eggs, and onion in large bowl. Mixture will be runny. Mix in all the ground meat, salt, pepper, and any optional addition you choose to use. If mixture is too stiff, add a little more liquid until manageable. Roll into small meatballs, using about 1 rounded teaspoon of meat for each Swedish meatball, or 1 rounded tablespoon for Italian meatballs. Sauté meatballs in butter in large frying pan, turning frequently to brown evenly and to keep meatballs rounded. (It will probably take 3 full pans to use up all the meat. It makes a lot, but you will be amazed how fast they disappear.) Lift out meatballs carefully when done and do next panful in the same butter, especially if you are going to freeze them.

If you want to freeze raw meatballs, paper plates work well as a base, but be careful not to freeze them in a lump—they'll be almost impossible to get apart. Put raw meatballs in a bull's-eye pattern on the plate, slip into a freezer bag or cover with plastic wrap, and freeze. Makes 48 small meatballs. *Serves 6 for dinner, 8 for buffet.*

Doris E. Berndtson, Woodmont United Church of Christ, Milford, Connecticut

Meatball Sauces

Sour Cream Sauce

¼ cup flour
¼ cup melted butter or pan drippings
1 cup water

2 cups sour cream
1 tablespoon dillweed
Salt and pepper

Add flour to melted butter or drippings over low heat, blending well until smooth. Gradually add water, stirring, then sour cream and dill, stirring constantly until mixture bubbles and thickens. Do not boil. Season to taste with salt and pepper. Add meatballs and simmer gently until heated through. *Serves 8.*

Kathy Paranya, The Unitarian Church, Franklin, New Hampshire

Brown Sauce

¼ cup butter
¼ cup flour

2 cups broth
Celery leaves or flakes

Melt butter and blend smoothly with flour. Gradually add broth, stirring constantly until smooth. Add several celery leaves or flakes. Put in meatballs and simmer gently to heat through. Remove and discard celery leaves before serving. *Serves 6.*

Cream Gravy

3 tablespoons butter
½ cup flour
3 cups beef stock

1 cup cream
Salt and pepper

Melt butter and add flour, stirring to golden paste. Add stock gradually, stirring briskly to avoid lumps. Add cream and season to taste with salt and pepper. Simmer 4–5 minutes. Add meatballs and let cook in gravy over low heat for 40 minutes. *Serves 8–10.*

Sweet and Sour Sauce

1 tablespoon cooking oil
¾ cup pineapple juice
2 tablespoons cornstarch
1 teaspoon soy sauce
¼ cup vinegar

½ cup water
½ cup sugar
2 slices pineapple, cut into pieces
1 large green pepper, cut into strips lengthwise

Mix oil with pineapple juice and cook over low heat for a few minutes. Mix cornstarch with soy sauce, vinegar, water, and sugar. Add to hot pineapple juice and stir until thickened. Add meatballs, pineapple pieces, and green pepper. Simmer until meatballs are hot. *Serves 6–8.*

Mrs. Albert F. Porter, Chocorua, New Hampshire

Mushroom Sauce

¼ cup minced onion
3 tablespoons cooking oil
3 tablespoons flour

1½ cups chicken broth
1 can (6 ounces) mushrooms, drained

Sauté onion in oil until golden. Add flour and blend to smooth paste. Gradually add broth, stirring. Cook, stirring, until sauce thickens. Add mushrooms and meatballs and simmer gently until heated through. *Serves 6.*

Barbara Lockhart, United Church of Christ, Keene, New Hampshire

Jackpot Pie

2 pounds ground beef
1 tablespoon butter
½ cup chopped onion
   Salt and pepper
2 cans (10¾ ounces each) tomato
   soup
3 cups water

8 ounces egg noodles
2 tablespoons Worcestershire
   sauce
½ cup sliced stuffed olives
2 cans (20 ounces each)
   cream-style corn
1 cup grated cheese (any kind)

Brown beef in butter. Remove from pan and sauté onion until tender. Add to meat along with salt and pepper to taste, soup, and water. Add uncooked noodles and simmer 10 minutes. Add Worcestershire sauce, olives, corn, and cheese. Bake at 350°F for 40 minutes. *Serves 8.*

Ruth Higgins, Tenney United Methodist Church, Salem, New Hampshire

Italian Delight

1 pound ground beef
½ pound bulk sausage
1 large onion, chopped
   Pinch of garlic powder
½ teaspoon salt
⅛ teaspoon pepper

1 can (4 ounces) mushrooms
8 ounces egg noodles
1 can (10¾ ounces) tomato soup
1 can (6 ounces) tomato paste
1 can (17 ounces) tomatoes
1 cup grated Cheddar cheese

Combine beef, sausage, onion, garlic powder, salt, and pepper. Steam 3–5 minutes in covered heavy skillet, until redness disappears from beef. Do not brown. Add mushrooms (with juice). Transfer to greased 2-quart baking dish. Cook noodles and drain. Add soup, tomato paste, and tomatoes (with juice) to noodles. Stir well. Add noodles and half the cheese to meat, mixing well. Sprinkle remainder of cheese over top. Bake at 350°F for 30 minutes, or until casserole bubbles and cheese is melted. *Serves 6.*

Marcia Fletcher, St. Anne's Episcopal Church, Calais, Maine

Beef or Pork Chow Mein

A Chinese delight.

1 pound ground beef
    or pork
1 medium onion, chopped
2 tablespoons butter
1 teaspoon salt
2 cups diced celery
1 cup water
1 can (16 ounces) mixed Chinese
    vegetables, drained

1 can (16 ounces) bean sprouts,
    drained
1 can (4 ounces) sliced
    mushrooms, drained
1 can (13½ ounces) pineapple
    tidbits or chunks
2 tablespoons cold water
2 tablespoons cornstarch
1 tablespoon soy sauce

Cook meat and onion in butter until lightly browned. Add salt, celery, and 1 cup water. Bring to boil. Cover and simmer until celery is crisp but soft (about 10 minutes). Drain pineapple, reserving ¼ cup of juice. Add Chinese vegetables, bean sprouts, mushrooms, and pineapple, and cook until hot. Combine 2 tablespoons water and cornstarch. Stir in soy sauce and reserved pineapple juice. Add to meat mixture. Cook until slightly thickened, stirring constantly. Serve hot with cooked rice or chow mein noodles. *Serves 6.*

Carolyn Ramsbotham, St. Thomas More Church, Durham, New Hampshire

Burger Bundles

One good way to make meat go further.

2 pounds ground beef
⅔ cup milk
2 cups herb-seasoned bread
    stuffing
2 cans (10¾ ounces each)

condensed cream soup
(mushroom, celery, or your
choice)
4 teaspoons Worcestershire sauce
2 tablespoons ketchup

Mix beef with milk. Divide into 10 patties. On waxed paper, flatten each patty to form a 6" circle. Put equal amounts of stuffing in center of each. Draw edges over stuffing and seal. Place in 3-quart casserole. Combine soup, Worcestershire sauce, and ketchup, and heat gently until smooth and bubbly. Pour over meat. Bake uncovered at 350°F for 45–50 minutes. *Serves 10.*

Jill Child, The Unitarian Church, Franklin, New Hampshire

Snowtime Beef Casserole

This attractive dish is like a cannelloni without the pasta and the extra effort. Exceptional. This casserole will warm up even the coldest heart in wintertime.

1 **pound ground beef**	¼ **teaspoon pepper**
2 **cans (8 ounces each) tomato sauce**	2 **packages (10 ounces each) frozen chopped spinach, cooked and drained**
¼ **cup chopped onion**	1 **pint cottage cheese**
1 **teaspoon parsley flakes**	1 **package (8 ounces) mozzarella cheese slices**
½ **teaspoon oregano**	
1 **teaspoon basil**	
¾ **teaspoon salt**	

Brown beef in skillet; pour off fat. Stir in tomato sauce, onion, parsley, oregano, basil, ½ teaspoon salt, and pepper. Simmer uncovered 10 minutes, stirring occasionally. Combine spinach with cottage cheese and remaining ¼ teaspoon salt. Spoon spinach mixture around edge of baking dish (9" × 13"). Pour beef mixture into center. Cut each mozzarella slice into 3 lengthwise strips. Arrange in lattice design over meat. Bake at 375°F for 20 minutes. *Serves 8.*

Ruth Messer, Concord Unitarian Church, Concord, New Hampshire

Mouthwatering Tamale Pie

A longtime Southwestern favorite.

2 pounds ground chuck
1 large onion, chopped
1 can (16 ounces) whole tomatoes
1 can (16 ounces) whole-kernel corn, drained
2 tablespoons chili powder
Salt and pepper
1 can (6 ounces) pitted black olives, drained
3 cups milk
2 cups cornmeal
2 cups shredded Cheddar cheese

Brown together chuck and onion. Add tomatoes (with juice), corn, chili powder, and salt and pepper to taste. Simmer for 30 minutes. Remove from heat and add olives. Mix milk with cornmeal and cook until thickened. Line bottom and sides of greased 3-quart casserole dish with cooked cornmeal mush. Add meat mixture and top with grated cheese. Bake at 325°F for 30 minutes. *Serves 8.*

Phyllis Shattuck, All Saints Episcopal Church, Pasadena, California

Calorie Counter's Moussaka

Try this for something ethnic and different. Tastes good warmed up the next day, too.
This recipe has 378 calories per serving for 6, or 248 calories for 8.

1 pound lean ground beef
1 medium onion, chopped
5 cups peeled and cubed eggplant
1 can (8 ounces) tomatoes, cut up
1 can (16 ounces) mushrooms, drained
¼ cup chopped fresh parsley
1 clove garlic, minced
½ teaspoon oregano
½ teaspoon rosemary, crushed
¼ teaspoon cinnamon
Salt and pepper
2 eggs
8 ounces Neufchâtel cheese, cut up
1 cup plain yogurt
¼ teaspoon salt

In skillet cook beef and onion until meat is browned. Drain off fat. Stir in eggplant, tomatoes (with juice), mushrooms, parsley, garlic, oregano, rosemary, cinnamon, and salt and pepper to taste. Cook, uncovered, for 15 minutes, stirring occasionally. Turn into rectangular baking dish. Use electric mixer or blender to combine eggs, cheese, yogurt, and salt. Mix or blend until smooth. Pour over meat. Bake at 350°F for 15–20 minutes. ***Serves 6–8.***

Dorothea Ruggles, First Congregational Church, Littleton, New Hampshire

Classic Lasagna Plus 2

The eggs and zucchini are the two pluses—they make the "total" difference!

1 **pound ground beef**	1 **teaspoon garlic powder**
¾ **cup chopped onions**	½ **teaspoon pepper**
2 **tablespoons olive oil**	½ **teaspoon oregano**
1 **can (28 ounces) Italian tomatoes**	8 **ounces lasagna noodles**
2 **cans (6 ounces each) tomato paste**	1 **pound cottage or ricotta cheese**
2 **cups water**	8 **ounces mozzarella cheese, shredded**
4 **tablespoons chopped parsley**	1 **cup grated Parmesan cheese**
1 **teaspoon salt**	3 **hard-boiled eggs, sliced**
	2 **cups thinly sliced zucchini**

In large heavy pan, lightly brown beef and onion in oil. Add tomatoes (with juice), tomato paste, water, parsley, salt, garlic powder, pepper, and oregano, and simmer uncovered about 30 minutes. Meanwhile, cook lasagna noodles as directed. In 9" × 13" baking pan, spread about 1 cup of sauce. Then alternate layers of noodles, sauce, cottage or ricotta cheese, mozzarella, Parmesan, hard-boiled eggs, and zucchini, ending with sauce, mozzarella, and Parmesan. Bake at 350°F for 40–50 minutes, or until lightly browned and bubbling. ***Serves 6–8.***

Sally Hale, Dublin Community Church, Dublin, New Hampshire

Carry-Out Casserole

A creamy, lasagna-like dish with an unusual fillip—ripe olives.

8 ounces wide egg noodles
2 pounds ground beef
3 tablespoons butter
2 cups tomato sauce
2 tablespoons flour
2 cups cottage cheese
1 cup sour cream

1 teaspoon salt
½ teaspoon pepper
¼ cup chopped black olives
⅓ cup grated onion
½ cup chopped green pepper
⅓ cup grated Parmesan cheese (optional)

Cook noodles according to package directions in boiling salted water. Drain. Brown beef in 2 tablespoons butter. Mix tomato sauce with flour, add to beef, and simmer for 10 minutes. Mix cottage cheese with sour cream, salt, pepper, and olives. Sauté onion and green pepper in remaining 1 tablespoon butter and add to cottage cheese mixture.

Place half the noodles in greased 3-quart casserole dish. Spread with cottage cheese mixture, top with remaining noodles, and cover all with beef mixture. Sprinkle, if desired, with grated cheese. Bake at 350°F for 30–40 minutes, or until heated through. *Serves 12.*

Marjorie M. Stultz, Concord Unitarian Church, Concord, New Hampshire

Quick Hamburger and Potato Casserole

You can put this one together in a jiffy.

2⅔ cups instant mashed potato flakes
1½ cups sour cream
1 cup water
1 pound ground beef
3 tablespoons chopped onion, or 1 tablespoon dried minced onion
1 can (15 ounces) tomato sauce

1 can (12 ounces) corn (with sweet peppers if you can find it), *undrained*
1 teaspoon salt
¼–½ teaspoon pepper
⅛ teaspoon oregano
½ cup diced American or Cheddar cheese

In ungreased 9" × 13" baking dish, blend potato flakes with sour cream and ½ cup water. Mixture should be crumbly. If not, add more potato flakes. Pat firmly into bottom of pan. Brown beef (with onions, if using fresh). Add dried onion (if not using fresh), remaining ½ cup water, tomato sauce, corn, salt, pepper, and oregano. Spoon beef mixture over potatoes. Sprinkle with cheese. Bake at 350°F for 25–30 minutes. This recipe is easily doubled. **Serves 6.**

Margaret Johnson, Trinity Episcopal Church, Claremont, New Hampshire

One-Dish Ground Beef

The title says it all.

1 pound ground beef	1 can (6 ounces) mushrooms, drained
1 cup chopped onion	
1 can (10¾ ounces) cream of mushroom soup	⅓ cup soy sauce
	2 cups boiling water
2 cups chopped celery	½ teaspoon salt
1 cup uncooked long-grain rice	¼ teaspoon garlic powder

Brown meat and drain, reserving fat in skillet. Remove meat to 2-quart baking dish. Sauté onion in reserved fat. Drain off fat and mix onion with meat. Add soup, celery, rice, mushrooms, soy sauce, water, salt, and garlic powder, and stir to combine. Bake at 350°F for 1 hour, or until celery is tender. Cover dish for last half-hour of baking. **Serves 6.**

Bonnie Ridge, The Unitarian Church, Keene, New Hampshire

Beef 'n' Bean Roll-Ups

Children love these. Fun and filling.

¼ cup butter
2 cups flour
2 teaspoons baking powder
½ teaspoon salt
½ cup milk
¾ cup molasses

1½ pounds ground beef
2 cans (16 ounces each) pork and beans
½ cup chopped onion
¼ cup ketchup
Salt and pepper

Cut butter into flour, baking powder, and salt. Add milk and ¼ cup molasses, mix well, and form into large ball. Roll out dough on floured surface to 9" × 12" rectangle. Brown meat and add to it pork and beans, onion, remaining ½ cup molasses, ketchup, and salt and pepper to taste. Bring meat mixture to boil. Spread ¾ cup of meat mixture over rolled-out dough. Starting with 12" side, roll up dough with meat inside and cut the roll into twelve 1" slices. Pour rest of meat mixture into 9" × 13" baking dish and top with dough slices. Bake at 400°F for 20–25 minutes. *Serves 6–8.*

Janet M. Secchiaroli, First Church of Christ, New London, Connecticut

Arcadian Shepherd's Pie

A "soufflé" potato topping makes something special out of this shepherd's pie.

1½ pounds ground beef
2 onions, minced
3 tablespoons + ½ cup butter
1 tablespoon ketchup
1 teaspoon Worcestershire sauce
Salt and pepper
Beef stock

2 eggs, separated
½ cup cream
⅛ teaspoon garlic powder
8–10 potatoes, peeled, boiled, and mashed
⅓ cup grated Parmesan cheese

Brown beef in 3 tablespoons butter. Add onions and sauté until golden. Mix meat and onions with ketchup and Worcestershire sauce. Season to taste with salt and pepper. Add a little beef stock and cook, covered, over low heat for 15–20 minutes. Beat egg yolks until light, whites until stiff. Beat yolks, cream, remaining ½ cup butter, and garlic powder into mashed potatoes. Gently fold in beaten egg whites. Put meat mixture into casserole and top with potatoes. Sprinkle with Parmesan cheese and bake at 350°F until puffed and browned. *Serves 6–8.*

Babootie

Exotically and apricotically tasty.

2 pounds ground beef, or 1 pound ground beef and 1 pound ground pork	Salt
	2 firm bananas, sliced
2 onions, chopped	1 apple, peeled, cored, and diced
1 can (16 ounces) tomatoes	1 tablespoon apricot jam, or
1½ tablespoons sugar	4 canned apricots, sliced
2 tablespoons curry powder	¼ cup slivered almonds
2 tablespoons vinegar	Tomato juice for thinning

Brown meat and drain off fat. Add onions, tomatoes (with juice), sugar, curry powder, vinegar, salt to taste, bananas, apple, jam or apricots, and almonds. Simmer gently, stirring frequently, for 30 minutes. Add tomato juice if too thick. Serve over rice. *Serves 8.*

Mary Nichol, First Presbyterian Church, Monroe, New York

Spaghetti Pie

Similar to baked lasagna but less expensive and less effort.

8 ounces spaghetti, broken into 2" pieces
2 tablespoons butter
⅓ cup grated Parmesan cheese
½ teaspoon salt
¼ teaspoon pepper
1 egg, well-beaten
1½ pounds ground chuck
1 medium onion, chopped
¼ cup chopped green pepper

2 tablespoons vegetable oil
1 jar (15½ ounces) thick spaghetti sauce
1 teaspoon sugar
½ teaspoon leaf oregano, crumbled
½ teaspoon garlic salt
1 cup cottage cheese
4 ounces mozzarella cheese, shredded

Cook spaghetti in boiling water following label directions; drain. Place in 9" × 13" baking dish. Stir in butter, Parmesan cheese, salt, pepper, and egg until thoroughly combined. Spread mixture evenly in pan.

Sauté chuck, onion, and green pepper in oil in large skillet until meat is brown; drain. Stir in spaghetti sauce, sugar, oregano, and garlic salt.

Spread cottage cheese over spaghetti layer and top with meat mixture. Bake at 350°F for 30 minutes. Sprinkle mozzarella cheese over top and bake an additional 10 minutes, or until cheese is melted and just begins to brown. Let stand 15 minutes before cutting. *Serves 6.*

Mrs. Thomas E. Denman, Sr., The Congregational Church, East Hampton, Connecticut

Pastitsio (Greek Macaroni Pie)

This popular recipe happily doubles, triples, quadruples . . . or halves!

1 large onion, finely chopped
2 tablespoons butter or olive oil
1½ pounds ground beef
¾ teaspoon salt
  Freshly ground black pepper
¼ teaspoon cinnamon

¾ teaspoon oregano
2 cups tomato puree
2 tablespoons minced parsley
½ pound small elbow macaroni
1 tablespoon cooking oil

Sauté onion in butter or olive oil in large heavy pan or skillet until soft. Stir in beef and cook until lightly brown. Season with salt, pepper, cinnamon, and oregano. Stir in tomato puree and parsley. Cover and simmer gently for 20 minutes. Taste and add more salt if necessary. Cook macaroni in large kettle of well-salted boiling water until tender but still slightly firm. Drain, then rinse in lukewarm water. Mix cooking oil well through macaroni to prevent it from sticking together. Make Creamy Topping (see below).

Creamy Topping

3 tablespoons butter
3 tablespoons flour
3½ cups milk
3 egg yolks, lightly beaten

¼ teaspoon nutmeg
¼ teaspoon salt
¼ teaspoon white pepper
½ cup Parmesan cheese

Melt butter and blend in flour. Stir in milk and cook about 5 minutes, stirring constantly to make a thin white sauce. Dip out 1 cup of hot sauce and pour thin stream into yolks, stirring constantly until well-blended. Pour mixture back into rest of sauce and stir for a few minutes over low heat. Do not allow to boil. Season with nutmeg, salt, and pepper.

In greased 9" × 13" Pyrex casserole, put a thin layer of macaroni, a layer of meat sauce, a second layer of macaroni, and a second layer of meat sauce. Pour Creamy Topping over all. Jiggle the dish so that some sauce runs through all layers. Sprinkle Parmesan over top. Bake at 350°F for 45 minutes. Remove from oven and let stand 15–20 minutes. Cut into large squares and serve from pan. *Serves 8.*

Elizabeth F. Bauhan, All Saints Church, Peterborough, New Hampshire

Cannelloni

Pasta rolled around a filling of meat, onion, and spinach, doubly sauced red and white.
Takes time but is worth it.

Pasta

10 lasagna noodles   1 tablespoon olive oil

Add noodles and oil to boiling salted water and cook according to package directions to just al dente stage. Drain and spread noodles side by side on flat area covered with foil. (Noodles will not stick to foil.) Cover with another layer of foil until ready to use.

Filling

1 clove garlic, minced   1 tablespoon butter
1 large onion, finely chopped   5 tablespoons Parmesan cheese
2 tablespoons olive oil   2 tablespoons cream
1 package (10 ounces) frozen   2 eggs, lightly beaten
    spinach, thawed, squeezed dry,   ½ teaspoon oregano
    and rechopped   Salt and pepper
1 pound ground beef

Sauté garlic and onion in olive oil until onions are soft. Add spinach to pan and cook, stirring constantly, for 4–5 minutes, or until all water has boiled away and spinach shows tendency to stick to pan. Turn into large bowl. Brown beef in butter, turning and stirring to cook evenly and break up all lumps. Add to bowl with spinach, along with Parmesan, cream, eggs, and oregano. Mix well. Add salt and pepper to taste.

Tomato Sauce

3–4 cups tomato sauce

Besciamella (Cream) Sauce

6 tablespoons butter
6 tablespoons flour
1 cup milk

1 cup cream
1 teaspoon salt
⅛ teaspoon pepper

In heavy or enamel saucepan, melt butter over moderate heat. Remove from stove and stir in flour. Return to stove and add milk and cream all at once. Cook, stirring constantly, over medium heat until well-blended. Then turn up heat and bring to boil, stirring diligently to prevent sauce from scorching. Turn down heat and simmer, still stirring, for a minute or more longer until sauce is thick enough to coat spoon heavily. Remove from heat and add salt and pepper.

Assembling Cannelloni

Pour a thin film of tomato sauce over bottom of 9" × 13" baking dish. Cut lasagna noodles exactly in half with sharp knife. Place 1 rounded tablespoon of filling at one end of each lasagna half and roll up. Place in baking dish. You will have three rows of filled halves: the rolls on the two outer rows being lengthwise with longer sides parallel to 13" side of dish; the middle row being placed crosswise, longer sides parallel to 9" side of dish. Dish will contain 16 rolls. (Two extra lasagna noodles were in case any were torn during cooking or handling.) Spread Besciamella Sauce over filled lasagna rolls. Then spoon tomato sauce *over* all; do not mix sauces. Sprinkle with Parmesan cheese and dot with butter. Bake uncovered at 375°F for 20 minutes, or until bubbling. (Cannelloni may be made ahead, covered tightly with foil or plastic wrap, and refrigerated for a day or two. It will take a little longer to bake a refrigerated cannelloni. For variation, the saucing can be reversed: place rolls on film of tomato sauce as before, but cover rolls first with tomato sauce and top with cream sauce.) *Serves 6–8.*

Company Beef Ragout

Make sure you have some cheesecloth on hand for the herb bag (bouquet garni)
called for in this succulent stew.

2 pounds stew beef, cut into 1" cubes	2 bay leaves
¼ cup flour	1 clove garlic
1 teaspoon salt	6 potatoes, cut into ½" pieces
3 tablespoons fat for browning	½ cup celery, cut into 1" pieces
3 cups boiling water	1 package (10 ounces) frozen peas
1 can (16 ounces) tomato sauce	1 tablespoon butter
4 sprigs parsley	1 tablespoon sugar
½ teaspoon marjoram	4 small onions, cut in half
½ teaspoon thyme	4 medium carrots, cut into 1" slices
½ teaspoon rosemary	

Shake beef with flour and salt in paper bag. Brown meat on all sides in fat. Place in 4-quart Dutch oven and cover with water and tomato sauce. Simmer until meat is tender—about 2 hours.

Place parsley, marjoram, thyme, rosemary, bay leaves, and garlic on a square of cheesecloth and draw up edges to make a little bag. Tie tightly at neck with butcher's twine or thread. Add to Dutch oven along with potatoes, celery, and peas.

Melt butter with sugar in skillet and add onions and carrots. Cook over medium heat, stirring, until well-glazed. Add to meat mixture. Cook until vegetables are tender; check every 30 minutes, though it may take an hour or longer. Remove and discard herb bag. Refrigerate overnight and reheat in oven before serving. *Serves 10–12.*

First Congregational Church, Littleton, New Hampshire

Boeuf Bourguignonne

Marinating the meat before cooking makes the difference
in this version of a favorite French stew.

3 pounds stew beef, cut into
  1½" cubes
1 medium onion, sliced
2 cups red wine
1 bay leaf
4 sprigs fresh parsley or
  2 tablespoons dried
¼ teaspoon thyme
2 tablespoons cooking oil
½ teaspoon salt

¼ teaspoon pepper
1 carrot, peeled and sliced
1 clove garlic, mashed
3 tablespoons butter
1 tablespoon flour
½ cup consommé
¼ pound salt pork, diced
24 small white onions
1 cup sliced mushrooms, fresh,
  or canned and drained

Combine beef, onion, wine, bay leaf, parsley, thyme, oil, salt, pepper, carrot, and garlic in bowl. Marinate in refrigerator for at least 4 hours, turning meat from time to time. Remove meat and pat dry with paper towels. Strain and reserve marinade. Brown meat in 2 tablespoons butter. Add flour and cook 3 minutes, stirring. Add consommé and reserved marinade and bring to boil. Cover, turn down heat, and simmer for 2 hours, stirring from time to time.

Melt remaining 1 tablespoon butter in small saucepan. Add salt pork and onions. Cook over medium heat about 10 minutes, or until golden. Transfer salt pork and onions to stew pot. Add mushrooms. Bring to boil. Cover, turn down heat, and simmer 45 minutes longer, or until meat is tender. Remove and discard bay leaf. Serve with boiled potatoes, noodles, or macaroni. *Serves 8–10.*

Moira Burnham, Church of the Epiphany, New York, New York

Lazy Man's Beef Stew

One of the best and certainly the easiest. We couldn't believe that "there's no browning of the meat, yet a rich gravy and marvelous flavor develop during the long, slow cooking," and even doubted there would be enough liquid. Doubters no more—we believe!

2 pounds stew beef	1 cup red cooking wine
4 large carrots, quartered lengthwise and cut into pieces	2 onions, thinly sliced
1 can (10¾ ounces) tomato soup	1 package (10 ounces) frozen peas
1 bay leaf	1 cup fresh mushrooms, sautéed in butter and drained, or
3–4 medium potatoes, cut into quarters	1 can (6 ounces), drained (optional)

Grease large casserole dish. Add beef, carrots, soup, bay leaf, potatoes, ½ cup wine, and onions. Cover and bake at 275°F for 4 hours. Remove from oven and stir (meat will be a little dry). Add peas (still frozen), mushrooms, if using, and remaining ½ cup wine, and if necessary, a little water. Cook for 1 hour longer. Remove and discard bay leaf. *Serves 6.*

Ethel Innes, The Unitarian Church, Franklin, New Hampshire

Beef Chop Suey

Like most stews, tastes best made the day before and reheated.

1 pound stew beef, cut into 1" cubes	1 can (6 ounces) mushrooms
1 tablespoon cooking oil	2 tablespoons diced pimiento (optional)
Water	
5 medium onions, chopped	2 tablespoons (or more) soy sauce
2 large stalks celery, chopped	Pepper
1 can (16 ounces) bean sprouts, drained	2 tablespoons cornstarch, mixed with ¼ cup cold water

Brown beef in hot oil in large skillet or 2-quart Dutch oven. Cover with water and simmer until tender—about 2 hours, adding water as needed. Add onions, celery, bean sprouts, and mushrooms (with liquid), and continue to simmer for 30 minutes more, or until vegetables are tender. Add pimiento, if using, soy sauce, and pepper to taste. Stir in cornstarch mixture and cook, stirring, until thickened. Serve over rice or chow mein noodles—do not heat chop suey and rice or noodles together. *Serves 6–8.*

Sharon Rivard, Woodmont United Church of Christ, Milford, Connecticut

Louisiana Beef Stew

An interesting stew featuring molasses, raisins, and a hint of ginger.

3 tablespoons flour	2 tablespoons cooking oil
1 teaspoon salt	1 can (16 ounces) tomatoes
½ teaspoon celery salt	3 medium onions, sliced
¼ teaspoon garlic salt	⅓ cup red wine vinegar
¼ teaspoon pepper	½ cup molasses
½ teaspoon ginger	½ cup water
3 pounds beef chuck, cut into 2" cubes	6–8 carrots, cut on diagonal
	½ cup raisins

Combine flour, salt, celery salt, garlic salt, pepper, and ginger, and sprinkle over beef cubes. Brown beef in hot oil. Remove to Dutch oven and add tomatoes (with juice), onions, vinegar, molasses, and water. Bring to boil, cover, and simmer about 2 hours. Add carrots and raisins and simmer 30 minutes longer, or until carrots are tender. *Serves 8–10.*

Katharine D. Foster, United Church of Christ, Keene, New Hampshire

Boeuf Flamande

Beef stew in a rich sauce made with beer.

½ pound salt pork, cut into
   ¼" cubes
3 pounds stew beef, cut into
   2½" cubes
1 teaspoon salt
½ teaspoon pepper
6 large onions, thinly sliced
1 teaspoon minced garlic
½ cup flour
1½ cups dark beer

2 cups beef or chicken broth, or
   2 bouillon cubes dissolved in
   2 cups boiling water
1 bay leaf
½ teaspoon thyme
2 teaspoons sugar
3 tablespoons wine vinegar
2 tablespoons chopped fresh
   parsley

Brown salt pork cubes until crisp in large skillet. Lift out to small bowl and reserve. Sprinkle beef with salt and pepper and brown in hot fat over medium heat. Transfer browned beef to 2-quart baking dish or casserole. To fat remaining in skillet, add 3 tablespoons butter if necessary. Add onions and cook gently until golden. Add garlic and cook for 2–3 more minutes. Stir in flour, blending well with onions and garlic, and cook for 2–3 minutes. Gradually stir in beer, then broth or bouillon, stirring constantly over medium heat. Add bay leaf, thyme, and sugar, turn heat to high, and bring to boil. Then turn down heat immediately and simmer sauce for 5 minutes. Pour sauce over meat in casserole, cover casserole, and bake at 375°F for 1½ hours, or until meat is tender. Stir in vinegar and sprinkle stew with parsley and browned salt pork. Remove and discard bay leaf. Serve over noodles, rice, or boiled potatoes. *Serves 8–10.*

Chili con Carne

This recipe tastes even better after freezing.

2 pounds stew beef, cut into
   ¾" cubes
¼ cup cooking oil
1 cup minced onion
2 cloves garlic, mashed
2 tablespoons chili powder
1 tablespoon paprika

2 teaspoons oregano
1 teaspoon ground cumin
1 teaspoon salt
¼ teaspoon pepper
1 cup water, or 2½ cups canned
   tomatoes

Brown beef in oil on all sides. Add onion and garlic and cook 5 minutes, stirring constantly. Stir in chili powder, paprika, oregano, cumin, salt, pepper, and water or tomatoes (with juice). Simmer until meat is tender, from 3 hours to all day (improves with length of cooking time). Stir and add water from time to time to keep liquid at original level. Serve with rice or kidney beans. *Serves 8.*

Mary Nichol, First Presbyterian Church, Monroe, New York

Ham, Pork, and Lamb

Ham is a perennial favorite at church suppers. It's easy to fix, popular with crowds, and delicious! Here you'll find new twists on ham and cheese, ham loaf, and ham casserole. The recipes for pork chops, pork loin, and sausage are winners, too. One stand-out is the richly-flavored Cassoulet, made with both sausage and lamb cubes. It'll make any crowd happy. There are also two other fragrant lamb stews and a pair of blue-ribbon lamb casseroles.

Ham and Chicken Luncheon Dish

The naturally delicious combination of ham and chicken is enhanced by just a touch of curry.

¼ cup butter
¼ cup flour
1¼ cups milk
½ cup chicken broth
¼ cup white wine
½ teaspoon curry powder
  Salt and pepper

1 cup diced cooked chicken
1 cup diced cooked ham
¼ pound sliced fresh mushrooms,
  or 1 can (4 ounces), drained
2 tablespoons diced pimiento
  (optional)

Melt butter and blend in flour. Add milk and broth gradually, stirring constantly. Bring to boil, still stirring, and cook until thickened. Lower heat and stir in one at a time wine, curry powder, salt and pepper to taste, chicken, ham, mushrooms, and pimiento, if using. Simmer 10 minutes, stirring occasionally, until heated through. Serve in pastry shells or toast cups or over rice. *Serves 6.*

Ham in Cream Sauce

This versatile recipe can be ladled over English muffins or toast for brunch, served with noodles or rice, or served as a side dish with a cheese soufflé.

4 tablespoons + 2 teaspoons
  butter
4 tablespoons flour
2 cups milk
¼ teaspoon nutmeg

  Salt and pepper
1 pound cooked ham, diced
2 tablespoons chopped chives
6 tablespoons sherry

Melt 4 tablespoons butter in saucepan and add flour, blending well. Add milk, stirring well and cooking over medium heat until thickened. Add nutmeg and salt and pepper to taste. Remove from heat. Cook ham in 2 teaspoons butter for about 10 minutes, stirring, and add chives. Cook gently 3–4 more minutes. Add sherry and heat through. Combine ham with cream sauce and serve. *Serves 6–8.*

Ham and Cheese Almost Soufflé

Also referred to as a mock soufflé or strata casserole, this puffy delight can be made with diced chicken, shrimp, or tuna instead of ham. If you are planning to take one to a potluck supper, bake it at the church because it will fall slightly as it cools.

8 slices white bread	3½ cups milk
¾ pound Cheddar cheese, cubed	2 teaspoons Worcestershire sauce
3 cups diced cooked ham	1 teaspoon dry mustard
1 can (4 ounces) sliced mushrooms, drained (optional)	½ teaspoon paprika
	1 teaspoon salt
6 large or 8 small eggs	⅛ teaspoon pepper

In buttered 3-quart casserole dish, alternately layer bread, cheese, ham, and mushrooms, if using, until casserole is full, ending with layer of cheese. Beat together eggs, milk, Worcestershire sauce, mustard, paprika, salt, and pepper, and pour over casserole. If liquid does not show two-thirds of way up in dish, add more milk. Bake at 350°F for 1 hour. Serve immediately. *Serves 6–8.*

Women's Association of The Congregational Church, Amherst, New Hampshire

Ham and Rice Dinner

Ham and rice are the only ingredients you are sure of in this beguilingly different dish. The rest is a guessing game.

3 cups hot cooked rice	2 tablespoons dry white wine (optional)
2½ cups cooked ham, cut into julienne strips	1½ teaspoons prepared mustard
1½ tablespoons butter	¼ teaspoon dillweed
½ cup chopped onion	¾ cup sour cream
2 cups thinly sliced celery	⅓ cup sliced pimiento
1 can (10¾ ounces) cream of chicken soup	

While rice is cooking, sauté ham in butter for 2 minutes. Add onion and celery, and cook over medium heat until tender crisp. Stir in soup, wine, if using, mustard, and dillweed, and heat thoroughly. Add sour cream and pimiento. Heat but do not boil. Serve over rice. ***Serves 6.***

Diane Gularneau, The Unitarian Church, Franklin, New Hampshire

Governor's Casserole

The Governor of New Hampshire dropped by for lunch the day this was being tested and gave it his enthusiastic endorsement.

1 package (20 ounces) frozen cauliflower florets
1 package (20 ounces) frozen broccoli florets
4 tablespoons butter
3 tablespoons flour
3 cups milk
6 ounces (or 1½ cups) shredded Cheddar cheese

4 ounces (or 1 cup) grated Parmesan cheese
½ teaspoon salt
3 cups chopped ham
3 cups fresh bread crumbs, tossed with 4 tablespoons melted butter

Cook cauliflower and broccoli in boiling salted water until slightly underdone. Drain and set aside. Melt butter in 1-quart saucepan. Stir in flour and blend well. Gradually add milk, stirring constantly until thickened. Add Cheddar, Parmesan, and salt, and stir over low heat until cheese melts. Place vegetables in ungreased 4-quart casserole dish and sprinkle with chopped ham. Pour cheese sauce over all. Make a border of buttered crumbs around edge of casserole. Bake uncovered at 350°F for 20–30 minutes, or until crumbs are lightly browned. ***Serves 10–12.***

Mrs. Daniel Burnham, Community Church, Dublin, New Hampshire

Crêpes Fasnacloich

Crêpes stuffed with ham and chicken and baked in a sherried cream sauce.
Easy to make and fabulous to eat. Serve with green salad.

Crêpes

2 eggs, beaten
1 cup flour
1 cup milk

1 tablespoon cooking oil
½ teaspoon salt

Put eggs in bowl and beat in flour. Add milk, oil, and salt, beating batter until smooth. Refrigerate to allow ingredients to blend while you make sauce.

Sauce

4 tablespoons butter
4 tablespoons flour
3 cups milk
   Scant ½ teaspoon salt (if you

don't use salted cooking sherry,
use 1 teaspoon salt)
⅓ cup cooking sherry
   Pinch of tarragon (optional)

Melt butter in top of double boiler and blend in flour. Add milk, 1 cup at a time, cooking over medium heat and stirring constantly until sauce thickens. Stir in salt, sherry, and tarragon, if using. Cover sauce and keep warm over hot water while you cook the crêpes.

Place 1 tablespoon butter and 1 tablespoon cooking oil on griddle or skillet over high heat until butter is melted and dash of cold water thrown onto griddle bounces in drops rather than sits and boils. Pour off excess fat into measuring cup to leave thin coating on skillet. Turn heat down to medium and ladle batter, a scant ¼ cup at a time, onto griddle. As soon as batter is on griddle, pick up griddle and rotate slowly and smoothly, tilting so that batter spreads evenly to form thin, round pancake 6"–7" in diameter. Return to heat and cook until top side of pancake is just set. Turn (loosen by sliding pancake flipper under, pick up edges of pancake with fingers, and flip). Cook a minute or so on other side (crêpe should be just golden on each side) and stack on plate. Add more of butter-oil mixture if crêpes start to stick. You should have 7–8 crêpes. (This step can be done ahead, as crêpes can be frozen and kept for up to a week.)

Meat Filling

1 cup diced cooked ham
2 cups diced cooked chicken or turkey

Parsley for final garnish

Mix ham and chicken or turkey together and add ¾ cup sauce, mixing well with meat. Grease 9" × 13" baking dish. Place about 2 rounded tablespoons of meat mixture on each crêpe and roll up. Arrange rolled-up crêpes in dish. Pour rest of sauce over filled crêpes and bake at 350°F for 20–25 minutes (longer if elements of dish are cold to start with), or until sauce is bubbling and filling is heated through. Sprinkle with parsley. *Serves 8.*

O. P. Valhalla, St. Matthew's Church, Bedford, New York

Pineapple Upside-Down Ham Loaf

3 tablespoons butter
⅓ cup light brown sugar
   Canned pineapple slices
   Maraschino cherries (optional)
1 pound (4 cups) ground cooked ham
⅔ pound freshly ground raw pork

2 cups bread crumbs
2 eggs, beaten
1 cup milk
1 teaspoon salt
⅛ teaspoon pepper
½ teaspoon dry mustard

Melt butter with brown sugar and place in bottom of 8" × 8" × 2" pan. Place layer of pineapple slices (with a cherry in the middle of each if desired) on top of sugar mixture. Mix together ham, pork, bread crumbs, eggs, milk, salt, pepper, and mustard, and spread evenly on top of fruit. Bake at 350°F for 1½ hours. Turn out onto platter and cut into squares. *Serves 6.*

Gladys Delay, Harwinton Congregational Church, Harwinton, Connecticut

Ham Pancake Pie

Sweet potatoes, apples, and ham under an unusual roof.

2 medium sweet potatoes, peeled and sliced thinly
3 cups (about ¾ pound) diced cooked ham
3 medium apples, peeled, cored, and sliced
½ teaspoon salt
¼ teaspoon pepper

3 tablespoons brown sugar
¼ teaspoon curry powder
⅓ cup water or apple juice
1 cup pancake mix
1 cup milk
½ teaspoon dry mustard
2 tablespoons melted butter

In 2-quart greased baking dish, layer half the potatoes, half the ham, and half the apples. Combine salt, pepper, brown sugar, and curry powder, and sprinkle half the mixture over layers in dish. Repeat the process with remaining potatoes, ham, apples, and brown sugar mixture. Pour water or apple juice over all. Cover dish and bake at 375°F until sweet potatoes are tender—about 40 minutes. Beat together pancake mix, milk, mustard, and butter. Take casserole from oven when potatoes are done and pour pancake batter over top. Bake 20 minutes more, uncovered, or until pancake is puffed and golden. *Serves 6.*

Sausage and Rice Casserole

Simple, inexpensive, and nourishing.

2 large onions, sliced
2 tablespoons cooking oil
1 pound sausage links
1 can (16 ounces) tomatoes

3 cups cooked rice
½ cup grated Cheddar or American cheese

Sauté onions in oil. Remove to bowl. Brown sausages in oil and cut each link into thirds. Mix onion and sausage with tomatoes (with juice) and rice. Pour into buttered casserole. Bake at 350°F for 1 hour. Fifteen minutes before hour ends, sprinkle with grated cheese. *Serves 8.*

Mary Wakefield, First Congregational Church, Rindge, New Hampshire

Sweet Ham and Pork Loaf

1 pound (4 cups) ground cooked ham	**1 cup dry bread or cracker crumbs**
⅔–¾ pound freshly ground raw pork	**1½ teaspoons dry mustard**
2 eggs, beaten	**½ teaspoon salt**
1 cup milk	**¼ teaspoon pepper**

Combine meats and add eggs. Stir in milk, crumbs, mustard, salt, and pepper, and mix well. Form into loaf and place on rack in baking dish, or pack into greased 9" × 5" loaf pan. Bake at 400°F until slightly browned (15–20 minutes). Meanwhile, prepare sauce.

Sauce

¼ cup vinegar	**1 teaspoon prepared mustard**
¼ cup water	**or ½ teaspoon dry mustard**
¾ cup brown sugar	

Combine vinegar, water, brown sugar, and mustard in saucepan and bring to gentle boil. Cook for 5 minutes.

Remove loaf from oven and pour half the sauce over it. Return to oven for 30 minutes. At end of this time, pour over rest of sauce. Place loaf pan on cookie sheet to catch any sauce that might boil over, and bake for 15 more minutes. When loaf is done, invert pan and remove loaf at once to prevent sticking. *Serves 6–8.*

Shirley T. Oladell, Harwinton Congregational Church, Harwinton, Connecticut

Ham Loaf with Cranberry Sauce

1 cup milk
1 cup soft bread crumbs (white)
1½ pounds cured ham, ground

1 pound freshly ground lean pork
2 eggs, beaten

Scald the milk and pour it over bread crumbs. Add to ham and pork and mix thoroughly until no bread crumbs show. Add eggs and mix again. Put into 9" × 5" loaf pan, then set loaf pan into shallow pan containing hot water at least 1" deep. Bake at 375°F for 2 hours. If loaf browns too much, cover meat with foil. Pour off fat and excess juice; serve plain or with Cranberry Sauce (see below). *Serves 8.*

Cranberry Sauce

1 cup canned jellied cranberry
   sauce
¼ cup light corn syrup

¼ cup water
Whole-berry cranberry sauce
for garnish

Boil jellied cranberry sauce, corn syrup, and water until thick. Cool; do not chill. Pour over loaf before serving and put under broiler a few minutes. Garnish platter with whole-berry cranberry sauce. Drain the berries if too juicy.

Nellie H. Crane, The United Church, Northfield, Vermont

Cajun Pork Meatloaf

Dishes from Louisiana's Cajun country are often very spicy, but the heat level in this main dish is moderate. For more heat, double or even triple the amount of cayenne and Tabasco sauce called for here.

2 tablespoons butter	1½ teaspoons salt
½ cup finely chopped green bell pepper	2 bay leaves
⅓ cup finely chopped celery	½ cup half-and-half
2 green onions, finely chopped	½ cup ketchup
3 tablespoons minced garlic	2 teaspoons Worcestershire sauce
1 teaspoon cumin	1½ teaspoons Tabasco sauce
½ teaspoon black pepper	1½ pounds ground pork
¼ teaspoon cayenne pepper	8 ounces ground turkey
⅛ teaspoon nutmeg	2 eggs, beaten

Melt butter in skillet over medium heat. Add green bell pepper, celery, green onions, and garlic. Sauté for 5 minutes or until golden. Reduce heat if vegetables brown too fast. Stir in cumin, black pepper, cayenne, nutmeg, salt, and bay leaves. Cook for 1 minute or until fragrant. Add half-and-half, ketchup, Worcestershire sauce, and Tabasco sauce; simmer, stirring to combine, for 2 minutes. Remove from heat to cool; remove and discard bay leaves.

Place pork and turkey in bowl. Add eggs and reserved vegetables. Mix until completely blended (mixture will be very moist). Spoon into greased 9" × 5" loaf pan and bake at 350°F for about 70 minutes or until an instant-read thermometer inserted in center registers 160°F. Cool for 10 minutes. Carefully pour off any liquid in pan. Turn loaf onto serving platter. *Serves 6–8.*

Melinda Ingalls, Gay Street United Methodist Church, Mount Vernon, Ohio

French Pork Pie (Tourtière)

Make this rich and savory Canadian specialty as one 10" pie
or as individual meat "pasties" or turnovers.

Crust

3 cups flour	1 cup shortening
1 teaspoon salt	⅔ cup water

Combine flour and salt. Cut in ½ cup shortening, then add remaining ½ cup shortening. Mix well and stir in water. Roll out. Makes enough pastry for one 10" two-crust pie.

Filling

2 pounds pork, trimmed of fat and ground or cut into ½" cubes	¼ teaspoon allspice
	2 teaspoons salt
1 pound ground beef	½ cup chopped onion
1 cup hot water	¼ teaspoon pepper
¼ teaspoon nutmeg	3 cups bread crumbs

Mix together pork, beef, water, nutmeg, allspice, salt, onion, pepper, and bread crumbs. Place in pastry-lined 10" pie plate and top with remaining pastry. Cut a few slits in top crust to allow steam to escape. Bake at 325°F for 1½ hours, or until pie is nicely browned. ***Serves 6–8.***

Diane Gularneau, The Unitarian Church, Franklin, New Hampshire

Pork Tenderloin with Granny Smith Apples

Warm spices and crispy apples make this pork main dish especially popular for autumn gatherings.

½ cup olive oil
1 tablespoon minced garlic
3 teaspoons cinnamon
1 teaspoon nutmeg
1 teaspoon cumin
3 pounds pork tenderloins, trimmed of fat

Salt and pepper
¼ cup butter
4 Granny Smith apples, unpeeled, cored, sliced ½" thick
3 tablespoons sugar

In large zipper-lock bag or bowl, combine oil, garlic, 1½ teaspoons cinnamon, ½ teaspoon nutmeg, and cumin. Add pork; rub to coat with marinade. Seal bag or cover dish. Refrigerate, turning occasionally, up to 8 hours.

Heat large non-stick skillet over medium-high heat. Remove pork and place in skillet; discard marinade. Brown on all sides, about 2–3 minutes per side. Season to taste with salt and pepper. Transfer to rectangular baking pan large enough to allow 2" between each tenderloin. (Do not wash skillet.) Roast at 400°F for 18–20 minutes or until an instant read thermometer inserted in thickest part of tenderloin registers 160°F. Remove and allow to rest 5 minutes.

Melt butter in same skillet over medium-high heat. Add apples and sauté for 5 minutes or until tender and browned. With spatula, scrape any browned bits on skillet bottom. Reduce heat if apples are browning too quickly. In small dish, combine sugar, remaining 1½ teaspoons cinnamon, and remaining ½ teaspoon nutmeg; add to skillet. Cook, stirring, about 2 minutes or until sugar melts. Slice pork at an angle into ½" thick slices. Arrange on large platter; spoon apples in center. *Serves 6–8.*

Bonnie Williams, New World United Methodist Church, Arlington, Texas

Pork Chop Roast
with Honeyed Sweet Potatoes

An enchanting blend of Hawaiian fruitiness and New England heartiness.

3 large sweet potatoes
6 pork chops, cut ¾" thick
¼ cup sifted flour
2 teaspoons salt
⅛ teaspoon pepper
  Melted fat
1 tablespoon prepared mustard

1 tablespoon brown sugar
6 pineapple slices
6 green pepper rings, ¼" thick
6 onion slices, ¼" thick
1 cup pineapple juice
1 cup honey
3 tablespoons melted butter

Boil potatoes until soft, then cut in half and peel. Meanwhile, coat chops with mixture of flour, salt, and pepper. Brown in melted fat. Arrange chops in shallow baking dish. Spread with mustard and brown sugar. Top each chop with pineapple, green pepper, and onion. Pour pineapple juice over chops. Coat sweet potatoes with honey and melted butter and arrange around chops. Bake covered at 350°F for 30 minutes; then remove cover and bake 30 minutes longer, or until chops are tender. *Serves 6.*

Woodmont United Church of Christ, Milford, Connecticut

Teriyaki Pork Loin

Good served with rice, peas combined with celery and water chestnuts, hot mustard, or horseradish applesauce.

1 4-pound pork loin (3 pounds if boned)
1 can (6 ounces) frozen pineapple or orange juice
⅓ cup soy sauce
3–4 cloves garlic, crushed

1 tablespoon cornstarch, mixed with 2 tablespoons water
½ cup drained pineapple chunks or diced fresh orange (optional)
  Pineapple or orange slices
  Parsley or watercress

Marinate loin 8 hours, turning from time to time, in mixture of fruit juice, soy sauce, and garlic. When ready to cook, preheat oven to 375°F. Drain pork, reserving marinade, and place in open roasting pan on rack. After 10 minutes, turn oven down to 325°F. Roast 35 minutes per pound (45 minutes per pound for boned roast), or until done—internal temperature should read 185°F—and pork is richly glazed. During last half-hour, brush several times with marinade.

Heat remaining marinade in saucepan and adjust seasonings. Add cornstarch and water mixture and cook, stirring, until thickened. Add pineapple chunks or diced orange if desired. Pour a little sauce over roast and garnish meat with fruit slices and a little parsley or watercress. Serve rest of sauce in gravy boat. *Serves 8–10.*

Evelyn H. Chase, Concord Unitarian Church, Concord, New Hampshire

Sausages Cooked in White Wine

This exquisite sauce is not hard to make, but what it does
to the lowly sausage link is hard to believe.

2 **pounds link sausage**	¼ **teaspoon thyme**
2 **tablespoons butter**	1 **bay leaf**
2 **tablespoons chives**	¼ **teaspoon marjoram**
1 **tablespoon flour**	3 **cups white wine, unsalted**

Brown sausages slowly in skillet, pricking skins first to prevent bursting. Remove and drain on paper. Discard fat in pan. Melt butter and add chives and flour. Cook over low heat for 2–3 minutes. Add thyme, bay leaf, marjoram, and wine, stirring to blend well, and simmer sauce for 20 minutes. Return sausages to skillet and heat in sauce until sauce thickens. Remove and discard bay leaf. Serve with mashed potatoes, omelet, or popovers. *Serves 6–8.*

Wagon-Wheel Sausage-Bean Casserole

Handsome and hearty fare with a Western flair.

1 pound dry lima beans
6 cups water
2 teaspoons salt
1 clove garlic
1 pound fresh link sausages
4 medium onions, sliced and broken into rings
1 medium green pepper, chopped (optional)

1 can (10¾ ounces) tomato soup
2 tablespoons brown sugar
¼ teaspoon pepper
½ teaspoon dry mustard
¼ teaspoon ground thyme
1 tablespoon celery flakes
⅓ cup white wine
½ cup grated Cheddar cheese

Bring beans and water to boil and boil for 3 minutes. Turn off heat and let stand 1 hour. Add 1 teaspoon salt and garlic and simmer until tender, or until bean skins wrinkle when you blow on beans gently—about 1 hour. Drain beans and remove garlic. Brown sausages lightly and remove from pan, along with all but 2 tablespoons fat. Drain sausage and set aside. In fat remaining in pan, sauté onion rings and green pepper (if using) until tender. In 2-quart casserole, mix well together the beans, onions, green pepper, if using, remaining 1 teaspoon salt, soup, brown sugar, pepper, mustard, thyme, celery flakes, and wine. Arrange sausages like wagon-wheel spokes on top of bean mixture. Cover and bake at 350°F for 1 hour. Remove cover and top with grated cheese. Melt cheese under broiler. *Serves 6–8.*

Cowboy Bob Beans

A tasty dish that's easy on both cook and pocketbook. Serve with salad and garlic bread.

1 can (28 ounces) yellow-eye beans
1 can (15 ounces) kidney beans
1 onion, chopped
1 green pepper, chopped

1 clove garlic, minced
1 pound frankfurters, sliced
3–4 tablespoons butter
1 can (20 ounces) chunk-style pineapple, drained, reserving juice

Combine beans. Sauté onion, green pepper, garlic, and frankfurters in butter and add the beans. Stir in pineapple chunks and half the juice from can. Bake at 350°F for 30 minutes. *Serves 6.*

Harriet E. Oinonen, The Congregational Church, New Ipswich, New Hampshire

Lamb-Rice Casserole

A traditional pilaf recipe—better than most.

3 pounds lamb—shoulder, loin,
  or leg
3 cups water
1 clove garlic, mashed
1 onion, halved
1 stalk celery with leaves, cut
  into large pieces

½ cup chopped onion
1 cup uncooked rice
2 tablespoons shortening or oil
1 teaspoon salt
½ teaspoon pepper

Place lamb, water, garlic, onion, and celery in heavy saucepan and bring to boil. Simmer 1 hour. Skim fat. Remove lamb from bones and cut into 1" cubes. Strain broth and reserve.

In large saucepan or flame-proof casserole, brown onion and rice in shortening or oil. Add lamb, 2½ cups reserved broth, salt, and pepper. Bring to boil and cook, covered, 30 minutes, or until rice is done and most liquid is absorbed. Serve immediately, or cool and store 1 or 2 days. To reheat, add a little lamb broth or water, and cook slowly over medium heat, stirring occasionally, until dish is hot. *Serves 8–10.*

Alice Halliday, St. Thomas's Episcopal Church, Hanover, New Hampshire

Slow-Cooker Middle-Eastern Lamb Shanks

Low, steady cooking makes lamb shanks as tender as butter. Serve cooked rice or orzo pasta with this richly flavored dish.

4½–5 pounds lamb shanks
1 carrot, thinly sliced
1 onion, quartered and sliced
¼ cup chopped parsley
2 large cloves garlic, minced
½ teaspoon oregano
½ teaspoon salt

½ teaspoon pepper
1 can (14 ounces) diced
   tomatoes with juice
1 cup dry red wine
1 cup beef broth
2 tablespoons fresh lemon juice

Place lamb, carrot, onion, parsley, garlic, oregano, salt, and pepper in 6-quart slow cooker. With hands or tongs, toss ingredients to coat evenly with seasonings. Add tomatoes with juice, wine, broth, and lemon juice. Set cooker to high. Cook for 30 minutes. Reduce setting to low and cook for 7 hours. *Serves 6–8.*

Rebecca Gale, Franklin Community Church, Franklin, Michigan

Cassoulet

You can make this French provincial classic in many variations on the same basic theme, depending on the kind of meats you add. Always a showstopper, though it does take time.

2 cups dry white beans, pea or great Northern
4 cups chicken or beef broth
2 carrots, diced
1 large onion, stuck with cloves
1 stalk celery with leaves, sliced
1 teaspoon salt
1 teaspoon sugar
2 bay leaves
2 tablespoons parsley flakes, or 3 sprigs fresh
5 peppercorns
½ teaspoon thyme
1 large onion, sliced
1 clove garlic, mashed
1 pound sausage (kielbasa, knockwurst, or salami), pork, or ham cut into 1" pieces
1 pound lean stewing lamb, cut into 1" cubes, or leftover roast lamb or other meat
4 tablespoons butter or fat
2 cups tomatoes, drained
   Large piece of bacon rind, slice of lean salt pork, ham bone, or ham hock
   Sliced cooked duck, goose or chicken meat (optional)

Soak beans overnight; drain. Simmer in broth with carrots, cloved onion, celery, salt, and sugar. At start of cooking, add to broth, bay leaves, parsley, peppercorns, and thyme tied up in cheesecloth bag. Cook beans until just tender—when skins wrinkle if blown upon. Sauté sliced onion; garlic; sausage, pork, or ham; and uncooked lamb in butter or fat. When meat is lightly browned, add tomatoes and simmer for 10 minutes. (If using *cooked* leftover meat, add now.) Place bacon rind, salt pork, or ham bone or hock in bottom of large casserole dish. Remove cloved onion and herb bag from bean pot. Drain beans, reserving broth. Layer casserole dish alternately with beans and mixed meats, ending with meat layer. Place sliced poultry meat, if using, on top. Pour bean broth over to just cover. Bake uncovered at 300°F for 2 hours. At the end of 2 hours, check liquid level; add more broth if necessary, replace cover, and return to oven for 1 more hour. (Good reheated, too.) *Serves 8–10.*

Mediterranean Lamb and Eggplant Bake

Earthy Mediterranean flavors meld in this easy-to-tote dish.
For a variation, ground beef may replace the lamb.

Salt
4 medium (3 pounds) unpeeled eggplants, sliced lengthwise into ¼"-thick slabs
2 cups chopped onion
2 tablespoons olive oil
2 teaspoons oregano
1½ teaspoons cinnamon
1½ teaspoons cumin
1 teaspoon black pepper

1 teaspoon cayenne pepper
2½ pounds ground lamb
1 can (28-ounces) crushed tomatoes in puree
½ cup chopped parsley or cilantro
12 tablespoons plain dry bread crumbs
½ cup grated Pecorino Romano cheese

Sprinkle salt generously over both sides of eggplant. Arrange in single layer on several thicknesses of paper toweling. Cover with paper toweling. Repeat layering. Set weighted tray atop paper towels. After 30 minutes, remove tray and press gently to squeeze any remaining bitter juices from eggplant. Rinse slices under cold water; pat dry.

Meanwhile, sauté onion in oil in large skillet over medium-high heat for 5 minutes. Add oregano, cinnamon, cumin, black pepper, cayenne, and 1½ teaspoons salt. Sauté for 3 minutes or until onions are soft. Crumble lamb into pan. Cook for about 5 minutes or until only traces of pink remain. Tilt pan and skim off and discard excess fat. Add tomatoes. Cook for 3 minutes or until heated. Stir in parsley or cilantro.

Mix 3 tablespoons breadcrumbs with cheese; set aside. Scatter 3 tablespoons breadcrumbs over bottom of greased 11" × 15" (5-quart) lasagna dish. Cover with one-third of eggplant slices topped with one-third of lamb mixture. Repeat two times with breadcrumbs, eggplant, and lamb mixture. Cover with aluminum foil. Bake at 375°F for 1 hour. Remove foil. Sprinkle with reserved cheese and breadcrumbs. Bake 10 minutes or until cheese bubbles. Allow to sit 15 minutes before serving. *Serves 8–10.*

Bonnie Beck, First United Church of Oak Park, Oak Park, Illinois

Swedish Lamb and Lentil Stew

1½ medium onions, sliced
1½ tablespoons butter or oil
1½ pounds lean lamb, cubed
 3 cups beef stock
    Salt and pepper

1½ cups red or brown lentils, soaked
    in water to cover for 3 hours
 1 bay leaf
 1 teaspoon marjoram
    Parsley

Sauté onions in butter or oil until tender. Remove and set aside. Turn up heat and brown lamb on all sides, stirring to prevent sticking. Return onions, add stock to cover and salt and pepper to taste, and simmer for 30 minutes. Drain lentils and add to pot with bay leaf and marjoram. Simmer 45 minutes longer, adding water or stock as necessary and stirring from time to time. Remove and discard bay leaf and bring slowly to boil. Sprinkle with parsley and serve hot. *Serves 6–8.*

Rosemary Lamb Stew

Serve with Lemon-Spinach Rice (page 117) for a gourmet meal.

 3 pounds lamb, fat removed and
    cut into 1½" cubes
1½ tablespoons cooking oil
1½ tablespoons butter
 ½ teaspoon rosemary
 2 cloves garlic, mashed
    Pinch of sage

 ½ teaspoon pepper
 1 tablespoon flour
 ¾ cup red wine
 1 cup chicken stock
 4 anchovy fillets, mashed
    Parsley

In Dutch oven, brown lamb in oil and butter. Add rosemary, garlic, sage, and pepper. Blend flour with a little wine to form a paste, then add rest of wine to paste and add to lamb. Add stock and cook, stirring, until slightly thickened. Cover and simmer for an hour or so, stirring from time to time, or until meat is tender. Dip out ½ cup sauce, combine with anchovies, then pour back into stew and blend. Simmer 5 minutes longer, garnish with parsley, and serve with rice, new potatoes, or noodles. *Serves 6.*

Lamb Poulette

The piquant, lemon-flavored sauce complements the lamb beautifully. Be sure you remove the stew from the heat before adding the egg yolks.

2 pounds lamb, shoulder or loin, trimmed and cut into 1½" pieces
Salt
3 cups boiling water
2 tablespoons butter
1½ tablespoons flour
2 cups boiling water, or 1 cup beef stock and 1 cup boiling water
1 teaspoon salt
¼ teaspoon pepper

Bouquet garni made up of 1 sprig parsley, 1 teaspoon thyme leaves, and 1 bay leaf tied into small square of cheesecloth
6–8 small white onions
10–12 fresh mushrooms, or 1 can (6 ounces), drained
Juice of ½ lemon
2 egg yolks

Sprinkle meat with salt and cover with 3 cups boiling water. Let stand 10 minutes and drain. Place meat in heavy saucepan with butter. Melt butter and stir in flour—do not let meat brown. Stir flour in well, then gradually add 2 cups boiling water, or beef stock and water, stirring constantly. Meat should be barely covered. Stir in salt and pepper, and add bouquet garni and onions. Simmer, covered, for 1 hour over low heat. Add mushrooms and simmer 30 minutes longer, or until meat is tender. Add more liquid if meat becomes dry.

When meat is tender, remove pan from heat and stir in lemon juice. Beat egg yolks in separate bowl and stir ½ cup hot sauce into them. Add yolks and sauce to meat, stirring in thoroughly. Sample sauce and add salt and pepper to taste. Place on serving dish and serve over rice or noodles. *Serves 6–8.*

Chicken and Turkey

Where *would* we all be without these two marvelous birds? Truly they are among the most versatile of all meats—*and* the least expensive. Talented cooks from across the country have provided here a marvelous array of classics and creations for just about every occasion. None are difficult, all are delicious, and all are different. Three remarkable stuffings are included at the end of the chapter.

Manicotti with Creamed Chicken and Almonds

Easier to make than it appears and very elegant.

1 chicken, cooked, skinned, boned, and cut into ½" cubes
1 tablespoon dry white vermouth
½ lemon
Salt and freshly ground pepper
2 tablespoons + 1 teaspoon butter
¼ cup finely chopped onion
3 tablespoons flour
1½ cups chicken broth
¾ cup heavy cream
½ cup grated Gruyère or Swiss cheese
3 tablespoons blanched almonds
1 small egg, lightly beaten
1 cup ricotta cheese
6 tablespoons Parmesan cheese
3 tablespoons chopped parsley
12 oven-ready manicotti shells*
½ teaspoon grated lemon rind

Place chicken in bowl with vermouth and squeeze lemon over meat. Sprinkle with salt and pepper to taste and set aside.

Melt 2 tablespoons butter in saucepan and add onion. Cook, stirring, until onion is wilted. Sprinkle with flour and cook, stirring with wire whisk or fork. Add broth, stirring rapidly with whisk. When thickened and smooth, add ½ cup cream. Simmer about 10 minutes, stirring occasionally; then add Gruyère or Swiss and salt and pepper to taste. Stir to blend and set aside.

Meanwhile, melt remaining 1 teaspoon butter in small ovenproof skillet and add almonds in one layer. Bake at 350°F until golden brown, shaking skillet and stirring almonds from time to time so they won't burn. Remove and let cool.

Mix chicken with almonds, egg, ricotta, 4 tablespoons Parmesan, and parsley, then add enough cheese sauce to bind chicken mixture.

To assemble, spoon equal amounts of chicken mixture inside each manicotti. In baking dish large enough to hold manicotti in one layer, spoon enough sauce into dish to cover bottom. Arrange filled manicotti over sauce. Mix remaining ¼ cup cream with cheese sauce and pour over manicotti. Bake, covered, at 350°F for 30–40 minutes until piping hot and bubbling. Sprinkle with remaining 2 tablespoons Parmesan and run briefly under broiler to glaze. Sprinkle with grated lemon rind and serve hot. *Serves 10–12.*

Helen D. Tawse, St. James' Episcopal Church, Keene, New Hampshire

*Regular lasagna noodles may be substituted for manicotti. Cook and fill as described in Cannelloni (see page 26). Crêpes (see Crêpes Fasnacloich on page 38) can also be used.

The Sultan's Favorite Chicken

An especially nice chicken divan. Goes well with fluffy, hot buttered rice.

2 broiler-fryers, or a 5-pound fowl
2 stalks celery
1 medium onion
2½ cups lightly salted water
6 tablespoons butter
½ cup flour
1 cup milk

2 cups strained chicken stock
1 teaspoon curry powder
1 teaspoon lemon juice
1 cup mayonnaise
2 packages (10 ounces each) frozen broccoli
Pimiento strips

Simmer chicken with celery and onion in water until tender. Remove meat from bones in large pieces. Strain and reserve stock. Melt butter in saucepan, blend in flour, and gradually add milk and stock. Cook over low heat until thick and smooth, stirring constantly. Remove from heat and add curry powder, lemon juice, and mayonnaise. Beat with rotary beater until very smooth. Cook and drain broccoli. Arrange in bottom of greased 3-quart casserole. Place pieces of chicken on top and pour sauce over all. Garnish with pimiento strips and bake at 400°F for 20 minutes, or until heated through. *Serves 8.*

Baptist Women's Fellowship, New London, New Hampshire

Asian-Style Chicken

An interesting combination of tastes and textures. Serve with extra soy sauce on the side.

1 package (10 ounces) frozen
  peas
1 cup diced cabbage
1 can (5 ounces) water chestnuts,
  drained
¼ cup cooking oil
6 tablespoons flour
½ teaspoon ground ginger
2½ cups chicken stock

1 tablespoon soy sauce
2 cups cooked, diced chicken
1 can (4 ounces) sliced
  mushrooms, drained
1 can (5 ounces) bamboo shoots,
  drained
1 can (16 ounces) mixed Chinese
  vegetables, or 2 cups fresh
  bean sprouts

Boil peas and cabbage together 2 or 3 minutes until crisp. Slice water chestnuts. In large skillet, heat oil, blend in flour and ginger, and stir until smooth. Add chicken stock slowly, stirring constantly until sauce thickens and bubbles. Add soy sauce, chicken, peas and cabbage, mushrooms, bamboo shoots, and Chinese vegetables or bean sprouts. Stir thoroughly until hot. Serve over hot rice or noodles. *Serves 6–8.*

Betty W. Doyle, United Church of Christ, Keene, New Hampshire

Layered Chicken

If you freeze this casserole, do not add the Chinese noodles until ready to bake.

3 chicken legs, cooked
1 can (10¾ ounces) cream of
  mushroom soup
1½ cups cooked rice
2 cans (4 ounces each) mushroom
  pieces, or ½ pound fresh, sliced

1 pint sour cream
½ package dry onion soup mix,
  crushed
1 can (5 ounces) chow mein
  noodles

Cut chicken meat from bones into large pieces. Place in bottom of greased 2-quart baking dish. Pour mushroom soup over chicken. Add layer of rice and layer of mushrooms. Pour sour cream over all and sprinkle with onion soup mix. Cover with noodles and bake at 350°F until hot and bubbly. *Serves 6.*

Charlotte Stone, First Congregational Church, Portland, Connecticut

Chicken Piquant

Chicken pieces cooked in spicy white wine sauce.

1 **broiler-fryer, cut into 6–8 pieces**	2 **teaspoons ground ginger**
¾ **cup white wine**	¼ **teaspoon oregano**
¼ **teaspoon salt**	¼ **cup soy sauce**
¼ **cup cooking oil**	1 **cup chicken broth**
	2 **tablespoons brown sugar**

Place chicken pieces in Dutch oven. Combine wine, salt, oil, ginger, oregano, soy sauce, broth, and brown sugar, and pour over chicken. Cover and bake at 375°F for 1 hour. Then uncover and bake at 400°F for 15 minutes more to brown and thicken sauce. Serve with rice. *Serves 6.*

Jill Child, The Unitarian Church, Franklin, New Hampshire

Lazy Chicken in Herbed Sauce

A Hollandaise-like sauce that makes itself. Cook a package of frozen broccoli right along with 1 cup raw rice, and serve chicken and sauce with or over this Broccoli-Rice.

1 broiler-fryer, cut into 6–8 pieces	¼ teaspoon oregano
2 tablespoons butter	2 tablespoons lemon juice
2 tablespoons cooking oil	1 can (10¾ ounces) cream of
1 teaspoon grated lemon rind	chicken or cream of mushroom
¼ teaspoon basil	soup

Skin chicken and brown lightly in hot butter and oil. Drain off fat and place chicken in baking dish. Mix together lemon rind, basil, oregano, lemon juice, and soup and spoon over top of chicken. Cover and bake at 325°F for 1–1¼ hours. Can be made the night before and reheated. *Serves 6.*

Evelyn H. Chase, Concord Unitarian Church, Concord, New Hampshire

Hot Chicken Salad

Crunchy and flavorful chicken dish. For variety, substitute ½ cup diced onion and ½ cup diced green pepper for 1 of the 2 cups of celery.

2 cups cubed cooked chicken	½ teaspoon salt
2 cups thinly sliced celery	½ cup grated cheese
1 cup mayonnaise	1 cup toasted bread cubes or
½ cup toasted slivered almonds	croutons
2 teaspoons lemon juice	

Combine chicken, celery, mayonnaise, almonds, lemon juice, and salt. Pile lightly into greased baking dish. Sprinkle with cheese and bread cubes or croutons. Bake at 450°F for 20 minutes, or until bubbly. *Serves 6.*

Shirley T. Oladell, Harwinton Congregational Church, Harwinton, Connecticut

Chicken Sour Cream Bake

Rich, different, and distinguished—but oh, so easy to do.
The chipped beef ends up tasting like Italian prosciutto ham.

6 chicken breast halves, skinned,
  boned, and halved again if too
  large to be wrapped in beef slice
1 jar (4 ounces) chipped beef,
  rinsed in boiling water and
  drained

12 slices bacon
2 cups sour cream
1 can (10¾ ounces) cream of
  asparagus or cream of
  mushroom soup
  Paprika

Wrap each breast section in slice of chipped beef, then wrap with bacon. Mix sour cream and soup. Place chicken in greased casserole dish and pour soup mixture over it. Sprinkle with paprika to taste. Bake uncovered at 325°F for 2 hours. *Serves 6–8.*

Catherine B. Anderson, United Methodist Church of the Hamptons, Hampton, New Hampshire

California Oven-Fried Chicken

Moist, tender, and habit-forming!

1 frying chicken, cut into 8 pieces
¼ pound melted butter
⅛ teaspoon garlic powder
⅛ teaspoon paprika

⅛ teaspoon thyme
1 teaspoon salt
1½ cups dry bread crumbs or
  finely crushed cornflakes

Dip chicken pieces in butter, then shake in paper bag containing garlic powder, paprika, thyme, salt, and crumbs or cornflakes. Place skin side up in lightly greased 9" × 13" baking dish, and bake at 350°F for 50 minutes or until done. *Serves 6–8.*

Mary Wakefield, First Congregational Church, Rindge, New Hampshire

Spring Chicken Maryland

A specialty of dining-car chefs during the Golden Age of Pullman travel that well deserves its fame. Easily divided.

3 broiler-fryers, cut up
6 tablespoons cooking oil
¼ cup flour
½ teaspoon salt
⅛ teaspoon pepper
3 slices (½" thick) salt pork, cut into square dice

3 pinches of nutmeg
¾ cup melted butter
3 cups cream or evaporated milk
Paprika
Parsley sprigs

Cut chickens into quarters. Brush with oil and dredge with flour, salt, and pepper. Fry salt pork in large skillet until brown. Add nutmeg. Place chicken on top of pork (without draining off fat) and baste with melted butter. Cover skillet and cook about 30 minutes over medium-low heat until tender. Turn chicken pieces over. Add 1 cup cream or evaporated milk, turn heat up to medium, and cook uncovered to let cream cook down. When sauce is fairly thick, add another cup of cream or milk, cook as before until thickened, and add the last cup of cream or milk. Cook until thick. To serve, spoon cream gravy over chicken pieces, sprinkle with paprika to taste, and garnish with parsley sprigs. *Serves 12.*

Chicken Pie with Crust

2 cut-up broiler-fryers
1 large onion, quartered
4 carrots, peeled and cut into pieces
2–3 cups water
¼ teaspoon rosemary
½ teaspoon thyme
¼ teaspoon marjoram

2 teaspoons salt
1 teaspoon pepper
1 package (10 ounces) frozen peas
⅓ cup butter
⅓ cup flour
1 cup cream

Put chicken into pot with onion and carrots. Add water to cover, rosemary, thyme, marjoram, 1 teaspoon salt, and ½ teaspoon pepper. Bring to boil and simmer, covered, for about 45 minutes, or until chicken is cooked. Drain chicken and reserve broth. Remove bones and skin from chicken pieces and cut meat into bite-sized chunks. Return chicken to vegetables and add frozen peas. Remove 1½ cups broth from pot. Melt butter in saucepan and blend in flour. Gradually add hot broth and cream, stirring constantly until thickened and smooth. Add remaining 1 teaspoon salt and ½ teaspoon pepper. Pour sauce over chicken and vegetables, adding more broth if necessary.

Pastry

1 cup shortening
3 cups flour

½ teaspoon salt
½–¾ cup cold water

Cut shortening into flour mixed with salt. Add water. Mix well to form ball. Roll out top and bottom crusts.

Place bottom crust in 9" deep-dish pie plate. Pour in chicken mixture and cover with top crust. Brush with milk. Pierce three small holes in top crust to let steam escape and put ring of foil around edge to prevent overbrowning. Bake at 350°F for 35–40 minutes, or until brown, removing foil after about 10 minutes. *Serves 6–8.*

Crust: Evelyn Shaw, Pilgrim Congregational Church, New Haven, Connecticut

Chicken Pie with Biscuit Topping

Use the recipe on page 58 for chicken, vegetables, and sauce.
Place in 9" × 13" baking dish and top with Baking Powder Biscuits.

Baking Powder Biscuits

2 cups flour
4 teaspoons baking powder
1 teaspoon salt

⅓ cup shortening
¾ cup milk

Sift together flour, baking powder, and salt, and cut in shortening. Add milk to make soft dough. Knead a few times on floured board. Lightly roll out to ½" thickness and cut with 2" cutter. Bake at 450°F for 10–15 minutes, or until chicken mixture is hot and biscuits are well-browned. *Serves 6–8.*

Biscuits: Susie Cleveland, The United Church, Northfield, Vermont

Chicken Loaf or Ring

Like its first cousin, meat loaf, good cold or hot.
Fill a hot chicken ring with rice or macaroni, a cold ring with fresh salad.

2 cups scalded milk
2 eggs, lightly beaten
1 cup soft bread crumbs
½ teaspoon salt
¼ teaspoon paprika

1 teaspoon Worcestershire sauce
3 cups diced cooked chicken
½ cup chopped celery
1 green pepper, chopped
1½ tablespoons lemon juice

Pour hot milk slowly in a thin stream onto eggs, stirring constantly. Add bread crumbs, salt, paprika, Worcestershire sauce, chicken, celery, pepper, and lemon juice. Mix well, and pour into buttered loaf pan or ring mold. Bake at 300°F until knife inserted in center comes out clean—45–60 minutes, approximately. The ring will cook in less time than the loaf. Do not overbake. Remove from oven and let stand 10 minutes before unmolding. *Serves 6–8.*

Nutty Chicken Pie

Chicken, mushrooms, and almonds in a velvety cream sauce under a pastry cover.

¼ cup butter
¼ cup flour
1 cup light cream
½ teaspoon salt (omit if you use
  bouillon cube to make broth)
¼ teaspoon pepper
1 cup chicken broth

¼ teaspoon dillweed
1 teaspoon chopped parsley
2 cups cooked diced chicken
1 can (4 ounces) sliced
  mushrooms, drained
½ cup toasted slivered almonds
  Pastry for single-crust 9" pie

Melt butter and blend in flour. Gradually stir in cream and cook, stirring, until smooth and thick. Add salt, pepper, chicken broth, dillweed, and parsley, and cook until smooth and thick once more. Stir in chicken, mushrooms, and almonds. Pour into 9" deep-dish pie plate and cover with pastry. Slash top and bake on cookie sheet in oven preheated to 450°F for 10 minutes. Reduce heat to 350°F and bake 15 minutes more. *Serves 6.*

Chicken Spaghetti Dinner

Spaghetti with a difference. The secret is the long simmer.

1 green pepper, chopped
1 cup diced celery
2 large onions, chopped
3 cloves garlic, chopped
½ cup cooking oil
1 can (16 ounces) tomato puree
2 cans (6 ounces each) tomato paste

2 puree cans water (32 ounces)
1 cup-up broiler-fryer, or 3 large chicken breasts, halved
1 teaspoon cinnamon
1 teaspoon salt
½ teaspoon pepper
½ teaspoon allspice
8 ounces spaghetti

Sauté green pepper, celery, onions, and garlic in ¼ cup cooking oil. Add tomato puree, paste, and water. Simmer 1½ hours, uncovered, stirring from time to time. Brown chicken pieces in remaining ¼ cup oil. Add with cinnamon, salt, pepper, and allspice to simmering sauce and continue to simmer, covered, for 1½ hours longer, or until chicken is tender. Cook spaghetti as directed and drain. Place in serving dish. Pour chicken and sauce over spaghetti. *Serves 6.*

Virginia Colivos, Greek Orthodox Church of the Annunciation, Dover, New Hampshire

Chicken Rice Casserole

An elegant version of a hot chicken salad.

2 cups diced cooked chicken
1 cup sliced celery
2 teaspoons finely chopped onion
½ cup chopped walnut meats
2 cups cooked rice
1 can (10¾ ounces) cream of chicken soup

½ teaspoon salt
¼ teaspoon pepper
1 tablespoon lemon juice
½ cup mayonnaise
½ cup water
3 hard-boiled eggs, sliced
2 cups crushed potato chips

In large bowl, combine chicken, celery, onion, walnuts, rice, soup, salt, pepper, and lemon juice. Mix mayonnaise with water until smooth and add to chicken mixture. Gently fold in egg slices. Turn mixture into greased 9" × 9" pan. Bake at 450°F for 25 minutes. Remove and top with potato chips. Return to oven for another 5 minutes. *Serves 6–8.*

Emilie C. Bugbee, The Congregational Church, Somers, Connecticut

Rich Chicken Noodle Casserole

Tabasco lends a special touch to this creamy invention.

3 cups uncooked medium egg noodles	1½ teaspoons salt
1 cup cottage cheese	¼ teaspoon Tabasco Sauce
1 cup sour cream	¼ cup sliced pitted ripe olives
6 tablespoons grated Parmesan cheese	2½ cups diced cooked chicken

Cook noodles according to package directions. Combine cottage cheese, sour cream, 4 tablespoons Parmesan, salt, and Tabasco. Stir in olives, noodles, and chicken. Turn into greased 2-quart casserole and sprinkle with remaining 2 tablespoons Parmesan cheese. Cover and refrigerate. One hour before serving, bake, covered, at 350°F for 35 minutes. Uncover and bake for 25 minutes longer. *Serves 6.*

Woodmont United Church of Christ, Milford, Connecticut

Peachy Chicken

A fruitful combination of flavors; good served over rice.

3	chicken breasts, halved	2	tablespoons vinegar
½	cup flour	2	tablespoons brown sugar
	Salt and pepper	1	teaspoon basil
2	tablespoons butter	½	teaspoon nutmeg
2	tablespoons cooking oil	1	can (16 ounces) peach (or
1½	cups orange juice		apricot) halves, drained

Shake chicken pieces in bag with flour and salt and pepper to taste; brown in butter and oil. Place browned chicken in greased 3-quart casserole dish. Combine orange juice with vinegar, sugar, basil, and nutmeg, and pour mixture over chicken. Cover and bake at 375°F for 1 hour and 15 minutes, or until tender. Baste often. Then place peach or apricot halves between chicken pieces, baste well, and bake uncovered for 15 minutes longer. *Serves 6.*

Barbara Pasichuke, First Congregational Church, Littleton, New Hampshire

Chicken à la King

This used to be *the* dish for special occasions, but somehow you don't run into it as often these days. Still good, though.

1	cup sliced mushrooms	2	cups milk or chicken stock
4	tablespoons butter	2½	cups cooked diced chicken
4	tablespoons flour	1	cup cooked peas
½	teaspoon salt	3	tablespoons diced pimiento
¼	teaspoon pepper		

Sauté mushrooms in butter. Blend in flour, salt, and pepper. Gradually stir in milk or stock. Cook over medium heat, stirring, until thickened. Add chicken, peas, and pimiento. Heat well and serve in pastry shells or Toast Cups. *Serves 8.*

Toast Cups

Cut crusts from bread slices. Press slices into muffin tins so 4 points of bread stick up. Bake at 400°F about 10 minutes, or until toasted and brown. Allow to cool a few minutes in pan so cups will hold their shape. If making these ahead, warm them for a few minutes on a cookie sheet before using.

Chicken Soufflé

This recipe has been multiplied to serve over a hundred for a church luncheon or dinner. Just as good warmed up.

16 slices white bread, buttered on one side, with crusts removed	5 eggs
3–4 whole chicken breasts, cooked, boned, skinned, and sliced	2 cups milk
½ cup mayonnaise	1 teaspoon salt
1 cup grated Cheddar cheese	1 can (10¾ ounces) cream of mushroom or cream of chicken soup

Butter a 9" × 13" baking dish. Line bottom with 8 slices bread. Cover with sliced chicken meat, spread slices with mayonnaise, and sprinkle with ½ cup Cheddar cheese. Top with remaining 8 slices bread. Beat together eggs, milk, and salt, and pour over entire casserole. Refrigerate overnight or all day. When ready to bake, spread soup over top. Bake at 350°F for 45 minutes. Sprinkle with remaining ½ cup Cheddar cheese, return to oven, and bake for 15 minutes longer. *Serves 10.*

Joan Dean, Grace Congregational Church, Rutland, Vermont

Chicken Potato Casserole

Thyme-touched scalloped potatoes topped and cooked with chicken.

4 cups thinly sliced peeled
potatoes
4–5 medium onions, sliced
Salt and pepper
Ground thyme
½ cup hot water

1 can (13 ounces) evaporated milk
2 slices bacon
2 tablespoons butter
2 broiler-fryers, about 3 pounds
each, cut up
Paprika

Put potatoes and onions in large roasting pan and sprinkle with salt, pepper, and thyme to taste. Add water. Reserve ¼ cup milk and pour remainder over vegetables. Put in 400°F oven while preparing chicken.

In large skillet, cook bacon until browned; remove and drain. Add butter to skillet, then chicken, and brown on all sides, removing pieces as they brown. Put chicken in pan with potatoes and sprinkle lightly with more salt, pepper, and thyme. Crumble bacon and sprinkle over top. Cover tightly with foil and bake at 400°F for 1 hour. Uncover, pour reserved milk over top, and sprinkle with paprika to taste. Bake 30 minutes longer. *Serves 8.*

Don Wyant, Woodmont United Church of Christ, Milford, Connecticut

Chicken and Corn Pudding

A smooth taste that goes well with other casseroles and with salads.

2 cups diced cooked chicken
3 eggs, well-beaten
3 cups milk
2 tablespoons flour
1½ teaspoons salt

⅛ teaspoon pepper
¼ cup minced onion
¼ cup minced green pepper
1¾ cups canned whole-kernel
corn, drained

Place chicken in greased casserole dish. Beat eggs, milk, and flour together in bowl, and add salt, pepper, onion, green pepper, and corn. Pour over chicken. Bake at 325°F for 1 hour or longer—until custard is set and knife inserted in center comes out clean. *Serves 6–8.*

Alma L. Hedrick, Harwinton Congregational Church, Harwinton, Connecticut

Chicken Enchiladas

- 3 tablespoons olive oil
- 3 stalks celery, chopped
- 1 large onion, chopped
- 3 large cloves garlic, minced
- 2 jalapeños, minced (optional)
- 3 cups (1 pound) coarsely chopped cooked chicken
- 1 can (8¾ ounces) corn kernels, drained, or 1 cup frozen corn kernels
- 2 teaspoons chili powder
- ½ teaspoon salt
- ½ teaspoon pepper
- 6 cups canned red or green enchilada sauce
- 1 can (14 ounces) black olives, drained and chopped
- 2 tablespoons minced fresh parsley
- 2 tablespoons minced fresh cilantro + ½ cup cilantro leaves for garnish
- 2 dozen flour tortillas (8" in diameter)
- 2 bags (8 ounces each) shredded Cheddar-Jack cheese mix
- 1 carton (16 ounces) sour cream
- 6–8 cups chopped lettuce

Heat oil in 6-quart pot over medium-high heat. Add celery, onion, garlic, and half the jalapeños, if using. Sauté for 10 minutes or until browned. Reduce heat if mixture is browning too quickly. Add chicken, corn, chili powder, salt, pepper, 1½ cups enchilada sauce, and all but ½ cup olives. Stir and reduce the heat to low. Simmer, stirring occasionally, for about 1 hour or until chicken is in shreds and sauce is thickened. Stir in parsley and 2 tablespoons minced cilantro.

Divide 1 cup of remaining enchilada sauce among two greased 11" × 15" (5-quart) lasagna pans, spreading sauce to cover bottom. Pour remaining 3½ cups sauce in shallow container wide enough to hold a tortilla. One at a time, dip both sides of a tortilla in sauce; shake off excess. (Canned sauces vary in thickness; if sauce is thick, use a pastry brush to lightly coat both sides.) Place tortilla in one lasagna pan. Place 2 tablespoons chicken mixture and 2 tablespoons cheese in center. Roll, then tuck in ends and place seam-side down at end of pan. Continue until all filled tortillas are placed, two per row, divided equally between the pans. Cover with sauce remaining in shallow container. Sprinkle with reserved olives and cheese. Bake at 350°F for about 20 minutes or until sauce bubbles and cheese melts. Allow to cool for 10 minutes. Garnish with sour cream, lettuce, and cilantro leaves. Pass remaining jalapeños, if using, at the table. ***Serves 12–16.***

Taunya L. DeLuca, St. Daniel the Prophet Catholic Community, Scottsdale, Arizona

Guisado de Pollo

This hearty Mexican-style chicken stew is subtly and intriguingly spiced.

4 tablespoons cooking oil
2 broiler-fryers, cut into serving pieces
2 chorizos (Spanish sausages), or 2 hot Italian sausages
½ pound cooked ham, diced
2 cups tomatoes, or 1 can (16 ounces)
1 clove garlic, finely minced
½ cup chopped onion

¼ cup finely chopped parsley
¼ pound almonds, roasted and ground
¼ teaspoon cloves
¼ teaspoon cinnamon
Salt and pepper
¾ cup dry white wine
¼ cup capers
3 yellow wax peppers, cut into strips (optional)

Heat oil and brown chicken on all sides. Transfer browned pieces to large Dutch oven or casserole dish. Remove sausage meat from casing and sauté with ham in oil until lightly browned. Pour off most of oil and add tomatoes (with juice), garlic, onion, parsley, almonds, cloves, and cinnamon. Add salt and pepper to taste. Bring to boil and pour over chicken. Cover and simmer about 15 minutes. Add wine, replace cover, and simmer 45–60 minutes longer, or until chicken is thoroughly cooked. Serve garnished with capers and wax peppers (if using) over cornbread or rice. *Serves 8–10.*

Helen D. Tawse, St. James Episcopal Church, Keene, New Hampshire

Never-fail Chicken Delicious

An unusual combination of potatoes, chicken, and sausage.
Our recipe tester reported, "Makes the potatoes taste fabulous."

6 medium potatoes, peeled and quartered
1 teaspoon oregano
1 teaspoon paprika
½ teaspoon garlic powder
1 teaspoon salt

½ teaspoon pepper
1 frying chicken, cut up
1 pound sweet Italian sausage links, cut up
¼ cup vegetable oil

Arrange potatoes in large, shallow 3-quart casserole. Mix oregano, paprika, garlic powder, salt, and pepper, and sprinkle half the mixture over potatoes. Arrange chicken and sausage on top. Pour oil over and sprinkle with remaining seasonings. Cover and bake at 425°F for 1 hour. Uncover, and bake at 375°F for 30 minutes, or until a nice brown. *Serves 6.*

Joanna Miller, Dublin Community Church, Dublin, New Hampshire

Chicken Marengo

Marengo is the name of a small Piedmontese village where Napoleon's chef, on the eve of the battle of Marengo, purportedly invented this famous dish to tempt his general's lagging appetite.

1 cup sliced fresh mushrooms	1 clove garlic, minced
2 tablespoons butter	½ cup consommé or dry white wine
1 broiler-fryer (3–4 pounds), cut into 6 serving pieces	2 tomatoes, cut into wedges and seeded
Salt and pepper	¼ teaspoon thyme
2–3 tablespoons cooking oil	1 tablespoon chopped parsley
4 green onions, with tops removed, sliced	

Sauté mushrooms in butter for 2 minutes; set aside. Sprinkle chicken pieces with salt and pepper to taste, and sauté in hot oil until brown. Remove chicken from skillet and set aside. Reserve drippings. Sauté onions and garlic in drippings until onions are soft. Stir in consommé or wine, tomatoes, and thyme, scraping bottom of skillet well. Add chicken to skillet. Cover and simmer 30 minutes, or until chicken is tender. Add sautéed mushrooms. Sprinkle with parsley and serve. *Serves 6.*

Joan Young, The Unitarian Church, Franklin, New Hampshire

Coq au Vin

Chicken in a rich red wine sauce.

1 tablespoon flour
Salt and pepper
3 chicken breasts, halved
1 tablespoon minced onion
2 tablespoons cooking oil
12 small white onions

1 cup sliced mushrooms
½ cup red wine
½ cup chicken broth
1 clove garlic, minced
1 bay leaf
½ teaspoon thyme

Mix flour with salt and pepper to taste. Dredge chicken in flour mixture. In large skillet, brown chicken and minced onion in oil. Place chicken in 4-quart casserole. Sauté small white onions and mushrooms in skillet until lightly browned. Add wine, broth, garlic, bay leaf, and thyme. When liquid starts to boil, stir well, pour into casserole, cover, and bake at 350°F for about 40 minutes. Before serving, remove and discard bay leaf. *Serves 6.*

Joan Young, The Unitarian Church, Franklin, New Hampshire

Easy Chicken Cacciatore

A bachelor's delight!

1 chicken (3 pounds), or the
equivalent in parts
1 jar (15½ ounces) spaghetti sauce

½ package Good Seasons Garlic
Mix

Cut up chicken into 6 serving portions. Combine spaghetti sauce with garlic mix. Dip each piece in sauce. Place in baking pan, and pour remaining sauce over all. Cover with aluminum foil and bake at 350°F for about 1 hour, or until tender. After removing chicken, use sauce in pan to pour over cooked noodles to accompany chicken. *Serves 6.*

Rev. Eugene B. Navias, Concord Unitarian Church (1957–1963), Concord, New Hampshire

Paella Valenciana

As the French do with cassoulet, the Spanish make their justly famed paella in all sorts of different ways, depending on the meat or seafood locally available.

1 **pound chorizo or Italian sweet or hot sausage**
½ **cup diced cooked ham**
1 **onion, chopped**
1 **clove garlic, minced**
4 **tablespoons cooking oil**
1 **can (4 ounces) mushrooms, liquid reserved**
1 **can (8 ounces) minced clams, liquid reserved**
1 **package (10 ounces) frozen peas, cooked with liquid reserved**
1 **can (6 ounces) tomato paste**

2 **bay leaves**
¼ **teaspoon pepper**
½ **teaspoon sugar**
1½ **cups white wine**
¾ **teaspoon salt**
2 **cups chicken stock**
1½ **cups uncooked long-grain rice**
½ **teaspoon ground saffron or yellow food coloring (optional)**
2 **cups cooked chicken, cut into julienne strips**
1 **tablespoon chopped parsley**

Cut sausage in ½" slices and sauté along with ham, onion, and garlic in 2 tablespoons oil. Drain mushrooms, clams, and peas and reserve liquid. If necessary, add enough water to liquid to equal 1½ cups. Set aside mushrooms, clams, and peas. Add tomato paste, bay leaves, pepper, sugar, wine, reserved liquid, and salt. Simmer for 30 minutes. Heat chicken stock to boiling. In large casserole or Dutch oven, brown rice in remaining 2 tablespoons oil, stirring. Add hot stock and saffron or food coloring, if using, to rice. Add ham and sausage mixture and chicken and stir. Cover tightly and bake at 375°F for 30 minutes, or until rice is cooked. Check at end of 30 minutes and add more liquid if necessary. When rice is done, stir in mushrooms, clams, parsley, shrimp, and peas. Bake uncovered at 375°F for 15–20 minutes to fluff rice and heat through. *Serves 8–10.*

Turkey Curry

This is a wonderful way to re-present the Thanksgiving turkey!

1 cup sliced sautéed fresh (or canned and drained) mushrooms
⅓ cup minced onion
1 large apple, peeled, cored, and diced
3 cups diced cooked turkey

6 tablespoons butter
3 tablespoons flour
½ teaspoon salt
1–1½ teaspoons curry powder
1½ cups turkey stock, mixed with a little cream

Sauté mushrooms, onion, apple, and turkey in butter until apple and onion are tender. Remove from heat and stir in flour, salt, and curry powder. Blend in ½ cup liquid and return to stove. Cook, stirring and gradually adding remaining 1 cup liquid, over medium heat until sauce has thickened. Put in top of double boiler and cook over boiling water 15 minutes longer. Taste to adjust seasoning. Serve with hot rice. *Serves 6.*

Italian Turkey Casserole

A different way to use turkey or chicken—with Italian cornmeal mush, or polenta.

1½ quarts water
1 teaspoon salt
½ cup yellow cornmeal
2 Italian hot sausages, cooked and sliced (optional)
3 cups diced cooked turkey or chicken

1 pound sliced mushrooms
3 tablespoons butter
2–2½ cups meatless tomato sauce
¾ cup grated Parmesan cheese
Pepper

Place water and salt in large saucepan. Bring to boil and gradually add cornmeal, stirring constantly with wooden spoon. Cook over medium heat until consistency of mashed potatoes (about 30 minutes). Put into 10" × 10" buttered baking dish and level off with spoon. Spoon sausage, if using, and turkey or chicken over polenta layer. Sauté mushrooms in butter and lay on top of turkey or chicken. Spread tomato sauce over all. Sprinkle with Parmesan and a little pepper to taste. Bake at 350°F for 45 minutes. *Serves 6–8.*

Clorinda C. Duke, United Church, East Calais, Vermont

Turkey Terrapin

For luxurious leftovers.

4 tablespoons butter	mushrooms (or use canned and
2 cups minced cooked turkey	drained)
or chicken	2 hard-boiled eggs
½ cup flour	Salt and pepper
Chicken stock	Paprika
1½ cups thin cream	½ cup sherry
1 cup sliced sautéed fresh	Parsley

Melt butter in frying pan. Dredge turkey or chicken well with flour and add to butter along with enough stock to blend well, stirring to keep mixture smooth. Add cream, mushrooms, and eggs with whites cut into strips and yolks sieved. Season to taste with salt, pepper, and paprika. Cook slowly until thick and creamy, and just before serving stir in sherry. Spoon over toasted and buttered English muffins, and garnish with chopped parsley. *Serves 6.*

Turkey Florentine

Turkey, spinach, and mushrooms in a smoothly delicious sauce.

8 tablespoons butter
1 chicken bouillon cube
3 cups diced cooked turkey
1 cup canned, drained mushrooms
¼ cup flour
2 cups milk
1 cup grated Colby or Cheddar
  cheese

1 teaspoon salt
3 tablespoons sherry
  Dash of nutmeg
2 packages (10 ounces each)
  frozen chopped spinach,
  cooked and drained

Melt 4 tablespoons butter and crush bouillon cube into hot butter. Sauté turkey in butter for 2–3 minutes, stirring to heat evenly. Remove turkey and add mushrooms to butter. Sauté for 2–3 minutes and add to turkey. Keep turkey and mushrooms hot. In same pan used to sauté, melt remaining 4 tablespoons butter and blend in flour. Gradually add milk, stirring until sauce is smooth and thick. Add cheese, salt, sherry, and nutmeg, stirring until cheese is melted. Butter a 9" × 13" baking dish. Spread spinach over bottom. Cover with turkey and mushroom mixture. Pour sauce over all and bake at 350°F for 30 minutes, or until heated through and bubbly. *Serves 8.*

Special Stuffing

The blue cheese in this elegant stuffing enhances the flavor of almost any poultry.

¼ cup butter
½ cup chopped celery
1 cup sliced mushrooms
½ cup chopped onion
4 cups croutons
¼ cup chopped parsley
½ cup sliced water chestnuts

½ cup crumbled American blue
  cheese
1 tablespoon poultry seasoning
¾ teaspoon sugar
  Dash of pepper
  Broth from giblets

In butter, sauté celery, mushrooms, and onion. In large bowl, combine croutons, parsley, water chestnuts, blue cheese, poultry seasoning, sugar, and pepper. Add celery and onion mixture. Blend well, tossing lightly. Add enough broth to dampen ingredients. Mix well. *Makes 8 cups.*

Parsley-Lemon Stuffing

The lemon rind and parsley endow this stuffing with a clean, light flavor all its own.

6 tablespoons butter + ¾ cup melted butter
1 medium onion, chopped fine
3 cups fresh bread crumbs

Grated rind of 3 lemons
1½ cups chopped parsley
3 eggs, well-beaten
Salt and pepper

Melt 6 tablespoons butter and sauté onion until tender and golden. In mixing bowl, combine bread crumbs, lemon rind, parsley, and onion. Add eggs and ¾ cup melted butter, and mix well. Season with salt and pepper to taste. ***Enough to stuff 1 large or 2 small chickens.***

Turkey Dressing

A really imaginative stuffing—enough to stuff into a 21-pound holiday turkey.

1 pound bulk pork sausage
8 cups bread cubes
½ cup butter
2 cloves garlic, minced
2 cups chopped celery and leaves
1 cup chopped onion
1 cup coarsely chopped mushrooms
¼ cup chopped parsley

¼ cup chopped green pepper
½ cup sliced almonds
2 teaspoons salt
½ teaspoon pepper
¼ teaspoon nutmeg
1 teaspoon poultry seasoning
Pinch of cayenne pepper
½ of 10½-ounce can consommé
½ cup dry sherry

Sauté sausage until light brown. Drain, reserving fat, and remove to large bowl. To pork fat, add bread cubes and stir. Remove to bowl with pork. In butter, sauté garlic, celery, onion, mushrooms, parsley, green pepper, and almonds until tender. Season with salt, pepper, nutmeg, poultry seasoning, and cayenne. Add consommé and sherry. Heat through. Add to bread cubes and pork mixture. Toss thoroughly.

Marcia Gehrke, United Methodist Church of the Hamptons, Hampton, New Hampshire

Eggs, Cheese, Fish, and Seafood

Egg-and-cheese casseroles are some of the best loved. And they can be served at any meal—from breakfast to a midnight supper. From omelettes to quiches, these dishes are sure to please family and friends.

Despite the sometimes-high price of fish and seafood, the importance of this food to our diet has not changed. The seafood recipes here range from the delicious to the absolutely extraordinary, including several inventive fish casseroles and tasty shrimp dishes.

Baked Omelet

The North Madison Congregational Church has served this omelet to 100 people at Easter sunrise breakfasts. Multiply recipe given below by number of persons to be served. Rises high in oven but will fall when taken out. Don't worry—it is supposed to.

1½ tablespoons butter	⅛ teaspoon salt
1 tablespoon cream	Dash of pepper
⅛ teaspoon dry mustard	¼ teaspoon sweet basil
1 tablespoon grated cheese	1 egg
Dash of onion powder	

In pan, melt ½ tablespoon butter. In bowl, combine cream, mustard, cheese, onion powder, salt, pepper, basil, remaining 1 tablespoon butter, and egg. Beat until frothy and pour into 6" ovenproof skillet or 1-quart casserole (mixture should be ¼" deep in pan). Bake at 350°F for 20–25 minutes, or until firm and beginning to brown. Cut into squares and serve.

Sonja Gibbs and Jan Woerheide, North Madison Congregational Church, North Madison, Connecticut

Easy Eggs and Tomato Benedict

The sauce—mayonnaise, milk, lemon juice, basil, and pepper— is a very acceptable substitute for hollandaise and easily made.

2 medium tomatoes	Dash of pepper
½ cup mayonnaise	4 English muffins, split and
¼ cup milk	toasted
½ teaspoon lemon juice	Salt
¼ teaspoon dry basil	8 eggs, poached and drained

Cut each tomato into 4 slices and set aside. In small saucepan, combine mayonnaise, milk, lemon juice, basil, and pepper. Heat. Keep warm. Cover each muffin half with a tomato slice. Sprinkle lightly with salt. Top with poached egg and pour sauce on top. *Serves 4 or 8.*

Mrs. Henry Johnson, Swanzey Congregational Church, Swanzey, New Hampshire

Scrambled Eggs in Mushroom and Cheese Sauce

The richest scrambled eggs in the world! May be prepared up to the broiling point and kept at room temperature for an hour ahead of time.

¾ cup butter
1 pound fresh mushrooms, quartered
2 tablespoons minced scallions or shallots
6 tablespoons flour
2 cups milk, scalded

1 cup heavy cream
Salt and pepper (season both sauce and eggs separately; use in all about ½ teaspoon salt and ⅛ teaspoon pepper)
16 eggs
½ cup grated Parmesan cheese

Melt 3 tablespoons butter in large frying pan and sauté mushrooms until just beginning to brown. Add scallions or shallots and cook for 2 minutes. Drain and set aside.

Make sauce by melting 3 tablespoons butter in 2-quart saucepan over medium heat. Blend in flour, and add milk gradually, stirring until smooth and thickened. Add ½ cup cream and let simmer, stirring, for about 5 minutes. Stir in remaining ½ cup cream to thin sauce so that it definitely coats a spoon but is not too thick. Add salt and pepper to taste. Set aside.

Scramble eggs in 4 tablespoons butter until just set. Add salt and pepper to taste.

Pour thin layer of sauce over bottom of buttered 9" × 13" baking dish. Sprinkle with 2 tablespoons cheese. Cover with half the scrambled eggs, then the mushrooms. Pour 1 cup sauce on top. Sprinkle 3 tablespoons more cheese over sauce and remaining eggs. Pour rest of sauce over all, sprinkle with remaining cheese, and dot with remaining butter. Brown lightly under *preheated* broiler for 1–2 minutes. ***Serves 12.***

Moira Burnham, Church of the Epiphany, New York, New York

Three-Cheese Deviled Eggs

This recipe can easily be doubled. For a flavor variation, replace the mustard with curry powder.

6 **hard-boiled eggs, cooled,**
   shells removed
½–¾ **cup mayonnaise**
2 **tablespoons grated Cheddar**
   cheese
2 **tablespoons grated Swiss cheese**

2 **tablespoons minced chives**
¼ **teaspoon stone-ground**
   prepared mustard
⅛ **teaspoon pepper**
¼ **cup (2 ounces) cubed Velveeta**
   cheese

Cut eggs in half lengthwise. Remove yolks and place in bowl; set whites aside. Mash yolks with ½ cup mayonnaise, Cheddar, Swiss, 1 tablespoon chives, mustard, and pepper. In microwaveable bowl, cook Velveeta on high for 1 minute, until melted; stir until smooth. Stir into yolk mixture. For creamier texture, add up to ¼ cup more mayonnaise. Pipe yolk mixture through pastry bag fitted with large decorative tip or spoon into egg-white halves. Sprinkle with remaining 1 tablespoon chives. Refrigerate until serving. *Makes 12.*

Lynne S. Froning, Saint Paul United Methodist Church, Lincoln, Nebraska

Brunch Eggs

A delicious Mediterranean version of poached eggs—similar to pipérade.
Double the recipe to serve 6 for supper.

2 **medium onions, sliced**
3 **tablespoons butter**
3 **green peppers, thinly sliced**
½ **cup chopped parsley**
½ **cup water**
½ **teaspoon salt**

¼ **teaspoon pepper**
3 **medium tomatoes, skinned and**
   cut into wedges
6 **eggs**
½ **cup shredded Muenster or**
   mozzarella cheese

Sauté onions in butter for 5 minutes. Add green peppers and parsley and sauté, stirring. Add water, salt, and pepper. Cover pan and cook, stirring occasionally, for about 10 minutes, or until liquid evaporates. Reduce heat. Add tomato wedges. With back of tablespoon, make 6 depressions in vegetables. Break 1 egg in each depression. Cook, covered, for about 4 minutes. Uncover, sprinkle with cheese, and cook another 1–2 minutes longer until set. *Serves 6.*

Mrs. Henry Johnson, Swanzey Congregational Church, Swanzey, New Hampshire

Eggs, Cheese, Fish, and Seafood   83

Deviled Egg and Spinach Casserole

Easily divided or multiplied. *The* answer to all those leftover Easter eggs!

12 hard-boiled eggs
 6 tablespoons mayonnaise
 ¼ teaspoon dry mustard
 ⅛ teaspoon pepper
 4 packages (10 ounces each)
    frozen chopped spinach
 ½ cup butter

 ¼ cup flour
 4 cups milk
 2 cups grated sharp cheese
 1 teaspoon Worcestershire sauce
 1 teaspoon salt
 ¼ teaspoon Tabasco Sauce

Cut eggs in half lengthwise and remove yolks. Mash yolks with mayonnaise, mustard, and pepper. Blend until smooth and fill egg whites with mixture. Cook spinach, drain, and squeeze out all moisture. Melt butter in saucepan and blend in flour. Add milk gradually to flour and butter paste, stirring constantly while cooking over medium heat until sauce thickens. Reserve ¼ cup grated cheese, and stir remaining cheese into sauce until cheese melts. Add Worcestershire sauce, salt, and Tabasco Sauce. Place spinach in greased 3-quart baking dish or casserole dish with half the cheese sauce. Mix spinach and sauce together with fork. Place deviled egg halves on top of spinach and cover with remaining cheese sauce. Sprinkle reserved grated cheese over all. Bake at 375°F for 20–25 minutes, or until bubbly and lightly browned. (Can be reheated at 325°F in covered dish.) *Serves 8–10.*

Ham and Eggs Brunch Casserole

This comforting dish can be assembled the night before serving. Cool the potatoes, onions, and peppers before adding the egg mixture, then refrigerate and bake the next morning.

 2 cups (8 ounces) frozen hash
    brown potatoes
1½ cups chopped onions
1½ cups chopped green or red bell
    peppers
 1 tablespoon vegetable or olive oil
 1 pound ham steak, cut into
    small cubes

 1 cup shredded Cheddar cheese
12 eggs
 1 cup milk
 1 teaspoon salt
 1 teaspoon pepper
 1 teaspoon dry mustard
 ½ teaspoon thyme (optional)

Press potatoes into 9" × 13" greased baking dish; place in oven broiler 6" from heat source, stirring occasionally, for about 8 minutes to brown. Remove.

Sauté onions and peppers in oil in large skillet over medium-high heat for 5 minutes or until golden. Spread onions, peppers, and ham evenly over potatoes. Sprinkle with cheese. In bowl, beat eggs, milk, salt, pepper, mustard, and thyme (if using). Pour into baking dish. Bake at 350°F for about 45 minutes or until eggs are cooked in center. *Serves 6–8.*

Lynne S. Froning, Saint Paul United Methodist Church, Lincoln, Nebraska

Mushroom Business

An interesting version of the ever-popular strata that vegetarians and mushroom fans will love.

1 **pound fresh mushrooms, coarsely sliced**	¾ **teaspoon salt**
3 **tablespoons butter**	⅛ **teaspoon pepper**
8 **slices buttered white bread**	2 **eggs**
½ **cup chopped onion**	⅓ **cup milk**
½ **cup chopped celery**	1 **can (10¾ ounces) cream of**
½ **cup chopped green pepper**	**mushroom soup**
½ **cup mayonnaise**	1 **cup shredded Cheddar cheese**

Sauté mushrooms in butter until aroma is released. Cut 3 of the bread slices into cubes and place in buttered 2-quart casserole dish. Combine onion, celery, green pepper, and mayonnaise. Add salt and pepper and spread over bread cubes. Add mushrooms. Top with 3 more cubed bread slices. Beat eggs slightly with milk and pour over. Refrigerate for at least 1 hour or overnight. Before baking, spread soup over top and sprinkle with last 2 cubed bread slices. Bake at 300°F for 60–70 minutes or at 350°F for 50–60 minutes. About 10 minutes before end of baking time, sprinkle with cheese. *Serves 8.*

Elizabeth K. Macrum, St. Stephen's Episcopal Church, Bucksport, Maine

Spaghetti Carbonara

This marvelous dish has been described as "Italian scrambled eggs and bacon."
If so, it is scrambled eggs and bacon taken to the nth power. Easily multiplied
or divided for breakfast, brunch, lunch, or dinner.

1 pound thin bacon slices	1 cup heavy or sour cream,
2 large onions, chopped	warmed slightly
fine	2 cups grated Parmesan cheese
1 cup dry white wine	½ cup chopped parsley
6 large or 8 medium eggs	2 pounds spaghetti or linguine
¼ pound butter, softened	Black pepper

Cook bacon slices until crisp. Drain on paper towels. Leave 3 tablespoons bacon fat in skillet. Sauté onions in bacon fat until golden and soft. Add wine and cook until it evaporates. Beat together eggs, butter, cream, Parmesan, and parsley. Add onions. Cook spaghetti in boiling salted water as directed on package. Transfer with slotted spoon to large warmed bowl. Add egg and cheese mixture and toss. Crumble bacon and sprinkle over top. Grind black pepper liberally over all and serve. *Serves 8.*

Adele Mac Veagh, Emmanuel Church, Webster Groves, Missouri

Quiche, that delectable French invention, is a treat at any meal, hot or cold, can be sold
at bazaars by the slice, served in bite-size pieces as an hors d'oeuvre, or taken in a brown
bag to work. Quiche can be made in a number of ways. Here are several.

Quiche Lorraine

¼ pound bacon strips	½ teaspoon salt
1 baked 9" pastry shell	Pinch of pepper
½ cup chopped onion (optional)	¾ cup grated Gruyère or Swiss
3 eggs	cheese
1½ cups cream	2 tablespoons butter

Cook bacon until crisp. Drain and break up into small pieces. Scatter pieces evenly on bottom of pastry shell. Sauté onion, if using, in bacon fat until soft, then distribute evenly in bottom of pastry shell with bacon. Beat eggs, cream, salt, and pepper together. Add cheese. Pour egg mixture into shell on top of bacon pieces. Cut butter into tiny dots and scatter over top of custard. Set pie plate on cookie sheet and place in 375°F oven. Bake for 40–50 minutes, checking after 25 minutes and thereafter every 10 minutes or so. Quiche is done when a silver knife inserted into center comes out clean. Cool on cake rack and serve warm. Reheats well. *Serves 6.*

Spinach Quiche

½ cup finely diced cooked ham
1 baked 9" pastry shell
1 package (10 ounces) frozen
  chopped spinach, cooked,
  drained, and rechopped
2 tablespoons chopped onion
3 tablespoons butter

3 eggs
1½ cups heavy cream
½ teaspoon salt
½ teaspoon pepper
½ teaspoon nutmeg
¼ cup grated Gruyère or Swiss
  cheese

Scatter ham evenly over bottom of pastry shell. Cook spinach and onion in 2 tablespoons butter, stirring from time to time, until *all* liquid has evaporated and spinach begins to stick to pan. Remove from heat. Beat eggs with cream, salt, pepper, and nutmeg. Add spinach and cheese and blend well. Pour into pastry shell. Cut the remaining 1 tablespoon butter into dots and sprinkle over top. Bake at 375°F for 40 minutes, or until set. Quiche is done when a silver knife inserted into center comes out clean. Cool slightly and serve. Reheats well. *Serves 6.*

Mushroom Quiche

Follow the preceding recipe for Spinach Quiche, substituting 1 cup cooked sliced mushrooms (drained, if you use canned) for spinach. Cook with onion in butter until onion is golden.

Corn Flan

Like a crustless corn quiche.

3 eggs
1 cup whole milk or half-and-half
4 tablespoons melted butter
1 package (16 ounces) frozen
  corn niblets, thawed
½ teaspoon salt
¼ teaspoon pepper

Pinch of cayenne pepper
¼ teaspoon nutmeg
½ pound Vermont Cheddar
  cheese, thinly sliced
2 tablespoons grated Parmesan
  cheese

Beat together eggs, milk or half-and-half, and butter. Stir in corn, salt, pepper, cayenne pepper, and nutmeg. Place half of mixture in buttered pie pan or 1½-quart baking dish. Spread with Cheddar cheese, top with remaining corn mixture, and sprinkle with Parmesan cheese. Bake at 325°F for approximately 45 minutes, or until set. Let stand a few minutes before cutting. *Serves 6.*

Margaret Michaelsen, North Bennington Congregational Church, North Bennington, Vermont

Clam Casserole

Easy to make and good to eat.

2 cans (8 ounces each) minced
  clams
24 crushed saltines

2 eggs, beaten
1½ cups milk
¼ cup melted butter

Combine clams (with juice), saltines, eggs, milk, and butter. Season to taste with salt, pepper, and/or herbs. Pour into 1½-quart casserole. Bake at 400°F for about 45 minutes. *Serves 6.*

Catherine B. Anderson, United Methodist Church of the Hamptons, Hampton, New Hampshire

Crab and Corn Bake

Delicious and rich. May be prepared ahead.

¼ cup butter
2 tablespoons flour
½ cup milk
½ teaspoon salt
Dash of pepper
1 tablespoon lemon juice
1 teaspoon prepared mustard
½ teaspoon horseradish
½ teaspoon Worcestershire sauce

1 can (6½–7½ ounces) crabmeat, flaked
2 hard-boiled eggs, chopped
1 can (16 ounces) whole-kernel corn, drained
1 can (16 ounces) cream-style corn
½ cup grated Parmesan cheese
½ cup buttered bread crumbs

Melt butter in saucepan and blend with flour. Gradually add milk and cook over medium heat, stirring, until white sauce thickens. Stir in salt, pepper, lemon juice, mustard, horseradish, and Worcestershire sauce. Mix together crabmeat, eggs, and corn. Add sauce and turn into greased 1½-quart casserole. Top with cheese and crumbs. Bake at 400°F for 15 minutes, or until heated through and bubbly. *Serves 6.*

Shirley Doherty, The Unitarian Church, Franklin, New Hampshire

Scalloped Clams

A quick and tasty seafood supper.

32 Ritz crackers, crushed
1 can (6½ ounces) minced clams
1 can (10 ounces) baby clams
¼ teaspoon thyme
2 eggs

1 cup milk
1 can (10¾ ounces) cream of mushroom soup
2 tablespoons melted butter

Cover bottom of greased 9" × 13" baking dish with some cracker crumbs. Mix together minced and baby clams and thyme and spoon some over layer of crumbs. Repeat layers of crumbs and clams and top with layer of crumbs. Beat eggs and combine with milk, soup, and butter. Pour over crumbs and clams. Bake at 350°F for 1 hour. *Serves 8.*

Rachel Seaward, The Unitarian Church, Franklin, New Hampshire

Mock Lobster Casserole

Marvelous way to make the relatively inexpensive haddock
into something much fancier. It works!

2 pounds haddock fillets	½ teaspoon minced onion
¼ teaspoon salt	⅛ teaspoon garlic powder
1 cup canned (or frozen and thawed) cream of shrimp soup	¼ cup melted butter
	½ teaspoon Worcestershire sauce
1 tablespoon lemon juice or sherry	¾ cup bread crumbs or crushed Ritz crackers

Place fish in greased 2-quart casserole. Sprinkle with salt. Mix soup with lemon juice or sherry. Pour over fish. Bake uncovered at 375°F for 20 minutes. While baking, sauté onion and garlic in butter. Remove from heat and add Worcestershire sauce. Then blend with crumbs or crackers. Sprinkle over fish and bake 10 minutes more. *Serves 6.*

Cheryl Tutt, Ascutney Union Church, Ascutney, Vermont

Kedgeree

The English eat kedgeree for breakfast, but it's good for supper, too.
Spinach—salad, creamed, or soufflé—is a natural with kedgeree.

6 tablespoons butter	4 hard-boiled eggs
1 teaspoon curry powder	Juice of ½ lemon
1½ cups raw rice	½ cup chopped fresh parsley
2 pounds white fish fillets (such as cod or haddock)	Pepper
	Dash of Worcestershire sauce
2 cups water	¼ cup milk (optional)
1 teaspoon salt	

Melt butter in saucepan; add curry powder and blend well. Add rice, stirring to coat well. Set aside. Poach fish in water for 10 minutes, or until done. Reserving broth, remove fish and set aside. To fish broth, add enough water to bring liquid up to 3 cups. Add with salt to rice in saucepan and bring to boil. Simmer, covered, until rice is tender and liquid is absorbed. Flake fish and chop eggs finely. In large mixing bowl, toss rice with fish. Add chopped egg, lemon juice, parsley, pepper to taste, and Worcestershire sauce. Toss well. If mixture seems dry, add milk. Spoon mixture into lightly greased 3-quart baking dish. Bake, covered, at 300°F for 25–35 minutes, until thoroughly heated. *Serves 10.*

Gaye S. LeBoutillier, St. Dunstan's Episcopal Church, Ellsworth, Maine

Marit's Fish Casserole

Fish and macaroni in a nutmeg cream sauce.

1 **pound uncooked white fish fillets**	2 **eggs, separated**
4 **teaspoons butter**	1 **cup elbow macaroni**
3 **tablespoons flour**	4 **American or provolone cheese slices**
1½ **cups milk**	3 **tablespoons plain dry bread crumbs**
½ **teaspoon salt**	
1½ **teaspoons nutmeg**	

Cut fish into small pieces. Melt butter in saucepan over medium heat. Add flour and stir 1 minute. Whisk in ¾ cup milk until lumps disappear. Whisk in salt, nutmeg, and remaining ¾ cup milk. Cook until thick. Remove from heat and stir in beaten egg yolks.

Cook and drain macaroni. Mix fish, macaroni, and white sauce together. Fold in stiffly beaten egg whites. Pour into buttered 1½ quart casserole and top with cheese slices and bread crumbs. Bake at 350°F for 30 minutes.

Sauce

¼ **cup melted butter**	1 **tablespoon lemon juice**
2 **tablespoons minced parsley**	

Combine butter, parsley, and lemon juice, and keep warm until fish is done. Pour over casserole and serve. *Serves 6.*

Rebecca Ulrich, Concord Unitarian Church, Concord, New Hampshire

Salmon Pudding

1 can (8 ounces) salmon, boned
  and flaked
⅛ teaspoon paprika
⅛ teaspoon dillweed
2 tablespoons lemon juice
¼ teaspoon salt

⅛ teaspoon pepper
2 dashes of Tabasco Sauce
  Dash of Worcestershire sauce
½ cup bread crumbs
½ cup milk, warmed
3 eggs, separated

Mix salmon with paprika, dillweed, lemon juice, salt, pepper, Tabasco Sauce, and Worcestershire sauce. Soak bread crumbs in milk and add to salmon. Add well-beaten egg yolks. Fold in stiffly beaten whites. Bake in greased 2-quart casserole at 350°F for 40 minutes, or until golden brown. *Serves 6.*

Elizabeth Hughes, Old Brick Church, Clarendon, Vermont

Flounder Crowns with Florentine Stuffing

This one could make you famous.

3 pounds flounder fillets, fresh
  or frozen
¾ teaspoon salt
½ cup chopped celery
½ cup butter, melted
1 box (6½ ounces) onion- and
  garlic-salted croutons (4 cups)

1 egg, beaten
1 package (10 ounces) frozen
  chopped spinach, thawed
½ teaspoon salt
¼ teaspoon thyme
⅛ teaspoon pepper

Divide fillets in half lengthwise. Sprinkle with salt. Cook celery in ¼ cup butter until tender. Combine with croutons, egg, spinach, salt, thyme, and pepper, and mix thoroughly. (Makes 4½ cups stuffing.) Place approximately ¾ cup filling on each fillet half. Roll fish around stuffing and secure with toothpicks. Place stuffed fish rolls—"crowns"—in shallow, well-greased 9" × 13" baking dish. You'll have about 16 crowns. Drizzle with remaining ¼ cup butter. Bake at 350°F for about 25 minutes, or until fish flakes easily when tested with fork.

Sauce

2 tablespoons butter	2 tablespoons heavy cream
2 tablespoons flour	½–1 cup small cooked shrimp
1 cup milk	Salt and pepper
1 egg yolk	

Melt butter and blend with flour. Add milk gradually, stirring constantly and cooking until thickened. Remove from heat. Beat egg yolk and mix with a little sauce. Add egg to remainder of sauce, stirring to blend well. Add cream, shrimp, and salt and pepper to taste. Heat through over double boiler and pour over flounder crowns. *Serves 8.*

Woodmont Congregational Church, Milford, Connecticut

Fish Casserole

Served at the Maundy Thursday Supper of Northfield's United Church,
this casserole can be changed by varying the herbs used to flavor it.

1½ pounds haddock fillets, cut into 2" strips	basil, thyme, savory, marjoram, rosemary
3 cups soft fresh bread, diced and pushed down in cup (about 7 slices)	2 cans (10¾ ounces each) cream of mushroom soup
1 medium onion, minced	½ cup milk
Pinch of salt	¾ cup cracker crumbs
Pinch(es) of one herb or combination of herbs: sweet	2 tablespoons butter, cut into small pieces

Lay half the fish on bottom of greased 9" × 13" casserole. Mix bread crumbs with onion, salt, and a pinch or so of herbs. Top fish layer with half this stuffing. Mix 1 can soup with ¼ cup milk and pour over stuffing. Repeat layers, ending with second can of soup mixed with remaining ¼ cup milk. Cover with cracker crumbs and dot with butter. Bake uncovered at 350°F for 1 hour. *Serves 8.*

Doris Seal, The United Church, Northfield, Vermont

Fabulous Flounder Fillets

Absolutely fantastic!

6 large flounder fillets (about 2 pounds)	6 slices tomato
½ teaspoon salt	12 slices (approximately 4" × 4") Gruyère or Swiss cheese

Sprinkle fillets on both sides with salt, then roll each up. In 9" × 13" greased baking dish, place flounder roll, beside it a tomato slice, and next to that a pair of cheese slices. Begin next row with tomato slice, then cheese, then flounder roll, and start third row with cheese, then flounder, and then tomato. Continue to make total of 6 rows. After all ingredients are used up, there should be a diagonal pattern in the way the flounder, tomato, and cheese line up. Preheat oven to 400°F.

Sauce

1 can (4 ounces) sliced mushrooms	¼ cup minced parsley + ¾ cup snipped parsley
2 medium onions, sliced	
2 tablespoons butter	1 cup light cream
1½ tablespoons flour	6 tablespoons sherry
1½ teaspoons salt	1½ cups uncooked long-grain rice

Drain mushrooms, reserving liquid. In 2-quart saucepan, sauté mushrooms and onion in butter until golden. Stir in flour, salt, and minced parsley, then add cream, reserved mushroom liquid combined with enough water to make ½ cup, and sherry. Stir until all is well-mixed. Bring to boil. Pour over fish, tomato, and cheese. Bake 15–20 minutes, or until fillets are golden and easily flaked with fork but still moist.

Meanwhile, cook rice. Stir snipped parsley into cooked rice. When fish is done, spoon rice along sides of dish. *Serves 6.*

Don Wyant, Woodmont Congregational Church, Milford, Connecticut

Shrimp and Rice Casserole

The dill makes the difference.

1 cup rice, cooked and drained
½ pound sharp Cheddar cheese, grated
2 cups cooked shrimp
4 eggs, separated
¾ cup milk
¼ teaspoon pepper
¼ teaspoon onion salt
¼ teaspoon dillweed

Mix rice, cheese, and shrimp (reserve about 1 cup cheese for top). Mix egg yolks and milk and combine with shrimp mixture. Season with pepper, onion salt, and dillweed. Beat egg whites until stiff and fold in. Turn into greased 2-quart casserole. Sprinkle reserved cheese on top. Bake at 375°F for 30 minutes. *Serves 8.*

Catherine B. Anderson, United Methodist Church of the Hamptons, Hampton, New Hampshire

Gourmet Shrimp

A good dish if you feel like splurging on shrimp without going to a lot of trouble.

2 pounds shelled, deveined medium shrimp (fresh or frozen)
3 quarts boiling water
1¼ teaspoons salt
1 tablespoon + 1 teaspoon lemon juice
3 tablespoons butter
1 cup chopped onion
1 cup chopped green pepper
1 can (10¾ ounces) cream of mushroom soup
1 cup sour cream
⅓ cup ketchup
1 can (6 ounces) sliced mushrooms, drained
⅛ teaspoon pepper
¼ cup dry white wine

Add shrimp to boiling water seasoned with 1 teaspoon salt and 1 tablespoon lemon juice. Boil 3 minutes. Drain and set aside. Melt butter in large skillet over medium heat. Add onion and green pepper. Sauté until onion is transparent. Add soup, sour cream, ketchup, mushrooms, remaining 1 teaspoon lemon juice, remaining ¼ teaspoon salt, pepper, wine, and cooked shrimp. Reduce heat, stir, and simmer gently for 5 minutes. Serve over hot rice. *Serves 8.*

Lillian Gerlander, Woodmont United Church of Christ, Milford, Connecticut

Spicy Shrimp with Mango-Fennel Salsa

This vibrant appetizer looks as good as it tastes. The recipe can easily be doubled.
If you can't find mango, use sweet ripe peaches instead.

8 ounces shelled, deveined raw
  shrimp
  Salt and pepper
2 tablespoons olive oil
4 garlic cloves, minced
1 fennel bulb, trimmed and diced
6 plum tomatoes, seeded and diced

1 mango, diced
1 cup fresh cilantro, chopped
½ cup fresh basil leaves, coarsely
  chopped
2 tablespoons fresh lime juice
1 tablespoon capers, rinsed and drained
½ teaspoon crushed red pepper

Season shrimp with salt and pepper; set aside for 10 minutes. In wok or large skillet, warm 1 table-spoon oil and garlic over medium heat for 1 minute or until sizzling. Turn heat to high. Add fennel; stir-fry for 1 minute. Add tomatoes and mango, stir-fry for 1 minute or until mixture is hot. Season to taste with salt and pepper. Remove and set aside. Add remaining 1 tablespoon oil to wok or skillet and turn heat to high. Add shrimp and stir-fry for 1½ minutes or just until opaque. Return fennel mixture to wok. Add cilantro, basil, lime juice, capers, and crushed red pepper. *Serves 6–8 as appetizer.*

Amy Chao, Lord's Grace Christian Church, Mountain View, California

Deviled Eggs, Shrimp, and Mushrooms in Cheese Sauce

Serve spooned over toast, English muffins, biscuits, noodles, or rice,
depending on what meal you are serving—breakfast, brunch, lunch, or supper.

6 hard-boiled eggs
3 tablespoons mayonnaise
  Pinch of dry mustard
  Dash of Tabasco Sauce

Dash of Worcestershire sauce
Salt and pepper
1 cup cooked, drained shrimp
1 cup sliced, cooked, drained mushrooms

Cut shelled eggs in halves and remove yolks. Mix yolks with mayonnaise, mustard, Tabasco Sauce, Worcestershire sauce, and salt and pepper to taste. Refill whites with mixture and place in buttered 1-quart casserole dish, along with shrimp and mushrooms.

Cheese Sauce

2 tablespoons butter
2 tablespoons flour
1 cup milk

½ cup cheese, diced
Salt and pepper

Melt butter over low heat and gradually blend in flour. Cook gently for a minute or so, then add milk a little at a time, stirring constantly throughout. When sauce has thickened, add cheese and salt and pepper to taste, continuing to stir until cheese is melted.

Pour Cheese Sauce over eggs, shrimp, and mushrooms and bake at 350°F until thoroughly heated and bubbling, about 10–15 minutes. *Serves 6.*

Shrimp and Blue Cheese Casserole

Mrs. Miller contributed a number of recipes that rated "superb." This one is an incredible combination of ingredients that really works. Very subtle and delicious taste. Try it!

1 pound cooked shrimp, or 1 can (12 ounces) rinsed and drained
1 can (16 ounces) cream-style corn

½ cup thinly sliced celery
1 green onion, sliced
1½ tablespoons melted butter

Combine shrimp and corn in greased 2-quart casserole. Sauté celery and onion in butter until tender. Add to shrimp.

Sauce

2 tablespoons butter
2½ tablespoons flour
1 cup milk

½ teaspoon salt
⅛ teaspoon pepper
3 ounces American blue cheese

Melt butter and blend in flour. Gradually add milk, stirring constantly, until thickened. Stir in salt, pepper, and blue cheese. Cook until cheese is melted. Pour over corn and shrimp and bake at 375°F for 30–40 minutes. Serve with rice or noodles. *Serves 6.*

Jeannette M. Miller, Morris Congregational Church, Morris, Connecticut

Sesame Scallops and Salmon with Cucumber

Use an English or "hothouse" cucumber for this recipe. This long, slender cucumber tends to have fewer seeds and be less bitter than regular cucumbers.

1 pound jumbo scallops
1 tablespoon soy sauce
2 teaspoons toasted sesame oil
½ teaspoon salt
1 tablespoon rice wine or white wine

1 teaspoon pepper
1 pound salmon fillet
3 tablespoons vegetable oil
1 English cucumber, thinly sliced
Rice wine vinegar (optional)

Cut scallops in half horizontally through middle. In shallow dish, combine soy sauce, sesame oil, and ¼ teaspoon salt. Add scallops; toss to coat. Marinate 30 minutes. In another shallow dish, combine wine, pepper, and remaining ¼ teaspoon salt. Add salmon; toss to coat. Marinate 30 minutes.

Place salmon on baking sheet. Broil 6" from heat source for about 6 minutes or until cooked. Meanwhile, heat vegetable oil in large skillet over high heat. Place scallops in single layer in pan. Fry about 1½ minutes each side or until golden. Arrange salmon in center of platter. Surround with scallops. Arrange cucumber slices in ring around outside; sprinkle lightly with vinegar, if using. *Serves 12–16 as appetizer.*

Lisa Chen, Allentown Chinese Christian Church, Wescosville, Pennsylvania

Salmon Mousse with Cucumber Sauce

A cool summer entrée that can also be made with water-pack tuna,
½ cup chopped celery, and ¼ cup chopped green pepper for variety.

1 tablespoon plain gelatin	2 teaspoons dillweed
2 tablespoons lemon juice	1 teaspoon grated horseradish
1 small onion	(optional)
½ cup boiling water	Dash of Tabasco Sauce
½ cup mayonnaise	1 can (16 ounces) salmon
¼ teaspoon paprika	1 cup sour cream

Empty gelatin into blender and soak for 3–5 minutes in a little cold water. Add lemon juice, onion, and water, and cover blender. Blend 40 seconds. Then add mayonnaise, paprika, dillweed, horseradish, if using, Tabasco Sauce, and salmon, and blend again. Add sour cream and blend once more. Pour into oiled mold and refrigerate until firm. Unmold on lettuce and serve with separate bowl of Cucumber Sauce. *Serves 8.*

Cucumber Sauce

½ cup heavy cream	Dash of pepper
2 tablespoons vinegar	1 cucumber, peeled, chopped,
¼ teaspoon salt	and drained

Beat cream until thick but not stiff. Add vinegar gradually while beating. Season with salt and pepper and fold in cucumber.

Baptist Women's Fellowship, New London, New Hampshire

Crispy Tuna Balls
with Spicy Cheddar Dip

Easy to prepare, these seafood starters are deliciously
different from the usual chips and dip.

1 can (6 ounces) tuna packed in
water, drained and flaked
½ cup plain dry bread crumbs
3 tablespoons mayonnaise
2 tablespoons minced onion
2 tablespoons minced parsley or
cilantro

1 egg, beaten
2 teaspoons dry mustard
¼ teaspoon Tabasco sauce
3 tablespoons butter, melted
¾ cup corn flakes, crushed

In mixing bowl, combine tuna, bread crumbs, mayonnaise, onion, parsley or cilantro, egg, mustard, and Tabasco sauce. Stir to combine. Shape into balls, about 2 teaspoons each. One at a time, use one hand to dip balls in butter and other hand to roll balls in corn flakes to coat. Place 1" apart on ungreased baking sheet. Bake at 450°F for 8–10 minutes or until hot and crispy. Serve with Spicy Cheddar Dip (see below).

Spicy Cheddar Dip

1 can (10¾ ounces) Cheddar or
Pepper-Jack cheese soup

¼ cup salsa, mild or hot

In bowl, combine soup and salsa. For warm dip, use a microwaveable bowl and heat in microwave until warm, about 30 seconds. ***Serves 6 (3 tuna balls per serving).***

Melinda Ingalls, Gay Street United Methodist Church, Mount Vernon, Ohio

Meatballs with Sweet and Sour Sauce, page 14

Snowtime Beef Casserole, page 17

Arcadian Shepherd's Pie, page 22

Cannelloni, page 26

Ham and Chicken Luncheon Dish, page 35

California Oven–Fried Chicken, page 61

Chicken Pie with Crust, page 63

Chicken Marengo, page 73

Paella Valenciana, page 75

Three-Cheese Deviled Eggs, page 83

Kedgeree, page 90

Flounder Crowns with Florentine Stuffing, page 92

Baked Beans, page 118

Pennsylvania Dutch Green Beans, page 121

Carrot Casserole, page 124

Autumn Leaves, page 133

Vegetable Sides and Casseroles

Most cooks spend the majority of time in the kitchen fixing an entrée of meat, poultry, or fish, and allow only a few minutes for the vegetables. But some of the vegetable casseroles in this chapter are interesting enough in their own right to consider building a meal around.

Baked Apple and Carrot Casserole

A perfect companion for baked beans, ham, or pork.

6 apples, cored, peeled, and
  thinly sliced
2 cups cooked carrot slices
⅓ cup brown sugar

2 tablespoons flour
Salt
¾ cup orange juice

Place half the apples in greased 2-quart baking dish and cover with half the carrots. Mix brown sugar, flour, and salt to taste, and sprinkle half the mixture over carrots. Repeat layers and pour orange juice over top. Bake at 350°F for 45 minutes. *Serves 6.*

Alma L. Hedrick, Harwinton Congregational Church, Harwinton, Connecticut

Baked Beans

Some require an onion in their baked beans; to others, this is heresy.
Include it or not, as you will, in this fine recipe.

1 pound dry navy or pea beans
6 cups water
½ pound salt pork, cut into
  ½" dice
1 small onion, peeled

⅓ cup molasses
¼ cup sugar
1 teaspoon dry mustard
¼ teaspoon pepper

Soak beans overnight in water. Place beans with soaking water in large kettle (add water to cover if necessary). Bring to boil; lower heat and simmer until beans are tender. Drain, reserving liquid. Place salt pork, onion, and beans in 2-quart bean pot or casserole. Combine molasses, sugar, mustard, pepper, and 1 cup of reserved bean liquid. Pour over beans. Stir thoroughly. Add just enough bean liquid to cover beans. Cover pot or casserole and bake at 300°F for 2 hours. Add liquid if necessary and stir. Continue baking 1½–2 hours longer, or until beans are tender. Bake uncovered for last half-hour. *Serves 8.*

Mary Nichol, First Presbyterian Church, Monroe, New York

Grace Manney's Baked Beans

Both Grace and her recipe are well-known at the Mendon Community Church.

1 **pound yellow-eye beans**	1 **teaspoon dry mustard**
1 **cup sugar**	⅓ **pound salt pork, thinly sliced**
1 **teaspoon salt**	

Soak beans overnight. Leave in soaking water and add sugar, salt, and mustard. Add water as necessary to cover beans. Cook until beans are tender. Turn into bean pot or Dutch oven, arranging salt pork slices on top. Cover and bake at 275°F for 6–8 hours, adding water from time to time when dry. *Serves 6–8.*

Ruth French, Mendon Community Church, Mendon, Vermont

Black Beans and Rice

Use any of this interesting dish left over to make a super soup.

1 **pound black beans, washed and dried**	2 **teaspoons salt**
6 **cups water**	¼ **teaspoon pepper**
1 **cup chopped onion**	1 **smoked ham bone (optional)**
1 **green pepper**	1 **slice bacon, minced**
1 **clove garlic**	¼ **cup wine vinegar**
½ **cup olive oil**	**Cooked rice**
2 **bay leaves**	1 **hard-boiled egg, sliced**
	Raw onion rings

Cover beans with water. Bring to boil, and boil 2 minutes. Cover. Let stand 1 hour. Sauté onion, green pepper, and garlic in olive oil for 5 minutes. Add to beans with bay leaves, salt, pepper, ham bone, if using, and bacon. Bring to boil and simmer, covered, for 2 hours. Add water if necessary. Add wine vinegar. Before serving, remove and discard bay leaves. Serve with hot cooked rice. Garnish with hard-boiled egg slices and onion rings. *Serves 8.*

Beth Bartlett, Concord Unitarian Church, Concord, New Hampshire

Stewed Green Beans

Beans in a minty tomato sauce.

2 pounds fresh green beans
½ cup olive oil
2 cans (6 ounces each) tomato
  paste
1 large onion, chopped

2 teaspoons minced fresh mint
  leaves, or ½ teaspoon (heaping)
  dried mint
1 teaspoon garlic powder
  Salt and pepper

Sauté beans in oil until bright green and tender. Stir in tomato paste, onion, mint, garlic powder, and salt and pepper to taste. Add enough water to cover beans. Simmer until cooked to preference. *Serves 8.*

Kathleen Adams, Park Street Baptist Church, Pittsfield, New Hampshire

Harvard Beets

Make with either canned or freshly cooked beets. If you use canned, reserve the liquid to use instead of the water below; if you use fresh, add the beets to the sauce immediately after slicing. Tangy and colorful.

2 tablespoons cornstarch
2 tablespoons sugar
1½ teaspoons salt
  Pinch of pepper

⅔ cup water
½ cup vinegar
2 cups sliced beets

In saucepan, mix together cornstarch, sugar, salt, pepper, water, and vinegar. Heat and cook, stirring, until mixture thickens and boils gently. Continue to cook, still stirring, for 1 minute more. Stir in beets, heat thoroughly, and serve. (Good cold, too.) *Serves 6.*

Edna W. Warner, Foxon Congregational Church, East Haven, Connecticut

Pennsylvania Dutch Green Beans

A fine way to renew interest in overabundant green beans from the garden.

1 pound fresh green beans, cut into short lengths and cooked, or 2 packages (10 ounces each) frozen cut green beans, cooked, or 2 cans (16 ounces each) cut string beans
6 slices bacon

2 medium onions, chopped
4 teaspoons cornstarch
1 teaspoon salt
½ teaspoon dry mustard
2 tablespoons brown sugar
2 tablespoons vinegar

Drain beans and reserve 1 cup water fresh or frozen beans were cooked in, or ½ cup liquid from can. Set aside. Fry bacon until crisp and drain on paper towel. Sauté onions in bacon fat until golden. In small bowl, mix cornstarch, salt, mustard, brown sugar, and vinegar. Add reserved liquid from beans and beat until smooth. Then add this mixture to bacon fat in pan and boil until thickened slightly. Add string beans and stir well. Crush bacon and sprinkle bacon bits on top of casserole. *Serves 8.*

Jeannette M. Miller, Morris Congregational Church, Morris, Connecticut

Orangey Beets

Similar to Harvard Beets, but uses orange juice instead of vinegar.

1½ tablespoons butter
⅓ cup brown sugar
1½ teaspoons cornstarch
⅔ cup orange juice

2 tablespoons grated orange rind
3 cups diced, cooked beets, or canned, drained
4 shakes each salt and pepper

Melt butter. Mix brown sugar and cornstarch. Stir into butter. Add orange juice gradually and cook, stirring constantly, until thickened. Blend in 1 tablespoon orange rind and beets. Shake salt and pepper and remaining 1 tablespoon orange rind over all. *Serves 8.*

Mary Wakefield, First Congregational Church, Rindge, New Hampshire

John Russell's Mushroom-Rice Casserole

This homey, baked side dish pairs well with chicken, ham,
roast beef, and other church supper mainstays.

½ cup butter or margarine

1½ cups chopped green onions,
white and light green parts

8 ounces fresh mushrooms, sliced

2 cups uncooked medium or long
grain rice

2 cans (14½ ounces each) beef
broth

2 cups water

1 teaspoon salt

1 teaspoon pepper
Paprika or minced parsley

In large skillet, melt butter or margarine over medium-high heat. Add green onions and sauté for 5 minutes or until softened. Add mushrooms and sauté for 5 minutes or until mushrooms are browned and no liquid remains. Stir in rice and cook until rice is lightly browned. Stir in broth, water, salt, and pepper; pour into greased 9" × 13" baking dish. Cover tightly with aluminum foil. Bake at 350°F for 50 minutes. Check rice doneness by carefully lifting foil away from you to avoid steam. If needed, re-cover and bake 10 more minutes or until rice is very tender. Sprinkle with paprika or parsley. *Makes 10–12 servings.*

Nancy Eichler, Roswell Presbyterian Church, Roswell, Georgia

Broccoli Casserole

Serve as a main dish, or halve to serve 8 as a side dish.

2 packages (10 ounces each)
frozen broccoli

1 can (10¾ ounces) cream of
mushroom soup

1 cup mayonnaise

2 eggs, beaten

1 cup grated sharp cheese
Pepper

4 tablespoons chopped onion
Crushed Ritz crackers for
topping

4 tablespoons butter

Cook broccoli for 5 minutes in boiling salted water. Drain well. Combine soup, mayonnaise, eggs, cheese, pepper to taste, and onion. Mix well. Add broccoli and turn into greased 2-quart baking dish. Sprinkle with crushed Ritz crackers and dot with butter. Bake at 350°F for 30 minutes, or until it bubbles and browns. *Serves 8.*

Kate Barnes, St. Paul's Episcopal Church, Fort Fairfield, Maine

Broccoli and Cheese Casserole

An unusual casserole that's a little like a soufflé, but not as fluffy.

3 eggs
1 cup cottage cheese
½ cup Cheddar cheese
3 tablespoons flour

2 teaspoons salt
Dash of pepper
2 packages (10 ounces each)
  frozen broccoli

Beat eggs, then add cottage cheese, Cheddar, flour, salt, and pepper. Beat well together. Cook broccoli as directed and drain well. Add to egg mixture. Pour into greased baking dish and bake at 350°F for 30–35 minutes. *Serves 6–8.*

Betty Fainelli, Harwinton Congregational Church, Harwinton, Connecticut

Stuffed Broccoli

Creamed broccoli with crunch and crumbs.

2 packages (10 ounces each)
  frozen chopped broccoli
4 tablespoons butter

¼ cup flour
2 chicken bouillon cubes
2 cups milk

Cook broccoli according to package directions. Drain and set aside. Melt butter. Add flour and mix. Add bouillon cubes and milk. Cook until sauce thickens. Grease 2-quart baking dish and place broccoli in it. Pour sauce over.

Topping

2 cups seasoned stuffing mix
6 tablespoons butter

⅔ cup water
⅔ cup chopped walnuts

Combine stuffing mix with butter, water, and walnuts. Place on top of sauce, and bake at 350°F for 20–30 minutes. *Serves 6–8.*

Lina Storrs, Center Congregational Church, Torrington, Connecticut

Carrot Casserole

Carrots enlivened with onion and horseradish. Fix ahead and heat when ready.

2 **bunches (2 pounds) carrots**	1 **teaspoon salt**
4 **tablespoons grated onion**	¼ **teaspoon pepper**
1½ **teaspoons horseradish**	1 **cup dry bread crumbs**
½ **cup mayonnaise**	½ **cup melted butter**

Scrape, dice, and boil carrots in salted water until crisply done. Drain, reserving ½ cup liquid. Place carrots in greased 2-quart casserole. In small bowl, mix reserved carrot liquid, onion, horseradish, mayonnaise, salt, and pepper. Pour over carrots. Top with bread crumbs and pour melted butter over all. Bake at 375°F about 20 minutes, or until slightly brown and bubbly. *Serves 6.*

Shirley T. Oladell, Harwinton Congregational Church, Harwinton, Connecticut

Carrots Excelsior

Colorful and custardy.

2½ **cups carrots, cooked, mashed, and seasoned with salt and pepper**	1 **cup bread crumbs**
	1 **tablespoon finely chopped onion**
2 **egg yolks, beaten**	2 **egg whites**
1½ **cups milk**	

Combine carrots, egg yolks, milk, bread crumbs, and onion. Beat egg whites until stiff, and fold lightly into carrot mixture. Turn into buttered 1½-quart casserole. Bake at 350°F for 45–60 minutes, or until knife inserted comes out clean. Serve hot. *Serves 6–8.*

Mrs. Albert G. Clark, United Church of Christ, Keene, New Hampshire

Far East Celery

Delicious served with steak or chicken.

4 cups celery, cut into 1" pieces
1 can (5 ounces) water chestnuts, drained and sliced
1 can (10¾ ounces) cream of chicken soup
1 small jar pimiento, drained and chopped
2 tablespoons butter
½ cup slivered almonds
½ cup bread crumbs

Cook celery in small amount of boiling salted water for about 8 minutes. Drain. In buttered 1-quart casserole, mix celery, water chestnuts, soup, and pimiento.

Melt butter in skillet and lightly brown almonds. Add bread crumbs and sprinkle mixture over casserole. Bake at 350°F for 35 minutes. *Serves 6.*

Eggplant Casserole

For a different note at a potluck supper.

½ of 10¾-ounce can golden mushroom soup
½ cup mayonnaise
1 egg, beaten
1 tablespoon grated onion
1 cup shredded cheese
1 medium eggplant, peeled, diced, and cooked in boiling salted water for 10–15 minutes
¾ cup crushed Ritz crackers (about 15 crackers)
1 tablespoon butter

Mix soup, mayonnaise, egg, onion, and cheese with eggplant. Place in greased 1½-quart casserole and cover with cracker crumbs. Dot with butter. Bake at 350°F for 25 minutes. *Serves 6.*

Betty C. Rollins, The Congregational Church, Atkinson, New Hampshire

Corn-Zucchini Bake

A nice combination. Also try topped with tomato sauce.

3–4 medium zucchini (1 pound)
¼ cup chopped onion
2 tablespoons melted butter
2 eggs, beaten
2 tablespoons flour
1 package (10 ounces) frozen whole-kernel corn, or 2 cups fresh corn cut from cob, cooked and drained
1 cup (4 ounces) shredded Swiss cheese

¼ teaspoon salt
¼ cup fine dry bread crumbs
1 teaspoon oregano or Italian seasoning (optional)
2 tablespoons grated Parmesan cheese
Tomato halves
Parsley

Wash zucchini; do not pare. Slice about 1" thick. Cook, covered, in small amount of boiling salted water until tender (15–20 minutes). Drain and mash with fork. Sauté onion in 1 tablespoon butter until tender. Combine eggs, flour, mashed zucchini, onion, corn, Swiss cheese, and salt. Turn into greased 1-quart casserole or 7" × 7" baking dish. Combine bread crumbs, oregano or Italian seasoning, if using, and Parmesan cheese with remaining 1 tablespoon melted butter. Sprinkle over corn mixture. Place on baking sheet. Bake at 350°F for 40 minutes if using 1-quart casserole, or for 25–30 minutes if using square baking dish—or until knife inserted comes out clean. Let stand 5–10 minutes before serving. Garnish with tomato halves and parsley. *Serves 6.*

Mrs. L. Bouchard, St. Paul's Church, Lancaster, New Hampshire

Eggplant Italiano

Cheese-filled battered eggplant rolls with a tomato-saucy flair.

Filling

1 cup grated mozzarella cheese
½ cup grated Parmesan cheese
⅓ cup cottage or ricotta cheese
½ teaspoon salt

¼ teaspoon pepper
½ teaspoon basil or oregano
1 tablespoon chopped parsley

Batter

1 egg
2 tablespoons flour

⅓ cup milk
1 tablespoon cooking oil

Other

2 small eggplants
¼ cup cooking oil
2 tablespoons butter

Flour
2 cans (6 ounces each) tomato
sauce

Combine mozzarella, Parmesan, cottage cheese or ricotta, egg, salt, pepper, basil or oregano, and parsley. Make smooth paste and chill. For batter, combine egg, flour, milk, and oil, and beat until smooth. Peel eggplants and cut lengthwise into thin slices. Heat oil and butter to 360°F. Dip eggplant slices in flour, then in batter, and sauté in hot oil until browned on both sides. Drain on paper towels. Place 2 tablespoons chilled filling mixture on each slice and roll loosely, placing seam-side down in buttered 9" × 13" baking dish. Cover with tomato sauce. Bake at 375°F for 15 minutes. *Serves 8.*

Margaret Michaelsen, The Congregational Church, North Bennington, Vermont

Scalloped Sweet Spanish Onions

Onions and cheese in a lovely crumb-topped custard.
Prepare a day ahead and bake when convenient.

¼ cup butter + 2 tablespoons
   butter, melted
3 medium Spanish onions, sliced
¼ cup chopped green pepper
2 tablespoons chopped pimiento
1 cup grated Swiss cheese

1 cup cracker crumbs
2 eggs, beaten
¾ cup light cream
1 teaspoon salt
⅛ teaspoon white pepper

Melt ¼ cup butter in skillet. Add onions and green pepper and cook until tender. Stir in pimiento. Place half of mixture in shallow greased baking dish. Sprinkle with ½ cup Swiss cheese and ½ cup cracker crumbs. Repeat layers of onions and cheese. Beat eggs with cream, salt, and pepper. Pour over onions in baking dish. Combine remaining ½ cup cracker crumbs with remaining 2 tablespoons melted butter. Sprinkle over top. Bake at 325°F for 25 minutes, or until set. Serve hot. *Serves 6–8.*

Mrs. Albert G. Clark, United Church of Christ, Keene, New Hampshire

Onion Pie

A marvelously hearty treat for onion fans. Serve with a fresh green salad.

Crust

6 tablespoons butter
1¼ cups flour

½ teaspoon salt
2–4 tablespoons ice water

Crumble butter into flour and mix with salt. Add ice water as necessary to form into ball. Spread pastry directly into 9" greased pie tin, pressing lightly into place with your fingers.

Filling

8 cups sliced onions
4 tablespoons butter
1 tablespoon cooking oil

Salt, pepper, and nutmeg
3 egg yolks, beaten until thick
½ cup heavy cream

Sauté onions in butter and oil in heavy frying pan. Cook, covered, over medium-low heat until onions are quite soft and pale gold (about 30 minutes). Stir occasionally to prevent sticking. Season to taste with salt, pepper, and nutmeg. Stir in egg yolks and cream. Pour into pastry shell and bake at 400°F for 30 minutes. *Serves 6–8.*

Moira Burnham, Church of the Epiphany, New York, New York

Savory Onion Kuchen

¾ cup warm water
1 package dry yeast
2 teaspoons sugar
1 teaspoon salt
4 tablespoons butter, softened
2¼ cups flour

3 cups sliced onions
1 egg
¼ cup sour cream
Sesame, caraway, celery, or dill seed

Measure warm water into large warmed bowl. Sprinkle in yeast and stir until dissolved. Stir in sugar, ½ teaspoon salt, and 1 tablespoon soft butter. Add 1 cup flour and beat until smooth. Then beat in enough additional flour to make a soft dough. Turn dough onto lightly floured board and knead until smooth (about 5 minutes). Place dough in greased bowl, turning to grease surface evenly. Cover and let rise in warm place for about 30 minutes.

Sauté onions in remaining 3 tablespoons butter. Cool. Beat egg with sour cream and remaining ½ teaspoon salt until smooth. Add cooled onions.

Punch down dough. Place in greased 9" × 13" pan. Pat out dough to cover bottom and 1" up sides of pan. Spread onion mixture on dough and sprinkle with your chosen seasoning seeds. Let rise in warm place for 20 minutes. Bake at 375°F for 45 minutes, or until crust is golden brown. Cool slightly on rack before cutting and serving. *Serves 6.*

Baked Potatoes Élégant

So much easier to eat in company than plain baked potatoes.

6 medium baking potatoes*
½ cup sour cream
1 package (3 ounces) cream
   cheese, softened
2 tablespoons milk

3 tablespoons butter, softened
1 teaspoon onion salt
   Salt and pepper
2 tablespoons chopped pimiento
   (optional)

Bake potatoes at 375°F until done. Cut slice from top of each and scoop out insides. Mash and mix with sour cream, cream cheese, milk, butter, onion salt, and salt and pepper to taste. Beat until smooth and fluffy. Stir in pimiento, if using. Fill potato shells. Return to oven and bake 15 minutes, or until potatoes are heated through. For variety, try topping stuffed potatoes with crumbled crisp bacon, chives, shredded cheese, or sour cream. **Serves 6.**

Barbara Lockhart, United Church of Christ, Keene, New Hampshire

*Do not use russets, or the filling will be gluey.

Spinach Rockefeller

A light and zesty dish to please all spinach lovers. Serve with sliced chicken or ham.

2 packages (10 ounces each)
   frozen chopped spinach
2 eggs, separated
½ cup melted butter
¾ cup cracker or bread crumbs
¼ cup grated onion

⅛ teaspoon thyme
½ teaspoon garlic powder
2 dashes of Tabasco Sauce
½ teaspoon salt
¼ teaspoon pepper
¼ cup Parmesan cheese

Cook spinach and drain well. Beat egg yolks and mix into spinach. Combine butter, crumbs, onion, thyme, garlic powder, Tabasco Sauce, salt, pepper, and Parmesan. Mix into spinach. Beat egg whites until stiff, and fold into spinach mixture. Pour into greased 2-quart casserole. Bake at 350°F for 30 minutes. *Serves 6.*

Betsy High, United Methodist Church of the Hamptons, Hampton, New Hampshire

Soft Clouds

A potato dish that lives up to its name.

6 medium potatoes, peeled, boiled, and drained	¼ cup grated Romano cheese
2 eggs, beaten	1 tablespoon parsley
4 tablespoons butter	½ teaspoon garlic salt
½ cup grated Velveeta cheese	Salt and pepper

In mixing bowl, combine potatoes, eggs, butter, Velveeta, Romano, parsley, garlic salt, and salt and pepper to taste. Whip with electric mixer until smooth. Transfer to greased 1½-quart baking dish. Bake at 350°F for 30 minutes. *Serves 6–8.*

Grace P. Van Etten, St. Mary's Church, Marlboro, New York

Spinach Squares

This easy semi-quiche is good served either as a vegetable dish
or with cheese sauce as a main course.

4 tablespoons butter
3 eggs
1 cup flour
1 cup milk
1 teaspoon salt
1 teaspoon baking powder

1 pound mild Cheddar cheese,
   grated
2 packages (10 ounces each)
   frozen spinach, thawed,
   drained, and chopped

Melt butter in 9" × 13" baking dish in 350°F oven and remove. In large bowl, beat eggs well. Add flour, milk, salt, and baking powder. Mix well. Add cheese and spinach. Mix well. Spoon into baking dish and level. Bake at 350°F for 35 minutes, or until top is slightly browned. Take out, cool for 45 minutes, and cut into squares. (This freezes well. After thawing, reheat at 325°F for approximately 12 minutes.) *Serves 8.*

Kathleen Adams, Park Street Baptist Church, Pittsfield, New Hampshire

Summer Delight

A happy choice for supper during that late-summer glut of garden squash.

6 cups (2 pounds) diced young
   summer squash
¼ cup chopped onion
1 can (10¾ ounces) cream of
   chicken soup
1 cup sour cream

1 cup shredded carrots
2 cups prepared stuffing mix
   (cornmeal is best)
¼ pound butter, melted
   Chopped parsley

Cook squash and onion in boiling water for 5 minutes. Drain. Combine soup, sour cream, and carrots. Gently fold in squash and onion. Combine stuffing mix with melted butter. Put ⅔ of stuffing mixture into greased 2-quart casserole, spoon in squash mixture, and top with rest of stuffing. Bake at 350°F for 25 minutes. Sprinkle with parsley. *Serves 6–8.*

Evelyn I. Johnson, Our Savior Lutheran Church, Hanover, New Hampshire

Autumn Leaves

This colorful casserole brings to mind the bright reds and yellows of fall.

2 cups diced summer squash	½ cup cream
1 cup finely chopped onion	1 teaspoon basil
6 medium tomatoes, skinned and cut up	1 tablespoon parsley
	Black pepper
6 tablespoons butter	4 cups cooked rice
¼ cup flour	¼ cup Parmesan cheese
2 cups chicken broth	

Sauté squash, onion, and tomatoes in 2 tablespoons butter until tender. Melt remaining 4 tablespoons butter in saucepan. Blend in flour. Gradually add chicken broth, stirring until thickened. Stir in cream, basil, and parsley. Season to taste with pepper. Mix vegetables with rice and sauce. Turn into buttered 2-quart casserole. Sprinkle with Parmesan cheese. Bake at 350°F until bubbling and heated through. *Serves 6–8.*

E. M. Charlton, St. Matthew's Church, Bedford, New York

Squash and Hominy Dish

Filling enough for the entrée; fine as a vegetable, too.

2 pounds zucchini or summer squash
1 large onion, chopped
4 tablespoons butter
½ cup water
2 cans (16 ounces each) hominy, drained

2 jalapeño peppers, seeded and chopped (wear plastic gloves when handling)
1½ cups sour cream
1 teaspoon salt
2 cups grated sharp cheese
Crushed corn chips for topping

Combine zucchini or squash, onion, butter, and water in skillet, and cook slowly until tender. Add hominy, peppers, sour cream, salt, and 1 cup cheese. Pour into greased 3-quart casserole, top with remaining 1 cup cheese, and sprinkle with crushed corn chips. Bake at 325°F for 1 hour. *Serves 8.*

Phyllis Shattuck, All Saints Episcopal Church, Pasadena, California

Tomato-Corn Rarebit

Tasty and easily transportable.

2 teaspoons chopped onion
1½ tablespoons butter
3 tablespoons flour
1 cup canned tomatoes
1 cup drained canned corn

½ teaspoon salt
1 package (8 ounces) processed cheese, shredded
6–8 slices toast or double-size saltines

Sauté onion in butter until onion is soft. Blend in flour; add tomatoes (with juice), corn, and salt. Cook slowly for 10 minutes. Add cheese and cook over low heat, stirring often, until cheese melts completely. (Too high heat will curdle it.) Serve on saltine crackers or toast points. *Serves 6.*

Mrs. Albert G. Clark, United Church of Christ, Keene, New Hampshire

Tomato-Cheese Crunch

Great with garden-ripe tomatoes.

6 medium tomatoes, peeled	1 cup grated Cheddar cheese
½ cup thinly sliced onion	2 cups crushed potato chips

Slice tomatoes ½" thick. Arrange half of slices in bottom of greased 2-quart casserole. Spread half the onion and half the cheese over tomatoes, ending with half the chips. Repeat layers, ending with remaining chips. Bake at 350°F for 30 minutes. ***Serves 6.***

Jean Cole, Concord Unitarian Church, Concord, New Hampshire

Mixed Vegetable Casserole

Vegetables in a mildly mustardy cream sauce.
Make with your own combinations of leftover vegetables, too.

1 package (10 ounces) frozen peas	⅓ cup flour
1 package (10 ounces) frozen lima beans	3 cups milk
1 cup chopped celery	1½ teaspoons salt
1 cup pared and sliced carrots	½ teaspoon paprika
⅓ cup + 2 tablespoons butter	½ teaspoon dry mustard
	1½ cups cracker crumbs

Cook frozen vegetables in one pot and celery and carrots in another, until almost tender. Drain and reserve. Melt ⅓ cup butter in saucepan. Add flour and blend; then, stirring constantly, gradually add milk and stir until thickened. Add salt, paprika, and dry mustard. Melt remaining 2 tablespoons butter and mix with crumbs in bowl. Turn vegetables into 2-quart buttered baking dish. Pour white sauce over and top with buttered crumbs. Bake at 375°F for 20 minutes, or until bubbling around edges. ***Serves 6.***

Mrs. Henry Delay, Harwinton Congregational Church, Harwinton, Connecticut

Vegetable Cobbler

Tasty and filling as a meatless but balanced meal.

4 cups cooked mixed vegetables
(limas, peas, string beans, corn,
and/or carrots)
1½ cups stock
1 teaspoon oregano, dillweed, or
thyme
½ teaspoon pepper

1½ cups whole wheat flour
2 teaspoons baking powder
1 teaspoon salt
½ cup cornmeal
2 eggs, beaten
1 cup milk or broth
¼–½ cup grated sharp cheese

Grease 9" × 13" dish. Heat vegetables in stock, and pour all into greased dish. Stir together oregano, dillweed, or thyme; pepper; flour; baking powder; salt; and cornmeal. Add eggs and milk or broth, and mix until well-distributed. Spread batter over vegetables. Bake at 425°F for 20–25 minutes. Immediately after removing from oven, sprinkle with grated cheese. *Serves 8–10.*

Stephanie Gross, Episcopal Church of St. John Baptist, Thomaston, Maine

Mixed Vegetables Italienne

Companionable contrasts. No need to peel young zucchini.

¼ cup salad oil
1 can (16 ounces) tomatoes
1 beef bouillon cube
4 cups zucchini, cut into
1" cubes (about 1¼ pounds)
1½ cups green pepper cut into
1" pieces (about ½ pound)
1 cup sliced carrots

1 cup peeled, diced potatoes
1 cup coarsely chopped onion
1 teaspoon oregano
1½ teaspoons salt
⅛ teaspoon pepper
1 cup frozen peas
½ teaspoon cornstarch, mixed
into 1 teaspoon water

In saucepan, combine oil, tomatoes (with juice), bouillon cube, zucchini, green pepper, carrots, potatoes, onion, oregano, salt, and pepper. Cover and bring to boil. Reduce heat and simmer. After 15 minutes, add frozen peas. Continue to simmer, covered, until vegetables are tender. Thicken with cornstarch. *Serves 6.*

Mary Nichol, First Presbyterian Church, Monroe, New York

Roasted Herbed Vegetables

Oven cooking caramelizes the natural sugars of root vegetables
and deepens their flavors. If the seasoning mix herbes de Provence is not available,
substitute one teaspoon each of thyme, sage, and rosemary.

3 cups 1" cubed carrots	2 tablespoons coarsely chopped
3 cups 1" cubed turnips	garlic (optional)
3 cups 1" cubed red potatoes	1 tablespoon herbes de Provence
2 large sweet onions, each cut	1 teaspoon salt
into 8 wedges	1 teaspoon pepper
⅓ cup olive oil	¼ cup minced parsley

Place carrots, turnips, potatoes, onion, oil, garlic (if using), herbes de Provence, salt, and pepper in 11" × 15" (5-quart) lasagna dish. Toss to coat vegetables with oil and seasonings. Roast at 375°F for about 1 hour, turning vegetables occasionally. If vegetables are browning too quickly, occasionally add 2 tablespoons hot water to pan.

Remove when vegetables are well browned and tender. Add parsley and toss. *Serves 8–10.*

T. L. C. Vegetable Casserole

Tomatoes, Limas, and Celery make a fine cold-weather supper.

1 cup dry lima beans	2 cups canned tomatoes
2 cups diced celery	Salt and pepper
½ cup minced green pepper	1 tablespoon butter
4 medium onions, sliced	2 slices bacon

Wash and soak beans overnight in cold water. In morning, add water as needed to cover, and simmer until tender or until bean skins shrivel when blown upon. Drain off water. Add celery, green pepper, onions, tomatoes (with juice), and salt and pepper to taste. Dot with butter. Place in greased 2-quart casserole. Top with bacon slices. Bake at 350°F for about 1 hour, or until bacon is crisp and vegetables are cooked. *Serves 6.*

Mrs. Albert Marcks, St. Mary's Church, Marlboro, New York

7-Minute Zucchini

A rapidly made and out-of-the-ordinary zucchini dish.

6 cups zucchini, peeled and coarsely grated (about 2 pounds)	¼ cup butter
	¼ cup chopped onions
	1 minced clove garlic
1 teaspoon salt	½ cup sour cream
½ pound sliced mushrooms, or 1 can (4 ounces), drained	1 tablespoon minced fresh basil, or 1 teaspoon dried basil

Combine zucchini and salt in strainer and let stand. Heat mushrooms in skillet, shaking over high heat until liquid evaporates. Add butter, onions, and garlic to mushrooms and sauté. Squeeze excess liquid from zucchini. Add to mushroom mixture and stir. Heat 5 minutes. Stir in sour cream and basil. Heat through, but do not boil. *Serves 6.*

Virginia Ritter Mesics, The United Church of Jaffrey, Jaffrey, New Hampshire

Italian Zucchini Casserole

Another reason to rejoice over a bountiful zucchini crop.

2½ pounds zucchini, thinly sliced
½ cup chopped onion
½ cup chopped green pepper
4 tablespoons butter
1 can (3 ounces) sliced mushrooms
1 package dry spaghetti sauce mix

1 cup water
1 can (6 ounces) tomato paste
4 ounces shredded mozzarella cheese
2 tablespoons grated Parmesan cheese

Cook zucchini in boiling salted water for 4–5 minutes. Drain. Sauté onion and green pepper in butter until tender. Remove from heat and add mushrooms, sauce mix, water, tomato paste, and mozzarella. Gently stir in zucchini. Transfer to greased 7" × 11" baking dish, and sprinkle with Parmesan cheese. Bake at 350°F for 30–35 minutes. *Serves 8.*

Evelyn Shaw, Pilgrim Congregational Church, New Haven, Connecticut

Lemon-Spinach Rice

Makes a wonderful partner to Rosemary Lamb Stew (page 49).

1½ cups uncooked long-grain rice
3 cups water
1 teaspoon salt
3 eggs, lightly beaten
1 package (10 ounces) frozen chopped spinach, cooked and drained

¾ cup grated Parmesan or Cheddar cheese
¼ teaspoon pepper
2 tablespoons parsley
2½ tablespoons lemon juice

Cook rice by simmering, covered, in boiling salted water until all water is absorbed. Stir spinach and salt into cooked rice. In a 2-quart casserole, mix egg with cheese, pepper, parsley, and lemon juice. Add rice mixture and mix well. Bake at 350°F for 30 minutes. *Serves 6.*

Spanish Rice

Smooth, creamy rice heated up with peppers. Olé!

1 cup chopped onions
¼ cup butter
4 cups freshly cooked rice
2 cups sour cream
1 cup creamed cottage cheese
1 large bay leaf, crumbled
½ teaspoon salt

½ teaspoon pepper
1 can (12 ounces) Tuscan
   peppers, or 2 cans (4 ounces
   each) chilies, chopped
2 cups grated sharp cheese
   Parsley

Sauté onions in butter. Stir in rice, sour cream, cottage cheese, bay leaf, salt, and pepper. In 2-quart crockery casserole or 9" × 13" baking pan, layer half the rice, the Tuscan peppers or chilies, and 1 cup grated cheese. Again layer remainder of rice and top with remaining 1 cup cheese and parsley. Bake in preheated 375°F oven for 25 minutes, or until hot and bubbly. *Serves 8.*

Catherine P. Newell, Concord Unitarian Church, Concord, New Hampshire

Spanish Rice II

A more traditional version.

3 slices bacon
1 cup uncooked long-grain rice
2 cups water
1 teaspoon salt
½ cup chopped onion
½ cup chopped celery

⅓ cup chopped green pepper
1 can (16 ounces) tomatoes
1 teaspoon sugar
1 teaspoon chili powder
½ teaspoon Worcestershire sauce
½ cup grated Cheddar cheese

Cook bacon until crisp and crumble. Reserve bacon fat. Set aside. Combine rice, water, and salt. Bring to boil. Stir briefly and reduce heat. Cover tightly and simmer until all liquid is absorbed—about 14 minutes. Sauté onion, celery, and green pepper in reserved bacon fat until tender. Add cooked rice, tomatoes (with juice), sugar, chili powder, Worcestershire sauce, and bacon bits. Transfer to greased casserole. Top with grated cheese. Bake at 350°F for about 20 minutes, or until bubbly. *Serves 6.*

Dorothy Freitag, Our Savior Lutheran Church, Hanover, New Hampshire

Soups and Salads

Nothing comforts the soul like a steaming bowl of soup. Three supremely satisfying ones are included here. If it's a heartier stew you're after, see the recipes in Beef (page 1); Ham, Pork, and Lamb (page 34); and Chicken and Turkey (page 51).

When it comes to salads, there are two schools of thought. One considers fruit with or without gelatin, marshmallows, or other sweet additions to be salads. The other believes that salads are vegetable rather than fruit. Period. To please both sides, this chapter includes both vegetable salads and fruit salads. No matter what side you take, you'll certainly find good things to eat.

French Onion Soup

An old favorite.

8 onions, thinly sliced
4 tablespoons butter
9 cups water
8 beef bouillon cubes

2 cups flavored croutons,
   or 8 slices toasted bread (any
   kind), crust trimmed
Sliced or grated Muenster or
   Swiss cheese

Sauté onions in butter until golden. Boil water and add bouillon cubes. Add onions and simmer for 1½ hours on top of stove. Just before serving time, pour soup into individual crocks or bowls, sprinkle in croutons or lay toasted bread on top of soup, and cover with cheese (any desired amount). Place crocks or bowls on cookie sheet. Heat at 350°F for 3–5 minutes, or put under broiler for 1–2 minutes—until cheese is melted. *Serves 8.*

Mark and Janet Dodge, Sacred Heart Church, Monroe, New York

Thick Spiced Lentil Soup

Hearty and lively.

½ pound dry lentils
5–6 cups water
2 onions, chopped
1 bay leaf
2 cloves garlic
1 can (8 ounces) tomato sauce

1 teaspoon pickling spice (tied up
   in cheesecloth bag)
¼ cup vinegar
¼ cup olive oil
Salt and pepper

Pick over and wash lentils. Add water to cover, onions, bay leaf, garlic, tomato sauce, pickling spice, vinegar, oil, and salt and pepper to taste. Simmer until lentils are cooked. Before serving, remove and discard bay leaf and pickling spice. *Serves 6–8.*

Virginia Colivos, Greek Orthodox Church of the Annunciation, Dover, New Hampshire

Sausage Chowder

A three-in-one dish: soup, stew, and chowder.

½ pound bulk sausage	¾ teaspoon salt
1½ cups cooked kidney beans	¼ teaspoon garlic salt
1½ cups canned tomatoes	¼ teaspoon thyme
2 cups water	¼ teaspoon pepper
1 small onion, chopped	½ cup diced potatoes
1 bay leaf	¼ cup chopped green pepper

Cook sausage in skillet until brown. Pour off fat. In large kettle, combine beans, tomatoes (with juice), water, onion, bay leaf, salt, garlic salt, thyme, and pepper. Simmer 1 hour covered. Add potatoes and green pepper. Cook until tender. Before serving, remove and discard bay leaf. *Serves 6.*

Bev McKeone, Center Congregational Church, Torrington, Connecticut

Bean Salad

A three-bean salad that can become four with chickpeas.

1 can (16 ounces) kidney beans, drained	1 can (16 ounces) chickpeas, drained (optional)
1 can (16 ounces) yellow string beans, drained	¾ cup sugar
1 can (16 ounces) green string beans, drained	½ cup vinegar
	½ cup salad oil

Combine kidney beans, string beans, and chickpeas, if using, in bowl. In saucepan, boil together sugar and vinegar for 10 minutes. Add salad oil and pour over vegetables. Let sit overnight in refrigerator. (Other vegetables may be added as desired, such as onions, peppers, and olives.) *Serves 12–16.*

Anne Gove, Concord Unitarian Church, Concord, New Hampshire

Molded Beet Salad

Colorful and handsome, with just enough "bite."

3 cups shredded canned or
  cooked beets
½ cup sugar
½ cup vinegar
2 tablespoons plain gelatin

½ cup cold water
1½ teaspoons salt
1½ cups finely chopped celery
2 tablespoons grated horseradish
1 tablespoon grated onion

Drain beets, reserving 1½ cups juice. Combine beets, sugar, and vinegar. Chill for 1 hour. Dissolve gelatin in water. Heat reserved beet juice and salt to boiling. Remove from heat and add gelatin. Stir until incorporated. Cool until syrupy. Add beets, celery, horseradish, and onion to gelatin mixture. Mix well. Pour into oiled 1½-quart mold. Chill until firm. Unmold on bed of lettuce or watercress. *Serves 8.*

Women's Association of The Congregational Church, Amherst, New Hampshire

Copper Pennies

A fitting name for a tasty carrot salad.

2 pounds carrots, pared and cut
  into round slices
1 green pepper, seeded and
  chopped

1 onion, chopped
½ cup chopped celery

Dressing

1 can (10¾ ounces) tomato soup
½ cup salad oil
¾ cup sugar
¾ cup vinegar

1 teaspoon Worcestershire sauce
1 teaspoon prepared mustard
  Salt and pepper

Boil carrot slices in salted water until almost tender. Drain and combine with green pepper, onion, and celery. Mix well together soup, oil, sugar, vinegar, Worcestershire sauce, mustard, and salt and pepper to taste. Pour over vegetables and refrigerate until well-chilled. Will keep in refrigerator a week or more. *Serves 8–10.*

Regina Stanhope, Our Savior Lutheran Church, Hanover, New Hampshire

Greek Cabbage Salad

Not a cole slaw, but just as refreshing.

1 medium head cabbage, shredded	½ pound feta cheese, crumbled
1–2 cloves garlic, crushed	Salt and pepper
2–3 teaspoons dillweed	¼–⅓ cup olive oil

Toss cabbage, garlic, dillweed, and feta. Season to taste with salt and pepper. Add enough oil just to coat ingredients (to make it look dressed but not soupy). Chill several hours. *Serves 6–8.*

Susan Cronewett, Our Savior Lutheran Church, Hanover, New Hampshire

Turkish Eggplant Salad

A real conversation piece and change of pace.

1 good-size eggplant
¼ cup olive oil
⅔ cup feta cheese, crumbled
Lemon juice

Salt and pepper
Parsley
Ripe black olives

Bake eggplant at 400°F until soft and skin crumbles. Peel, remove seeds, cool, and dice. Whip eggplant in blender with oil to make smooth paste. Add feta and lemon juice to taste and mix well. Season to taste with salt and pepper and spread mixture on flat serving dish (lined with lettuce or watercress, if desired). Garnish with parsley and olives. *Serves 6–8.*

Belkis H. Vassaf, Concord Unitarian Church, Concord, New Hampshire

24-Hour Layered Salad

A delightful mix of vegetables, cheese, and bacon.

1 head lettuce, torn into bite-size
pieces
1 head cauliflower, broken into
florets
¼ cup sliced green onions
and tips
1 package (10 ounces) frozen
peas, thawed

1 small sweet red pepper,
chopped
2 cups mayonnaise
2 tablespoons sugar
1 cup shredded Cheddar cheese
8 slices bacon, cooked and
crumbled

In large bowl, layer ingredients in order given; *do not mix.* Tightly cover bowl with plastic wrap or lid. Refrigerate overnight. Toss before serving. *Serves 8–10.*

Lina Storrs, Center Congregational Church, Torrington, Connecticut

Marinated Vegetable Salad

Use these vegetables or experiment with your own combinations.

½ cup salad oil
½ cup vinegar
½ cup sugar
2 cups whole cooked green beans
1 cup sliced cooked carrots

1 cup sliced celery
1 cup green pepper, sliced or cut into strips
1 medium Spanish onion, sliced

Prepare dressing of oil, vinegar, and sugar mixed together. Mix green beans, carrots, celery, green pepper, and onion into dressing and keep pressed down with plate on top. Refrigerate overnight. Drain well before serving. *Serves 8–10.*

Susan Cronewett, Our Savior Lutheran Church, Hanover, New Hampshire

Asian Wilted Greens Salad

A useful salad to serve with an Asian entrée.

3 cups torn lettuce
3 cups torn fresh spinach
1 cup bias-sliced celery
2 medium tomatoes, cut into wedges
¾ cup chopped green pepper
½ cup sliced radishes
⅓ cup sliced green onion

1 envelope (6 ounces) Italian salad dressing mix
⅓ cup salad oil
¼ cup vinegar
4 teaspoons sugar
½ teaspoon salt
1 can (16 ounces) Chinese chop suey vegetables, drained

In large salad bowl, combine lettuce, spinach, celery, tomatoes, green pepper, radishes, and onion. In saucepan, combine salad dressing mix, oil, vinegar, sugar, salt, and Chinese vegetables. Heat to boiling and pour over salad mixture. Toss gently to coat. Serve at once. *Serves 8.*

Betsy High, United Methodist Church of the Hamptons, Hampton, New Hampshire

Mixed Salad

A luncheon salad with plenty of protein.

1 small head lettuce	1½ cups cooked chicken or tuna
2 medium tomatoes, skinned	½ cup Cheddar cheese
1 small cucumber, pared	2 tablespoons chopped onion
2 hard-boiled eggs	1 cup garlic dressing
¼ pound crisp cooked bacon	

Rip lettuce leaves into small pieces and place in large salad bowl. Finely chop tomatoes, cucumber, eggs, bacon, chicken or tuna, and cheese. Arrange each in row across lettuce, ending with onion. Pour dressing over salad and toss lightly. *Serves 6.*

Carol Jensen, United Church of Hardwick, Hardwick, Vermont

Sauerkraut Salad

Most people feel strongly about sauerkraut . . . either you *love* it or you *hate* it. Here's a recipe for those who love it.

1¼ cups sugar	1 cup diced celery
½ cup salad oil	1 onion, chopped
½ cup vinegar	1 cup diced green
1 can (16 ounces) sauerkraut, drained, rinsed, and snipped	pepper

Mix sugar, oil, and vinegar. Pour over sauerkraut, celery, onion, and green pepper in bowl. Mix and let stand several hours or overnight in refrigerator. Drain before serving. *Serves 8–10.*

Joanna Miller, Dublin Community Church, Dublin, New Hampshire

Green Pea Salad

Serve as is or on lettuce.

2 packages (10 ounces each) frozen peas, defrosted
1 cup celery, finely cut
½ cup scallions, finely cut
1 pound bacon, cooked and crumbled
1 cup sour cream
Salt

Combine peas, celery, scallions, bacon, sour cream, and salt to taste. Chill thoroughly. *Serves 8.*

Catherine B. Anderson, United Methodist Church of the Hamptons, Hampton, New Hampshire

Super Salad Sandwich

Also good served on lettuce without bread and garnished with slices of lemon or avocado.

1 can (6½ ounces) tuna, drained and flaked
1 cup cottage cheese
2 chopped hard-cooked eggs
1 large tomato, chopped and drained
½ cup shredded natural Cheddar cheese
1 teaspoon lemon-pepper
marinade, or 1 teaspoon garlic salt + dash of lemon juice
¼ cup chopped celery
2 green onions, sliced
⅓ cup mayonnaise
¼ teaspoon salt
16 slices whole grain bread, toasted and buttered
½ cup fresh alfalfa sprouts

Mix together tuna, cottage cheese, eggs, tomato, Cheddar, marinade or garlic mixture, celery, onions, mayonnaise, and salt. Chill. Spread mixture on 8 slices of toast, then top with sprouts and remaining toasted slices. *Serves 8.*

Evelyn H. Chase, Concord Unitarian Church, Concord, New Hampshire

Salad Excelsior

Served for lunch with a creamy Italian, Caesar, or other cheesy dressing and hot garlic bread, this is a complete meal. Augment, if you wish, with soup and dessert.

1 pound fresh spinach
1 head garden lettuce
4 hard-boiled eggs, quartered
4 tomatoes, skinned and sliced
1 can (8½ ounces) artichoke
  hearts, drained
1 cup cooked (or canned, rinsed,
  and drained) medium shrimp

1 cup creamy Italian or Caesar
  dressing
½ pound bacon, cooked crisp and
  crumbled
1 cup toasted and buttered
  croutons

Wash spinach and garden lettuce leaves. Drain. Remove thick stems from spinach and tear into pieces. Tear garden lettuce into pieces. Put in clean towel or towels and refrigerate to crisp. Line large bowl with mixture of crisped lettuce and spinach. Add eggs, tomatoes, artichoke hearts, and shrimp. Toss with dressing, mixing well to coat all ingredients. Sprinkle bacon and croutons over top. *Serves 8.*

Spinach Salad

To ensure crisp spinach, wrap washed and stemmed leaves in a clean towel and refrigerate for at least an hour before using in salad.

1 pound fresh spinach
2 hard-boiled eggs, chopped
½ of 5-ounce can water
  chestnuts, sliced thin

5 strips bacon, cooked and
  crumbled

Dressing

½ cup sugar
1 cup salad oil
⅓ cup ketchup
½ cup vinegar

2 tablespoons Worcestershire
    sauce
1 medium onion, grated

Wash, drain, and remove hard stems on spinach. Combine spinach with eggs, water chestnuts, and bacon. Mix together sugar, oil, ketchup, vinegar, Worcestershire sauce, and onion and pour over spinach. Toss and serve. *Serves 6.*

Jean Cole, Concord Unitarian Church, Concord, New Hampshire

Golden Potato Salad

A cold potato salad with a creamy mayonnaise dressing.

6 cups peeled, diced, and boiled
    potatoes
½ cup diced cucumber
½ cup chopped onion
2 tablespoons chopped chives
⅔ cup mayonnaise

⅓ cup yogurt
2 tablespoons cider vinegar
1 tablespoon prepared mustard
1½ teaspoons salt
¼ teaspoon pepper
    Paprika

Combine potatoes, cucumber, onion, and chives in large bowl. Blend mayonnaise, yogurt, vinegar, mustard, salt, and pepper in small bowl. Pour over potato mixture and blend thoroughly. Refrigerate several hours. Sprinkle with paprika before serving. *Serves 6–8.*

Carol Jensen, United Church of Hardwick, Hardwick, Vermont

Main Dish Potato Salad

This salad recipe, over 50 years old and handed down from the Bedford Men's Club (now disbanded), is now served at the Unity Club Harvest Supper every October to 450–600 people. Here, it is cut down to serve 8.

2 pounds potatoes, peeled
3 stalks celery, chopped
1 pound rump veal (or lean pork)
1 large onion, grated

1 pimiento, diced
Salt and pepper
1 cup whipped salad dressing
1 head lettuce

Cook potatoes, cool, and dice. Mix in celery. Cook veal, cool, and dice. Add onion and pimiento with veal to potatoes. Season to taste with salt and pepper, then mix with salad dressing and serve on bed of lettuce. *Serves 8.*

Bedford Presbyterian Church, Bedford, New Hampshire

Hot Potato Salad

Made with onion and hard-boiled eggs.

6 medium potatoes, chopped
2 hard-boiled eggs, chopped
4 slices bacon, diced
¼ cup minced onion

1 egg, beaten
¼ cup cider vinegar
1¾ teaspoons salt

Cook potatoes. Add chopped eggs. Fry bacon and onion until delicate brown. Strain, reserving bacon fat. Add fat slowly to beaten egg and beat well. Add vinegar and salt and pour mixture over potatoes. Mix lightly to blend well; heat in double boiler. Serve hot. *Serves 6.*

Mary Kay Royer, Center Congregational Church, Torrington, Connecticut

Spaghetti Salad

Essentially a "potato" salad—but with pasta!

1 package (8 ounces) thin
  spaghetti
4 hard-boiled eggs
1 green pepper, finely cut
1 stalk celery, finely cut
1 teaspoon finely grated or
  minced onion

Salt and pepper
½ of 5-ounce jar green olives,
  finely cut, and a few slices for
  top of salad
½ cup whipped salad dressing
  (*not* mayonnaise)

Cook spaghetti, drain, and rinse with cold water. Drain again. Add eggs, green pepper, celery, onion, salt and pepper to taste, olives, and salad dressing. Mix thoroughly. Chill in refrigerator for a few hours before serving to allow flavors to blend. Top with remaining olive slices. ***Serves 6–8.***

Mrs. Albert G. Clark, United Church of Christ, Keene, New Hampshire

Hot German Potato Salad

"A New Year's tradition from my mother-in-law's family," featuring chicory.

14 medium potatoes, peeled and
  cut into large chunks
⅓ pound bacon, cut with kitchen
  shears into ¼" squares
¼ cup bacon fat

¼ cup cider vinegar
¼ cup water
2 cups snipped chicory
2 tablespoons sugar
  Salt and pepper

Boil potatoes until slightly firmer than required for mashing. Fry bacon pieces over medium-low heat until crisp (reserve ¼ cup fat). Mix vinegar and water. As soon as potatoes are done, drain, dump into large bowl, and immediately add chicory, bacon pieces, vinegar and water, hot bacon fat, and sugar. Toss well and season to taste with salt and pepper. ***Serves 8.***

Mary Wakefield, First Congregational Church, Rindge, New Hampshire

Danish Potato Salad

A cooked dressing without mayonnaise over a cold salad
with hard-boiled eggs and radishes.

¼ cup vinegar

¼ cup water

¼ cup sugar

¼ teaspoon salt

Dash of pepper

1 teaspoon prepared mustard

2 eggs, well-beaten

1 cup whipped salad dressing

4 cups peeled, cooked, diced potatoes

2 hard-boiled eggs, chopped

½ cup chopped cucumbers

1 tablespoon minced onion

1 tablespoon chopped green pepper

3–4 diced or sliced radishes

Combine vinegar, water, sugar, salt, pepper, and mustard in saucepan. Bring to boil. Reduce heat and gradually beat in eggs. Cook, stirring constantly, until slightly thickened. Remove from stove and beat in salad dressing. Toss together potatoes, hard-boiled eggs, cucumbers, onion, green pepper, and radishes. Pour dressing on potato mixture and toss gently. Adjust seasonings if necessary. Refrigerate for several hours. *Serves 6–8.*

Beatrice Benjamin, The United Church, East Calais, Vermont

Everlasting Cole Slaw

1 head cabbage

1 small onion, finely chopped

2 carrots, grated

2 stalks celery, diced

1 cup chopped black olives
(optional)

1 sweet pepper, diced

½ cup sugar

⅔ cup vinegar

1 cup salad oil

1 teaspoon mustard

1 teaspoon celery seed

1 tablespoon salt

Finely shred cabbage. Add onion, carrots, celery, olives, if using, and pepper. Add sugar and turn into 11" × 15" pan. Mix vinegar, oil, mustard, celery seed, and salt in saucepan. Bring to boil. Pour hot liquid over vegetables. Mix well, cover, and refrigerate. *Serves 8–10.*

Naomi Crook, Chocorua Community Church, Chocorua, New Hampshire

Cabbage Slaw

1 cup mayonnaise
½ cup milk
½ cup seedless raisins
½ cup drained crushed pineapple

1 medium dark green cabbage, shredded
1 red apple, or 3 red and 3 green cherries

In large mixing bowl, combine mayonnaise and milk to make thick dressing. Stir in raisins and pineapple. Add cabbage and mix well. Cut apple into wedges, leaving skin on. In decorative design, place apple wedges or cherries on cabbage. *Serves 8–10.*

Flora C. Hammond, Unitarian Universalist Church, Keene, New Hampshire

Dill Dip

1 cup mayonnaise
2 teaspoons dill seed
1 cup plain yogurt

1 tablespoon minced green onion
2 teaspoons salt

Beat together mayonnaise, dill seed, yogurt, onion, and salt until well-blended. *About 2 cups.*

Carolyn Ramsbotham, St. Thomas More Church, Durham, New Hampshire

3 Weeks Cole Slaw

3 pounds white cabbage, chopped
1 green pepper, chopped
  (optional)
2 white onions, chopped
1½–2 cups sugar

1 cup salad oil
1 cup cider vinegar
1 teaspoon celery seed
2 teaspoons salt

Combine cabbage, green pepper, if using, onions, and sugar. Mix well. Mix oil, vinegar, celery seed, and salt and bring to hard boil. Pour over cabbage mixture and stir very well. Store in refrigerator in airtight container. Let stand at least 3 days as flavor improves as it ages. Will keep refrigerated for a month. *Serves 10.*

Pauline Hammond, Free Will Baptist Church, Northwood, New Hampshire

Chili Dip

Use this dip with a crudité, or raw vegetable, platter. Arrange broccoli or cauliflower florets, slivered peeled carrots, celery ribs, quartered tomatoes, sliced cucumber, cut fresh green beans, cut-up green pepper, turnip strips, radishes, or mushroom slices on a large plate or platter with a bowl of dip in the center or on the side. Do the same with the recipe for Dill Dip (page 133).

1 cup mayonnaise or sour cream
2 tablespoons grated onion
2 teaspoons vinegar
2 teaspoons chives (dried or fresh)
2 teaspoons chili sauce

½ teaspoon curry powder
½ teaspoon salt
¼ teaspoon red-pepper flakes,
  crushed
½ teaspoon thyme

Combine mayonnaise or sour cream, onion, vinegar, chives, chili sauce, curry powder, salt, red-pepper flakes, and thyme. *About 1¼ cups.*

Janet Dodge, Sacred Heart Church, Monroe, New York

Astoria Salad

A fruit salad, but not sweet, except for the apples.

4 large red apples, cored and cut up into small pieces but left unpeeled
2 stalks celery, finely chopped

½ cup chopped walnuts
½ cup cubed cheese
½ cup raisins

Dressing

¼ cup yogurt
¼ cup mayonnaise

¼ cup sour cream

Combine apples, celery, walnuts, cheese, and raisins in bowl. Mix well together yogurt, mayonnaise, and sour cream and add to salad. Toss and serve on lettuce. *Serves 6.*

Carolyn Myrick, Temple Congregational Church, Temple, New Hampshire

Cranberry Salad

A can of whole-berry cranberry sauce can be used in this recipe, but then omit the sugar.

2 packages (3 ounces each) lemon gelatin
2 cups boiling water
1 cup sugar
2 cups ground fresh cranberries

1 cup drained crushed pineapple
1 cup finely diced celery
½ cup chopped nuts (any kind)
1 cup orange juice

Soak gelatin in a little bit of cold water for 3–5 minutes, then dissolve gelatin in boiling water. Add sugar and stir until sugar is dissolved. Add cranberries, pineapple, celery, nuts, and orange juice. Refrigerate until partially congealed. Stir and return to refrigerator until set. Serve on lettuce. *Serves 10–12.*

Jeannette M. Miller, Morris Congregational Church, Morris, Connecticut

Christmas Fruit Salad

Adds a colorful note to a holiday table setting.

1½ pounds red grapes, seeded and halved

1 can (8½ ounces) pineapple chunks

4 oranges, peeled, seeded, and cut up small

½ cup sugar

Dressing

1 tablespoon butter

1 tablespoon flour

½ cup sugar

¼ teaspoon dry mustard

1 egg, beaten

¼ teaspoon pepper

¼ cup vinegar

2 tablespoons water

1 cup cream, whipped

Combine grapes, pineapple (with juice), oranges, and sugar and let stand overnight in refrigerator. Meanwhile, melt butter in top of double boiler and add flour. Add sugar, mustard, egg, pepper, vinegar, and water. Cook, stirring, until smooth and thickened. Cool and refrigerate overnight. Drain juice from fruit in morning. Add whipped cream to dressing. Mix dressing and fruit, and serve on lettuce or as fruit cup. *Serves 6–8.*

Rosamond Wehrwein, Swanzey Congregational Church, Swanzey, New Hampshire

Blueberry Salad

A nifty idea for a fruit salad.

2 packages (3 ounces each) black raspberry gelatin

2 cups boiling water

1 can (20 ounces) crushed pineapple

1 can (16 ounces) blueberries, or 1½ cups fresh blueberries + ½ cup water

Topping

8 ounces soft cream cheese

8 ounces sour cream

½ cup sugar

1 teaspoon vanilla

½ cup chopped walnuts

Soak gelatin in a little bit of cold water for 3–5 minutes, then mix gelatin and boiling water and stir until gelatin is dissolved. Add pineapple (with juice) and canned blueberries (with juice) or fresh berries and water. Pour into 9" × 13" pan and chill until congealed. Cream together cream cheese, sour cream, sugar, and vanilla, and spread over gelatin. Sprinkle with chopped walnuts. Refrigerate. *Serves 8–10.*

Marcia Fletcher, St. Anne's Episcopal Church, Calais, Maine

Foam Over the Sea

An apt name for a pretty gelatin salad. The dressing is important to the dish.

1 package (3 ounces) lime gelatin

1 cup boiling water

1 cup pear juice (drained from canned pears)

½ teaspoon vinegar

½ teaspoon ground ginger, or 1 teaspoon chopped crystalline ginger

1 package (3 ounces) cream cheese, softened

2 cups drained and diced canned pears

2 tablespoons honey

1 cup mayonnaise

Soak gelatin in a little bit of cold water for 3–5 minutes, then dissolve gelatin in boiling water and add pear juice and vinegar. Pour half of gelatin into flat 6" × 10" glass dish and refrigerate until set. Cool remaining gelatin until syrupy and whip. Work ginger and cream cheese into gelatin as you whip. Fold in pears. Spread mixture over gelatin that has set in refrigerator. Chill. To make dressing, whip together honey and mayonnaise. Serve salad with lettuce and dressing. *Serves 6.*

Carolyn Buck, Wapping Community Church, South Windsor, Connecticut

5-Cup Salad

Vary this by using other fruits by the cupful as well—
apple wedges, banana slices, grapes, or whatever is in season.

1 cup drained crushed pineapple
1 cup grated coconut
1 cup drained mandarin oranges

1 cup miniature marshmallows
1 cup sour cream

In a large bowl, mix together pineapple, coconut, oranges, marshamallows, and sour cream. Let stand overnight. Serve on lettuce. ***Serves 6–8.***

Shirley T. Oladell, Harwinton Congregational Church, Harwinton, Connecticut

Spicy Peach Salad

Peachy keen. Serve on lettuce with cottage cheese or yogurt.

1 package (3 ounces) peach
   gelatin
¼ cup sugar
¼ teaspoon cinnamon
⅛ teaspoon cloves
1 cup boiling water

¾ cup peach syrup (drained from
   canned peaches)
2 tablespoons vinegar
1 can (16 ounces) sliced peaches,
   drained

Soak gelatin in a little bit of cold water for 3–5 minutes. Mix sugar, cinnamon, cloves, and gelatin and dissolve in water. Add peach syrup and vinegar. Chill, stirring occasionally, as spices are apt to settle. When *slightly* thickened, add peaches. Stir and chill until firm. ***Serves 6.***

Gladys Priest, Foxon Congregational Church, East Haven, Connecticut

Strawberry Nut Salad

A great combination of tastes.

2 packages (3 ounces each)
  strawberry gelatin
1 cup boiling water
2 packages (10 ounces each)
  frozen strawberries, thawed

1 cup drained crushed pineapple
3 medium bananas, mashed
1 cup chopped pecans
1 pint sour cream

Soak gelatin in a little bit of cold water for 3–5 minutes, then mix gelatin with boiling water in large bowl. Fold in strawberries, pineapple, bananas, and pecans. Pour half of mixture into 9" × 13" baking dish or metal mold. Refrigerate 1 hour. Spread sour cream over top. Layer balance of mixture on top of sour cream and refrigerate overnight or for several hours. Serve on lettuce or plain. *Serves 12.*

Elnor Hayward, First Baptist Church, Concord, New Hampshire

Jellied Vegetable Salad

Traditional at church suppers. Included in this section
because the vegetables are embedded in sweet gelatin.

1 package (3 ounces) lemon
  gelatin
½ teaspoon salt
1 cup boiling water

1 cup cold water
½ cup shredded cabbage
½ cup shredded carrots
2 tablespoons French dressing

Soak gelatin in a little bit of cold water for 3–5 minutes, then dissolve gelatin and salt in boiling water. Add cold water. Refrigerate until partially jelled. Meanwhile, marinate cabbage and carrots in French dressing for 15 minutes. Add vegetables to gelatin and stir to distribute evenly. Chill until firm. Cut into squares and serve plain or on lettuce. *Serves 6.*

Marcia Fletcher, St. Anne's Episcopal Church, Calais, Maine

Breads and Breadstuffs

This chapter has the most magnificently de-*luscious* ideas for pancakes, doughnuts, muffins, quick breads, yeast breads, coffee cakes, rolls, and biscuits. You won't find these recipes anywhere else. Some are quite surprising inventions—like Squash Biscuits, somewhere between a yeast and quick bread, and so light they are hard to believe; and Deli-Cakes, probably the most airborne pancake alive.

Deli-Cakes

Cooked like pancakes, but the stiffly-beaten egg whites folded in make these cakes unique. Incredibly light and tender, they are a perfect foil for creamed toppings or sweet fruit sauces, and the contributor's own invention.

½ cup flour
1 teaspoon baking powder
½ teaspoon salt
2 large or 3 medium eggs, separated

2 tablespoons melted butter
⅔ cup milk
1 tablespoon sugar or honey (optional)

Combine flour, baking powder, and salt. Beat egg yolks, and add along with butter and milk. If you plan to use as dessert cakes, you may add the sugar or honey. Beat egg whites until stiff. Fold into mixture. Drop in 3"–4" rounds on greased and heated griddle. Brown lightly on both sides over medium heat. Serve warm, topped with hot applesauce flavored with cinnamon and nutmeg, or with hot blueberries. Or serve with creamed mushrooms or ground ham, with sausages, and of course, with maple syrup. Or use to make strawberry shortcake. *Makes about 18 cakes.*

Walter Clement, United Methodist Church, Plymouth, New Hampshire

Bread Crumb Pancakes

Delicate and delicious pancakes that taste very much like French toast. You must use *fresh* bread crumbs.

1½ cups fresh bread crumbs
2 cups buttermilk or soured milk
1 cup flour
1½ teaspoons salt

2 eggs, beaten
1 teaspoon baking soda, dissolved in ¼ cup hot water

Combine bread crumbs, buttermilk or sour milk, flour, salt, and eggs. Mix well. Add baking soda just before frying pancakes. *Serves 6.*

Marcia Fletcher, St. Anne's Episcopal Church, Calais, Maine

Five-Grain Pancakes

2 cups buttermilk
1 cup sour cream
2 eggs
½ teaspoon salt
2 tablespoons sugar
¼ cup bran cereal
1 cup white flour

¼ cup rye flour
¼ cup soy meal flour
¼ cup buckwheat flour
¼ cup cornmeal
2 teaspoons baking soda,
  dissolved in ¼ cup warm water

In large bowl, combine buttermilk, sour cream, eggs, salt, and sugar. Add cereal. Sift flours and cornmeal together and beat into liquid mixture. Stir in baking soda. Cook as any pancake on hot skillet. Skillet is ready for pancakes when drops of cold water shaken onto it jump and bounce rather than just boil. Serve with butter and jam and/or maple syrup. *Makes about 36 pancakes 4" in diameter.*

Lillian Farrar, United Church of Christ, Keene, New Hampshire

Flora's Doughnuts

Even if you've never tried doughnuts before, these are "easy as pie" and scrumptious.

3 cups flour
½ teaspoon salt
3 teaspoons baking powder
½ teaspoon cinnamon

⅔ cup sugar
2 eggs, beaten
2 tablespoons shortening, melted
1 cup milk

Sift together flour, salt, baking powder, and cinnamon. Add sugar and mix to soft dough with eggs, shortening, and milk. Roll out to ½" thickness on well-floured surface. Cut out doughnuts. Fry in 2" hot (360°F) fat until brown on both sides. Drain and serve plain or sprinkled with sugar. For a fancier touch, frost when cool with mixture of maple syrup and confectioners' sugar. *Makes about 24 doughnuts.*

Flora C. Hammond, Unitarian Universalist Church, Keene, New Hampshire

Milk Chocolate Doughnuts

An oldie that's a real goodie.

2 squares unsweetened chocolate
1 cup sugar
1 egg
1 teaspoon baking soda

1 teaspoon baking powder
2–3 cups flour
1 teaspoon salt
1 cup soured milk

Melt chocolate over hot water and mix with sugar in large bowl. Add egg and mix well. Combine baking soda, baking powder, 2 cups flour, and salt, and add alternately with milk to sugar mixture. Add as much of remaining 1 cup of flour as needed to make soft dough. Roll to ½" thickness, cut out, and fry in deep fat (370°F) for total of 3–5 minutes, turning each doughnut as it rises. Roll in granulated sugar when hot and confectioners' sugar when cold. ***Makes 2 dozen.***

Mrs. Almond Hager, United Church of Christ, Keene, New Hampshire

Apple Muffins

A change from blueberry muffins and lighter than doughnuts.

1⅛ cups flour
1¾ teaspoons baking powder
¼ teaspoon salt
¼ teaspoon cinnamon
¼ teaspoon nutmeg
2 tablespoons shortening

¼ cup + 1 tablespoon sugar
1 egg, beaten
½ cup milk
1 cup apples, cored, peeled, and
     finely chopped

Sift flour, baking powder, salt, ⅛ teaspoon cinnamon, and ⅛ teaspoon nutmeg. Cream shortening with ¼ cup sugar. Add egg, then flour mixture, alternating with milk. Fold in apples and fill greased muffin cups two-thirds of the way. Combine remaining 1 tablespoon sugar, ⅛ teaspoon cinnamon, and ⅛ teaspoon nutmeg and sprinkle over tops. Bake at 375°F for 20–25 minutes. ***Makes 10 muffins.***

Ruth Colby, First Congregational Church of Pembroke, Pembroke, New Hampshire

Potato Doughnuts

Such a wonderful texture.

3 eggs
¾ cup sugar
3 tablespoons soft butter
⅓ cup milk
2¾ cups flour
4 teaspoons baking powder
1 teaspoon salt

½ teaspoon nutmeg
1 teaspoon mace
½ teaspoon cinnamon
1 cup plain mashed potatoes
 (containing no milk, butter, or
 seasonings)

Beat eggs well. Beat in sugar and butter. Stir in milk, flour, baking powder, salt, nutmeg, mace, and cinnamon, and beat in until smooth. Add potatoes and blend well. Chill 2–3 hours. Turn out about a third of the dough at a time onto a lightly floured board. Dust sparingly with flour. Roll out to ⅓" thickness and cut with floured cutter. Fry in deep fat or oil (375°F). As doughnuts rise, turn them. Cook 2–3 minutes total until light golden brown. Lift out and drain on paper toweling. Dust with sugar or cinnamon sugar. ***Makes about 3 dozen.***

Mary Wakefield, First Congregational Church, Rindge, New Hampshire

Corn Muffins

A real honey of a corn muffin.

¼ cup oil
1¼ cups milk
1 egg
¼ cup honey

1 cup yellow cornmeal
3 teaspoons baking powder
½ teaspoon salt
1¼ cups sifted flour

Blend oil, milk, egg, and honey into cornmeal, baking powder, salt, and flour. Do not overmix. Bake in greased muffin pans at 425°F for 20–25 minutes. ***Makes 12 large muffins.***

Carol Jensen, The United Church of Hardwick, Hardwick, Vermont

Blueberry Muffins

Blueberries can be fresh, frozen, or canned (drain canned blueberries before using), but of course right off the bush is best!

3 tablespoons butter, melted	1 tablespoon baking powder
3½ tablespoons sugar	½ teaspoon salt
1 egg, beaten	1 cup milk
2 cups flour	1 cup blueberries

Combine butter, sugar, and egg. Sift together flour, baking powder, and salt. Add alternately to egg mixture with milk. Beat until batter is full of bubbles. Stir in blueberries. Fill greased muffin tins three-quarters of the way and bake at 350°F for about 30 minutes. *Makes 12 muffins.*

Mildred D. Chamberlain, The Congregational Church, South Hero, Vermont

Apple Bread

A nice change from banana bread—good for showers and bake sales— or after school with milk!

4 cups flour	1 cup cooking oil
2 teaspoons baking soda	¼ cup sour cream
2 teaspoons cinnamon	2 teaspoons vanilla
1 teaspoon salt	2 cups chopped apples
2 cups sugar	1 cup chopped nuts (any kind)
4 eggs, beaten	

Sift flour and baking soda, cinnamon, and salt. Combine sugar with eggs, oil, sour cream, and vanilla. Beat well. Blend in flour mixture. Fold in apples and nuts and pour into 2 greased and floured loaf pans. Bake at 350°F for 1 hour, or until done. *Makes 2 loaves.*

Caroline Hunt, First Baptist Church, Hudson, New Hampshire

Patty's Pumpkin Muffins

Just as good without the raisins.

1 cup raisins	¾ teaspoon cinnamon
½ cup hot water	½ teaspoon salt
2 eggs	⅓ cup cooking oil
1 cup solid-pack canned pumpkin	1¾ cups flour
1¼ cups sugar	1½ teaspoons baking powder
¾ teaspoon cloves	½ teaspoon baking soda

Soak raisins in water for 5 minutes. Do not drain. In large mixing bowl, beat eggs; stir in pumpkin, sugar, cloves, cinnamon, and salt. Add oil, mixing well. Stir together flour, baking powder, and baking soda. Add to pumpkin mixture with half the raisin-water mixture. Mix well. Add remaining raisin mixture. Stir well. Fill greased muffin pans two-thirds of the way. Bake at 400°F for about 25 minutes. *Makes 12 large or 16 medium muffins.*

Gladys Priest, Foxon Congregational Church, East Haven, Connecticut

Beer Bread

Slices better when cool but is delicious hot from the oven. Especially good toasted.

4 cups flour	¼ cup sugar
2 tablespoons baking powder	1 can (12 ounces) beer
2 teaspoons salt	1 egg, slightly beaten

Mix flour, baking powder, and salt with sugar. Add beer and egg both at once and stir. You may have to knead last of flour in with hands. Place in greased 9" × 5" loaf pan and bake at 375°F until done—about 1 hour and 10 minutes. Remove from pan immediately and cool. *Makes 1 loaf.*

Dianne Johnson, Dublin Community Church, Dublin, New Hampshire

Blueberry Bread

We think perhaps it's the molasses that makes this so good—but does not darken it.

2 cups flour
¼ cup sugar
½ teaspoon baking soda
½ teaspoon salt
¼ cup molasses

1 cup soured milk or yogurt
2 tablespoons butter, melted
1 egg, beaten
1 cup blueberries

Sift together flour, sugar, baking soda, and salt. Combine molasses, sour milk or yogurt, butter, and egg and mix well. Stir in dry ingredients and beat to blend. Fold in blueberries. Turn into greased 9" × 9" pan and bake at 350°F for 40 minutes. *Serves 9.*

Blueberry-Pineapple Loaf

An attractive loaf for breakfast or tea. Good toasted, too, with butter or cream cheese.
Tastes more blueberry than pineapple.

¾ cup sugar
1 egg
2 tablespoons melted butter
¾ cup pineapple juice
2 cups flour

½ teaspoon salt
2 teaspoons baking powder
½ cup drained crushed pineapple
½ cup fresh or frozen blueberries
½ cup nuts (any kind)

Combine sugar and egg; cream with butter. Add pineapple juice. Combine flour, salt, and baking powder, and add to sugar mixture. Then stir in pineapple, blueberries, and nuts; pour into greased 8" × 4" loaf pan. Bake at 350°F for 1 hour. *Makes 1 medium loaf.*

Arlene Gilman, Woodstock Baptist Church, Woodstock, New Hampshire

Cornbread

Makes a big batch of sweeter-than-usual cornbread that children love.
Reduce the sugar to ½ cup for a standard cornbread.

¾ cup sugar
2 eggs, beaten
2 cups flour
1 cup yellow cornmeal

1 tablespoon baking powder
¾ teaspoon salt
2½ tablespoons melted butter
1½ cups milk

Mix sugar with eggs. Sift together flour, cornmeal, baking powder, and salt, and add to egg mixture. Stir in butter and milk. Beat up quickly. Bake in greased 9" × 13" pan at 350°F for about 30 minutes. *Serves 8–12.*

Evelyn Shaw, Pilgrim Congregational Church, New Haven, Connecticut

Irish Oatmeal Bread

A hearty oatmeal quick bread, chewy and moist.

3 cups flour
1½ tablespoons baking powder
1 teaspoon salt
1¼ cups rolled oats
½ cup raisins (optional)

1 egg
¼ cup honey
1½ cups milk
1 tablespoon melted butter

Sift together flour, baking powder, and salt. Add oats and raisins, if using. Beat egg lightly, then add honey and milk and beat until well-blended. Add dry ingredients and stir just until all is moistened. Turn into greased 9" × 5" loaf pan. Brush top of loaf with melted butter and bake at 350°F for 1 hour to 1 hour and 15 minutes. *Makes 1 large loaf.*

Mrs. Charles Wilson, Center Congregational Church, Torrington, Connecticut

Date Nut Bread

¾ cup cut-up dates
1 cup boiling water
1 cup brown sugar
1 egg, beaten
2 cups flour

½ teaspoon baking soda
½ teaspoon salt
½ teaspoon baking powder
¾ cup chopped walnuts
2 tablespoons cooking oil

Cover dates with boiling water. Add brown sugar and egg. Mix well. Sift flour, baking soda, salt, and baking powder together and add to date mixture, along with walnuts and oil. Turn into greased 9" × 5" loaf pan and bake at 350°F for 45 minutes. *Makes 1 large loaf.*

Priscilla Downing, Killingworth Congregational Church, Killingworth, Connecticut

Sausage Cake

Very similar to zucchini or pumpkin bread—and no, you cannot taste the sausage!

1 pound loose pork sausage
1½ cups brown sugar
1½ cups sugar
2 eggs, lightly beaten
3 cups sifted flour
1 teaspoon ginger

1 teaspoon pumpkin pie spice
1 teaspoon baking powder
1 teaspoon baking soda
1 cup strong cold coffee
1 cup raisins
1 cup chopped walnuts

Combine meat with brown sugar and sugar until well-blended. Add eggs and beat well. Sift together flour, ginger, pumpkin pie spice, and baking powder. Stir baking soda into coffee. Add flour mixture and coffee alternately to meat mixture, beating well after each addition. Pour boiling water over raisins to cover and let stand 5 minutes. Drain well and pat dry with paper towel. Fold raisins and walnuts into batter. Turn into well-greased and floured Bundt pan (9-cup size). Bake at 350°F for 1½ hours, or until done. Cool 15 minutes before turning out of pan. To store, wrap tightly in plastic wrap and refrigerate. *Makes 1 round loaf.*

Marcia Gehrke, United Methodist Church of the Hamptons, Hampton, New Hampshire

Zucchini Bread

One of the best.

3 eggs
¾ cup cooking oil
1½ cups sugar
2 cups chopped zucchini
(approximately ¼" dice)
2 teaspoons vanilla
3 cups flour
1 teaspoon salt

1 teaspoon baking soda
½ teaspoon baking powder
1 teaspoon cinnamon
¾ cup chopped nuts (any kind),
optional
¾ cup raisins or cut-up dates
(optional)

Mix eggs, oil, sugar, zucchini, and vanilla. Sift together flour, salt, baking soda, baking powder, and cinnamon, and add to egg mixture. Stir in nuts and/or raisins or dates, if desired. Turn into 2 greased 8" × 4" loaf pans and bake at 350°F for 50–60 minutes. *Makes 2 medium loaves.*

Barbara Lockhart, United Church of Christ, Keene, New Hampshire

Quick Graham Bread

Easy to make bread with a firm texture and a rich molasses-y taste. Perfect with baked beans.

3 cups graham flour
½ cup cornmeal
1 cup whole wheat flour
½ cup sugar
1 teaspoon salt
½ cup molasses

1 egg, beaten
2 teaspoons baking soda,
dissolved in 1 cup soured milk
2 cups milk
½ cup raisins (optional)

Combine graham flour, cornmeal, whole wheat flour, sugar, and salt. Combine molasses, egg, baking soda mixture, and milk. Stir in dry ingredients, adding raisins, if using. Turn into greased 9" × 5" loaf pan and bake at 350°F for 50–60 minutes. *Makes 1 large loaf.*

Florence Smith, Harwinton Congregational Church, Harwinton, Connecticut

Pineapple-Raisin Tea Ring

A real conversation piece until everyone takes the first bite—then just munching sounds!

2 yeast cakes	2 eggs
¼ cup lukewarm water	5–5½ cups sifted flour
1 cup scalded milk	6 tablespoons brown sugar
1 teaspoon salt	2 teaspoons cinnamon
½ cup sugar	2 tablespoons chopped nuts
4 tablespoons butter +	(any kind)
2 tablespoons melted butter	Maraschino cherry halves

Soften yeast in water. Combine milk, salt, sugar, and 4 tablespoons butter in large bowl. Cool to lukewarm. Stir in eggs and softened yeast. Gradually add flour. Knead on lightly floured board until smooth and satiny. Place in greased bowl; cover and let rise in warm place until doubled in size (1½ hours).

Divide dough in half. Roll out one portion on floured board to 20" × 12" rectangle. Brush with 1 tablespoon melted butter. Spread with half of Pineapple-Raisin Filling (see below). Combine brown sugar and cinnamon and sprinkle half over filling on dough. Roll dough the long way as for jelly roll. Shape into ring on greased baking sheet. With scissors, make cuts 1" apart through top of ring to within 1" from bottom. Alternate cut slices, bringing one to center and next to outside of ring. Cover. Repeat with remaining dough. Let rise in warm place until light and doubled in size—45–60 minutes. Bake at 375°F for 20–25 minutes. Let cool on racks. Frost with Confectioners' Sugar Glaze (see page 181) while warm; sprinkle with chopped nuts. Garnish with maraschino cherry halves. ***Makes 2 rings.***

Pineapple-Raisin Filling

1 can (20 ounces) crushed pineapple, well-drained	¾ cup sugar
1 tablespoon cornstarch	½ cup seedless raisins

Mix together pineapple, cornstarch, and sugar. Cook over medium heat until thickened. Add raisins.

Peg Rodenhiser, The Congregational Church, New Ipswich, New Hampshire

Julekage (Scandinavian Christmas Bread)

Brian Anderson shares this special bread each holiday season with his church.

1 package regular or Rapid Rise yeast	½ teaspoon salt
¼ cup warm water	1 egg, slightly beaten
1 cup warm milk	½ cup raisins
2 tablespoons vegetable shortening or softened butter	¼ cup fruitcake mix or chopped citron
½ cup sugar	¼ cup quartered red candied cherries
½ teaspoon cardamom	3½–3¾ cups flour
	Vegetable oil

In small measuring cup, dissolve yeast in water; set aside 5 minutes or until bubbly. In large bowl, combine milk with shortening or butter; stir to melt. Stir in sugar, cardamom, and salt. Stir in yeasty water, egg, raisins, fruitcake mix or citron, and cherries. Mix in 3 cups of flour, 1 cup at a time, mixing well after each addition.

Use remaining ¾ cup flour to generously coat work surface and scrape remainder to side. Turn dough onto surface. With well-floured hands, knead dough. Work in only enough remaining flour to prevent sticking. Continue kneading about 8 minutes or until dough is smooth ball. Place in large oiled bowl, cover and set aside 1 hour or until doubled in bulk. Punch down dough, knead lightly, shape into ball and place in bowl. Coat lightly with oil, cover and set aside 1 hour or until doubled in bulk again. Punch down dough and knead lightly. Shape into ball and place in oiled 9" round cake pan. Oil top lightly. Cover and set aside 1 hour or until doubled in bulk once more. Bake at 350°F for 40–45 minutes or until browned. Loaf will sound hollow when tapped. If top is browning too quickly, cover loosely with aluminum foil. Remove and transfer to cooling rack. Spread with Vanilla Glaze (see below).

Vanilla Glaze

1 cup sifted confectioners' sugar	1 teaspoon vanilla
1 tablespoon milk	Red and green candied cherries

In bowl, whisk confectioners' sugar, milk, and vanilla until smooth. Add a few drops more milk to make glaze that drips easily from a spoon. Pour glaze over loaf, spreading with back of spoon and allowing glaze to drip down sides. If desired, cut strips of red and green candied cherries. Arrange like poinsettias on top of loaf. Allow to set 30 minutes before slicing. ***Makes 1 round loaf.***

Brian Anderson, Evangelical Lutheran Church, Frederick, Maryland

Apple Coffee Cake

Make this for coffee hour on Sunday morning. Be sure cake is cold before turning out. If turned out hot, it will break up.

5 tablespoons sugar	¼ cup orange juice
2 teaspoons cinnamon	2½ teaspoons vanilla
3 cups flour	3 teaspoons baking powder
1 cup sugar	1 teaspoon salt
1 cup cooking oil	5 apples, peeled, cored, and
4 eggs	thinly sliced

Combine sugar and cinnamon and set aside. In large bowl, combine flour, sugar, oil, eggs, orange juice, vanilla, baking powder, and salt. Beat well. Grease 10" tube pan. Pour in one-third of the batter, half the apples, and one-third of the cinnamon and sugar alternately until all ingredients are used. Bake at 350°F for 1 hour and 10 minutes.

Laura Goodenough, The Congregational Church, Winchester Center, Connecticut

Cherry Coffee Cake

Pretty and cheery—really more a cake than a bread, but super with coffee.

1¾ cups flour	½ cup milk
1 cup sugar	1 egg
1 teaspoon baking powder	1 teaspoon vanilla
¼ teaspoon baking soda	¼ teaspoon lemon extract
¼ teaspoon salt	1 can (21 ounces) cherry pie
½ cup + 2 tablespoons butter	filling

Grease and flour 9" × 9" baking pan. Sift together 1¼ cups flour, ½ cup sugar, baking powder, baking soda, and salt. Add ½ cup butter, milk, egg, and vanilla and beat until well-mixed. Turn into baking pan, spreading batter evenly. In small bowl, combine remaining ½ cup flour, ½ cup sugar, and 2 tablespoons butter until mixture is like coarse crumbs. Sprinkle half on top of batter. Stir lemon extract into pie filling. Spread over crumbs on batter. Sprinkle rest of crumb mixture over top. Bake at 350°F for 1 hour, or until top is light golden. Cut into squares. ***Serves 9.***

Mrs. L. Bouchard, St. Paul's Church, Lancaster, New Hampshire

Danish Kringle

This rich Danish pastry—pronounced "KRING-la"—graces many a church table throughout the upper Midwest.

1 package (¼ ounce) active dry yeast	1 teaspoon salt
8 tablespoons sugar	1 cup vegetable shortening
½ cup warm water	1 cup warm milk
4 cups flour	3 egg yolks, beaten
	2 tablespoons butter, softened

Dissolve yeast and 1 tablespoon sugar in water. In mixing bowl, combine flour, salt, and 5 tablespoons of remaining sugar. With pastry blender or fork, cut shortening into flour mixture until reduced to pea-sized pieces. Add milk, egg yolks, and yeast mixture. Beat with spoon until mixture forms a thick batter. Transfer to large greased bowl; cover and refrigerate overnight.

With spatula, scrape dough onto a well-floured work surface. Dust dough with flour. Knead very lightly for about 1 minute or until dough forms a ball. (Dough will be very soft and fragile.) Divide into 4 balls. Place 3 balls back in refrigerator. Roll or pat remaining ball with well-floured rolling pin or hands into a 10" × 14" rectangle. With floured offset spatula, transfer to greased baking sheet. Spread ½ tablespoon butter lengthwise down center of dough. Sprinkle with ½ tablespoon of remaining sugar. Spread one-quarter of Almond Custard Filling (see below) lengthwise down center. Lift and fold one long edge to mid-line of filling. Repeat with other side. Fold short edges gently to form seal (it is not necessary to seal center seam). Repeat with remaining dough, butter, sugar, and filling on 3 greased baking sheets. Cover and set aside to rise for 2 hours or until doubled in bulk. Bake kringles at 325°F for 30–35 minutes or until golden. Remove from oven to cool. Drizzle Kringle Icing (see below) over kringles.

Almond Custard Filling

½ cup sugar	1 cup half-and-half
2 tablespoons cornstarch or 4 tablespoons flour	2 egg yolks, beaten
Dash of salt	2 tablespoons butter
	1½ teaspoons almond extract

In top of double boiler or metal bowl set over simmering water, combine sugar, cornstarch or flour, and salt. In mixing cup, combine half-and-half and egg yolks; whisk gradually into dry ingredients. Cook over medium heat, whisking constantly, about 4 minutes or until thickened. Remove from heat and whisk in butter and almond extract. Set aside to cool. Cover and refrigerate overnight.

Kringle Icing

1 cup confectioners' sugar   ¼ teaspoon vanilla
4–5 teaspoons milk

In bowl, whisk confectioners' sugar, 4 teaspoons milk and vanilla until smooth. Add 1 teaspoon milk if icing is too thick. *Makes 4 kringles.*

Darline Struve, St. Stephen's Lutheran Church, Clinton, Iowa

Crumb Cake

Good served either warm or cold, as a breakfast coffee cake, or as a dinner dessert.

¾ cup butter
1½–2 cups brown sugar (depending on sweetness desired)
2½ cups flour
1 teaspoon baking soda
1 cup buttermilk or soured milk

1 egg, beaten
1 teaspoon vanilla
½ teaspoon salt
½ cup chopped nuts (any kind), optional

Combine butter, brown sugar, and flour, and work together until crumbly. Reserve 1 cup of mixture for topping. Beat baking soda into buttermilk or soured milk and add to flour mixture along with egg, vanilla, and salt. Stir (do not beat) all ingredients together until batter is smooth. Pour into greased 9" × 13" cake pan. Sprinkle reserved crumb topping over batter. If desired, nuts can be added to crumbs before sprinkling. Bake at 350°F for 35–40 minutes. *Serves 24.*

Helen Michaels, St. Dominic's Catholic Church, Sheboygan, Wisconsin

Danish Puff

Danish pastry from "scratch." The only sugar is in the icing.

2 cups sifted flour
1 cup butter
2–3 tablespoons (approximately) + 1 cup water

3 eggs
1 teaspoon almond extract
   Chopped nuts (any kind) or coconut

Measure 1 cup flour into bowl. Cut in ½ cup butter. Sprinkle with 2 tablespoons water and mix with fork. (You may need to add 1 tablespoon more water.) Shape into ball and divide in half. Pat dough with hands into 2 long strips, 12" × 13" each. Place strips 3" apart on ungreased baking sheet.

Combine remaining ½ cup butter and 1 cup water in saucepan. Bring to rolling boil, and remove from heat. Stir in remaining 1 cup flour immediately to keep it from lumping. When smooth and thick, add 1 egg at a time, beating until smooth after each addition. Add almond extract and mix again. Divide in half and spread one-half evenly over each piece of pastry on the baking sheet. Bake at 350°F for about 60 minutes, or until topping is crisp and nicely browned.

Frost with Confectioners' Sugar Glaze (see page 181) or with Thin Chocolate Icing. (Melt 1 square unsweetened chocolate with 1 teaspoon butter. Remove from heat and add 1 cup confectioners' sugar and 2 tablespoons boiling water. Blend until smooth.) Sprinkle with chopped nuts or coconut. *Serves 8–10.*

Sara Houlberg, The Congregational Church, Sherman, Connecticut

Sour Cream Coffee Cake

This chef has a way with coffee cake.

½ cup butter
1 cup sugar
2 eggs
1 teaspoon vanilla
2 cups flour, sifted
1 teaspoon baking powder

1 teaspoon baking soda
1 cup sour cream
½ cup brown sugar
1 teaspoon cinnamon
½ cup chopped walnuts

Cream together butter, sugar, eggs, and vanilla. Combine flour, baking powder, and baking soda. Add alternately with sour cream to butter mixture. Mix well. Grease and lightly flour 10" tube pan. Put half of batter in pan. Combine brown sugar, cinnamon, and walnuts. Sprinkle batter with half of brown sugar mixture. Repeat. Bake at 350°F for 45 minutes. Serve hot with butter. *Serves 12.*

Thomas A. Nerbonne, United Baptist Church, Concord, New Hampshire

Rhubarb Coffee Cake

Mrs. Farr says, "This recipe always makes a big hit at our church breakfasts. It makes a large cake that is quite different and very moist."

2 cups sifted flour	¼ teaspoon cloves
1½ cups sugar	2 eggs
1 teaspoon baking soda	½ cup cooking oil
1 teaspoon salt	⅓ cup milk
1 teaspoon cinnamon	2 cups fresh rhubarb, cut into
¼ teaspoon allspice	½" pieces

Sift flour, sugar, baking soda, salt, cinnamon, allspice, and cloves together in mixing bowl. Place eggs, oil, and milk in another bowl and beat together. Then add to dry ingredients. Fold in rhubarb. Turn into greased 9" × 13" pan. Make Topping (see below) and spoon over batter. Bake at 350°F for 50 minutes. *Serves 18–24.*

Topping

⅔ cup flour	4 tablespoons butter
½ cup brown sugar	¼ cup chopped nuts (any kind)

Combine flour, brown sugar, and butter with fork. Add nuts and stir.

Lillian Farr, All Saints Episcopal Church, Wolfeboro, New Hampshire

Swedish Coffee Ring

A time-saving means to a handsome end.

Dough made from 1 package hot roll mix, or 1 roll frozen white bread dough, thawed	**½ cup firmly packed brown sugar**
	½ cup flaked coconut, or ½ cup chopped nuts (any kind)
¼ cup melted butter	**1 teaspoon cinnamon**

Turn out dough on floured breadboard and roll into rectangle ¼"–½" thick. Spread butter on dough. Combine brown sugar, coconut or nuts, and cinnamon. Sprinkle over dough. Roll up on long side as for jelly roll, wetting edges to seal. Place on greased baking sheet, bringing ends together to form ring.

With scissors, cut 1" slices almost through ring. Turn each cut piece on its side. Cover with clean towel and let rise in warm place until doubled in bulk, about 1 hour. Bake at 375°F for 25 minutes, or until golden brown. While still warm, brush top with Glaze (see below) and sprinkle with flaked coconut, if desired. ***Serves 8.***

Confectioners' Sugar Glaze

Gradually add about 1 tablespoon hot milk or water to 1 cup sifted confectioners' sugar in bowl. Blend well.

Mrs. Edward B. Riley, First Congregational Church, Concord, New Hampshire

Walnut-Raisin Coffee Cake

Quite impressive when done properly. For Christmas, make poinsettias with red and green slivered maraschino cherries put into pan first of all.

2 cups warm water
2 packages dry yeast
1 tablespoon salt
1 tablespoon + 2 cups sugar
　　Sprinkle of ginger
8 cups (approximately) flour
1 cup shortening

2 eggs, beaten
1 cup cold water
½ cup melted butter
1½–2 teaspoons cinnamon
　　Raisins
　　Chopped walnuts

Put warm water in large bowl and sprinkle with yeast, salt, 1 tablespoon sugar, and ginger. Let set until yeast rises to top of water. Add about 2 cups flour, enough to make a sponge dough that will drop from spoon in a mound. Let rise until bubbly. Combine shortening, 1 cup sugar, eggs, and cold water. Add to yeast mixture. Mix well. Add rest of flour (more if necessary) to make soft, nonsticky dough. Cover with cloth and let rise. Punch down and let rise again. With floured hands, roll dough into balls a little larger than a walnut. Roll balls in melted butter. Combine remaining 1 cup sugar with cinnamon and roll dough balls in this mixture. Place balls in layers in greased 10" tube pan, topping each layer with a few raisins and chopped walnuts. Fill pan one-half to two-thirds of the way. Let rise until doubled in bulk. Bake at 375°F for 40–45 minutes. (If top browns too fast, reduce heat to 350°F for remainder of baking time. Turn out of pan to cool. *Serves 8–10.*

Peg Rodenhiser, The Congregational Church, New Ipswich, New Hampshire

Dill Bread

Great for lunch or brunch. Best served warm from oven.

1 package dry yeast
¼ cup lukewarm water
1 cup cottage cheese, heated to warm
2 tablespoons sugar
2 tablespoons grated onion, or 1 tablespoon minced dry onion

1 tablespoon butter
2 teaspoons dill seed
1 teaspoon salt
¼ teaspoon baking soda
1 egg
2¼–2½ cups flour

Soften yeast in lukewarm water and combine in mixing bowl with cottage cheese, sugar, onion, butter, dill seed, salt, baking soda, and egg. Stir in flour. Knead well. Let rise in warm place until doubled in bulk (about 1 hour). Punch down and knead again. Form into loaf and place in greased and floured 9" × 5" loaf pan. Let rise in warm place for 30 minutes. Bake at 350°F for 50 minutes. *Makes 1 large loaf.*

Mrs. Burton Erickson and Eleanor Wells, First Congregational Church, Concord, New Hampshire

Maple Oatmeal Bread

A good substantial bread subtly flavored with maple. Terrific with peanut butter.
If you like your bread sweet, include the honey.

2 packages dry yeast
¼ cup lukewarm water
  Pinch of sugar
1 cup rolled oats (not quick)
1 cup maple syrup
1 cup hot strong coffee
¾ cup boiling water

¼ cup honey (optional)
⅓ cup shortening
2 teaspoons salt
4½ cups white flour
2 eggs, lightly beaten
2 cups whole wheat flour

Dissolve yeast in lukewarm water with sugar for 10 minutes or until foamy. In large bowl, combine oats, maple syrup, coffee, water, honey, if using, shortening, and salt. Stir until shortening is melted and let cool until lukewarm. Stir in 1 cup white flour, eggs, and yeast mixture, and beat with electric mixer until smooth. Add remaining 3½ cups white flour and whole wheat flour, 2 cups at a time, and beat dough until smooth and elastic. Form dough into ball, transfer to greased bowl, and turn to coat both sides. Let dough rise, covered, for 1 hour and 30 minutes, or until doubled in bulk. Punch down dough. Divide between 2 buttered 9" × 5" loaf pans, and let rise, covered, for 1 hour. Bake at 350°F for 45 minutes. Turn out on racks to cool. *Makes 2 large loaves.*

Carol Jensen, The United Church of Hardwick, Hardwick, Vermont

Molasses-Bran Bread

Easy to make and very good.

¾ cup bran cereal
½ cup molasses
2 tablespoons butter
2 teaspoons salt
2 cups boiling water

2 packages dry yeast
½ cup warm water
4 cups white flour
3 cups whole wheat flour

In large bowl, combine bran, molasses, butter, salt, and boiling water. Cool to lukewarm. Dissolve yeast in warm water and stir into bran mixture. Stir in white and whole wheat flours. Place dough in greased bowl and turn to coat evenly. Cover with damp cloth and let rise until double. Punch down. Divide dough in half. Place each half in well-greased 9" × 5" loaf pan. Cover with damp cloth and let rise until double. Bake at 400°F for 45 minutes. Turn out on wire rack and brush tops with melted butter. *Makes 2 large loaves.*

Carol Jensen, The United Church of Hardwick, Hardwick, Vermont

Oatmeal Bread

Light-textured and golden oatmeal loaves.

1 cup rolled oats	2 cups boiling water
½ cup molasses	1 package dry yeast
2 teaspoons butter	½ cup warm water
1 tablespoon butter	5–5½ cups flour

Combine oats, molasses, salt, butter, and boiling water. Stir and let stand until lukewarm. Mix yeast with warm water and stir into oatmeal. Add 4½ cups flour. Beat well and knead in bowl (dough will be sticky). Let rise until doubled in bulk. Punch down and add enough remaining flour to make dough firm enough to knead on floured board. Shape into loaves and put into 2 greased 8" × 4" loaf pans. Let rise until light and nearly doubled. Bake at 350°F for 50 minutes. *Makes 2 medium loaves.*

Helen Poole, Harwinton Congregational Church, Harwinton, Connecticut

Feather-Light Dinner Rolls

A well-named recipe. Makes 18 medium or 24 small rolls.

1 package dry yeast	¼ cup sugar
¼ cup lukewarm water	1 teaspoon salt
¼ cup shortening	1 egg, beaten
¾ cup scalded milk	3½–3¾ cups flour

Dissolve yeast in water. Melt shortening in scalded milk and add sugar, salt, and egg. When mixture has cooled to lukewarm, add dissolved yeast. Stir in flour and knead 5–10 minutes, or until dough is smooth. Let rise until doubled in bulk (45–60 minutes). Form rolls—18 medium or 24 small—and place on greased baking sheet. Let rise until light (about 45 minutes). Bake at 375°F for 10–15 minutes, or until done. *Makes 18–24 rolls.*

Liese Shewmaker, Our Savior Lutheran Church, Hanover, New Hampshire

Rindge Rye Bread

1 package dry yeast	2 tablespoons soft shortening
1¾ cups warm water	1 teaspoon salt
1 cup rye flour	2 tablespoons honey
2½ cups white flour	Melted butter

Dissolve yeast in water. Combine rye and white flours and set aside. Add shortening, salt, honey, and half of the flour to yeast and beat 2 minutes at medium speed. Add remaining flour and blend with spoon, scraping bowl frequently. Cover with cloth and let rise in warm place until doubled in bulk (about 30 minutes). Stir batter down by beating about 25 strokes. Spread batter into greased 8" × 4" loaf pan. (Batter is sticky—use floured hand to pat into shape.) Cover with cloth again and let rise to ¼" from top of pan (40–45 minutes). Bake at 375°F for 45 minutes, or until loaf sounds hollow when tapped on the bottom. Brush with melted butter and cool on rack. ***Makes 1 medium loaf.***

Mary Wakefield, First Congregational Church, Rindge, New Hampshire

Butter Dips

Tender tidbits of biscuit dough baked in butter.

½ cup butter	3½ teaspoons baking powder
2 cups + ¼ cup flour	1½ teaspoons salt
1 tablespoon sugar	1 cup milk

Preheat oven to 400°F. Place butter in 9" × 13" baking dish and melt in oven. Take dish out of oven when butter has melted. Meanwhile, sift flour, sugar, baking powder, and salt together. Add milk and stir with fork just until all is moistened. Turn onto floured board and roll into rectangle approximately 9" × 13". Score with knife into ¾" strips lengthwise and crosswise every 2", going almost but not quite through dough. Lift scored dough (in 2 halves is easiest) on pancake turners and place on melted butter in baking dish. Bake at 400°F for 15–20 minutes. ***Enough to serve 8.***

Flora C. Hammond, Unitarian Universalist Church, Keene, New Hampshire

White Bread

Nice flavor and texture. Can be used to make either rolls or one large loaf.

3½ cups hot water
½ cup sugar
1 tablespoon rendered chicken fat or soft shortening

1 tablespoon salt
2 packages dry yeast
8 cups flour

Combine hot water with sugar, chicken fat or shortening, and salt. Cool to lukewarm and stir in yeast. Let stand until foamy, then add 4 cups flour. Keep adding flour until mixture can be kneaded by hand and is not sticky but nice and smooth. Knead well and put in greased bowl covered with damp towel and set in warm place to rise until doubled in bulk. Punch down and shape into loaf (or rolls). Place in greased 9" × 5" loaf pan and let rise again until light. Bake at 400°F for about 20–25 minutes, or until done (loaf should sound hollow when tapped on bottom). *Makes 1 large loaf.*

Jan Shoup, Center Congregational Church, Torrington, Connecticut

Cinnamon Rolls

A nice surprise to serve for lunch.

1 yeast cake
4 tablespoons lukewarm water
1 cup scalded milk
½ cup shortening

½ cup sugar
2 eggs, beaten
1 teaspoon salt
4½ cups flour

Crumble yeast and add water. Let stand 5 minutes. Mix milk with shortening, cool to lukewarm, and add to yeast. Stir in sugar, eggs, salt, and 2 cups flour. Beat 3 minutes, then add remaining 2½ cups flour. Mix well, cover with cloth, and let stand until dough has doubled in bulk.

Filling

4 tablespoons butter, melted
½ cup sugar

1 teaspoon cinnamon

Roll dough ¼" thick and spread with melted butter. Mix sugar and cinnamon and sprinkle over buttered dough. Roll up dough tightly and cut roll into ⅓" slices. Flatten down and place flat side up in greased pan. Let rise until doubled in size. Bake at 400°F for 20 minutes.

Eva Day, The Unitarian Church, Peterborough, New Hampshire

Refrigerator Rolls

We think the melt-in-the-mouth quality of these superb rolls
has something to do with the built-in butter.

¼ cup sugar
½ teaspoon salt
13½ tablespoons butter
1 cup boiling water

1 package dry yeast
¼ cup warm water
1 egg, beaten
3½ cups flour

Mix sugar, salt, 1½ tablespoons butter, and boiling water. Cool to lukewarm. Dissolve yeast in water and add to sugar mixture. Add egg and stir in flour. Refrigerate overnight. Punch down and knead lightly on floured board. Shape into rolls. Cut remaining butter into teaspoon-size pieces and put 1 piece into center of each roll. Place on greased baking sheet. Let rise until doubled in bulk. Bake at 400°F for 10–12 minutes. ***Makes 3 dozen rolls.***

Edna Foss, Suncook United Methodist Church, Suncook, New Hampshire

Orange Bow Knots

Excellent coffee roll, and sure seller at bake sales, too.

1 yeast cake
¼ cup warm water
1 cup milk, scalded
½ cup shortening
⅓ cup sugar
1 teaspoon salt

5–5½ cups sifted flour
2 eggs, well-beaten
¼ cup orange juice
2 tablespoons grated orange
rind

Soften yeast in warm water. Combine milk, shortening, sugar, and salt. Cool to lukewarm. Stir in about 2 cups flour and beat well. Add eggs. Stir in yeast, orange juice and rind, and remaining flour. Mix well. Cover and let rest for 10 minutes. Knead on lightly floured board. Place in greased bowl and let rise in warm place until doubled. Punch down, cover, and let rest 10 minutes. Roll dough out ½" thick. Cut into 10" strips, ½" wide. Tie each strip in a knot. Arrange on greased baking sheet. Cover and let rise until doubled. Bake at 400°F for 12–15 minutes. Spread with Orange Topping (see below). **Makes about 24.**

Orange Topping

2 tablespoons orange juice
1 teaspoon grated orange rind

1 cup confectioners' sugar

Combine orange juice, orange rind, and confectioners' sugar. Blend well.

Raised Rolls

Serve plain or iced with a butter frosting.

½ cup scalded milk
¼ cup shortening
2 tablespoons sugar
1½ teaspoons salt

½ cup cold water
1 package dry yeast
1 egg
3 cups flour

Combine scalded milk, shortening, sugar, and salt. Cool to lukewarm by adding water. Add yeast and egg and mix well. Then add flour. Mix well and turn onto floured board. Roll dough out to ¼" thickness. Cut rolls with biscuit cutter and place in greased pan. Let rise until doubled in size. Bake at 400°F for 15–20 minutes. ***Makes 1 dozen rolls.***

Jeannette M. Miller, Morris Congregational Church, Morris, Connecticut

Squash Biscuits

An airy and flavorsome cross between a biscuit and a roll. "A must for Thanksgiving dinner."

½ cup milk
½ cup sugar
1 teaspoon salt
1 cup cooked, mashed winter
   squash
½ yeast cake

½ cup warm water
5 cups flour
½ teaspoon baking soda
⅓ cup melted shortening
½ cup melted butter

Scald milk. Add sugar, salt, and squash, and cool to lukewarm. Dissolve yeast in warm water and add to squash mixture. Sift 2 cups flour with baking soda. Combine with squash mixture, blending thoroughly. Add shortening and beat well. Stir in remaining 3 cups flour to make soft dough. Cover and let rise until doubled in bulk. Punch down and let rise again. Shape on floured board into biscuits, dip in melted butter, and arrange on baking pan. Let rise once more until light. Bake at 375°F for about 20 minutes, or until lightly browned. ***Makes 3 dozen.***

Priscilla Downing, Killingworth Congregational Church, Killingworth, Connecticut

Cinnamon Roll-Ups

A delightful snack to serve at coffee hour following a church service—
or at any other "coffee."

1 loaf thin-sliced white sandwich
  bread (about 20 slices)
  Milk
1 package (8 ounces) cream
  cheese, softened

½ cup melted butter
¾ cup sugar mixed with 1
  teaspoon cinnamon
  Sour cream

Remove crusts from bread slices. Roll each slice flat with rolling pin. Blend just enough milk with softened cream cheese to make it easily spreadable. Spread 1 side of each bread slice with cream cheese. Roll up each slice, cheese side in. Roll in melted butter, then roll in sugar mixed with cinnamon. Cut each roll into 2 pieces. Bake on cookie sheet at 400°F for 12–15 minutes. Serve warm with sour cream for dipping. Roll-ups can be made ahead of time, refrigerated, and baked just before serving. Can also be frozen. If freezing, freeze before cutting. *Yields 40 tidbits; serves 8 or more.*

Nancy A. Burton, St. Andrew's Church, Newcastle, Maine

Cakes

For a special occasion, or to make an ordinary occasion a little more special, what is more elegant than a cake? The recipes in this chapter will become traditions in your family—like Jeannette Miller's Birthday Cake, a light, white-frosted yellow cake; or the smoothly delectable, classic Red Velvet Cake.

From Apricot Pound Cake (so moist you can serve it for a week), to the one-pan Wacky Cake that takes only minutes to prepare, to the aristocratic high-rise Walnut Cake, each cake here is a family-pleaser that will command high praise—and high prices at bake sales, too!

Apple Upside-Down Cake

Serve with coffee and heavy cream, whipped or not, for dessert.

¾ cup butter
¾ cup brown sugar
½ teaspoon cinnamon
3 cups sliced apples
1¼ cups flour
1 cup sugar

1½ teaspoons baking powder
¾ cup milk
⅓ cup shortening
1 egg
1 teaspoon vanilla

In greased 8" × 8" cake pan, melt butter and mix in brown sugar and cinnamon. Put sliced apples in mixture and stir until apples are coated. Mix flour, sugar, baking powder, milk, shortening, egg, and vanilla, and spread over apple mixture. Bake at 350°F for about 35 minutes, or until cake mixture is light brown and firm to the touch. Let cool 20 minutes, then turn out on plate.

Joanne Earle, Old Brick Church, Clarendon, Vermont

Special Applesauce Cake

A fruitcake-textured spice cake that keeps well.

3½ cups flour
1 teaspoon baking soda
½ teaspoon salt
2 teaspoons cinnamon
1 teaspoon cloves
2 teaspoons nutmeg

1 cup butter
1 cup sugar
2 eggs, beaten
2 cups warm applesauce
1 cup coarsely chopped walnuts
1 cup raisins

Sift together flour, baking soda, salt, cinnamon, cloves, and nutmeg. Cream butter and sugar. Add eggs. Alternately stir in sifted dry ingredients and applesauce. Stir in walnuts and raisins. Mix well. Pour into well-greased 10" tube pan. Bake at 350°F for 60–70 minutes. Cool 20 minutes, then turn out of pan.

Karen Russo, The Congregational Church, East Hampton, Connecticut

Tempting Bishop's Cake

An enticing concoction somewhere between a fruitcake and a chocolate-chip cookie.

1½ cups flour
1½ teaspoons baking powder
½ teaspoon salt
1 package (6 ounces) chocolate bits
2 cups chopped nuts (any kind)

1 cup cut-up dates
1 cup halved maraschino or glacé cherries
3 eggs
1 cup sugar

Sift together flour, baking powder, and salt. Add chocolate bits, nuts, dates, and cherries. In another bowl, beat eggs and sugar. Add to dry ingredients and fold in. Fill two 8" × 4" greased loaf pans three-quarters of the way and bake at 325°F for 45 minutes, or until done.

Nancy A. Burton, St. Andrew's Church, Newcastle, Maine

Apricot Pound Cake

Dense, moist, and a bit different—keeps well, too.

1 cup butter
3 cups sugar
6 eggs
½ teaspoon rum extract
1 teaspoon orange extract
½ teaspoon lemon extract
¼ teaspoon almond extract

1 teaspoon vanilla extract
1 teaspoon butter extract
3 cups sifted flour
¼ teaspoon baking soda
½ teaspoon salt
1 cup sour cream
½ cup apricot nectar

Cream butter and sugar until light and fluffy. Add eggs, 1 at a time, beating well after each addition. Add rum, orange, lemon, almond, vanilla, and butter extracts. Then combine flour, baking soda, and salt, and mix together sour cream and apricot nectar. Add alternately to butter mixture and beat well. Pour into greased and floured 10" tube pan. Bake at 325°F for 60–70 minutes. Cool before serving.

Marcia Fletcher, St. Anne's Episcopal Church, Calais, Maine

Birthday Cake

Mrs. Miller has made generations of birthday cakes;
this is a fine yellow cake with a white boiled frosting that is good for birthdays—
and almost any other occasion.

1 cup butter	2¾ cups flour
2 cups sugar	3 teaspoons baking powder
4 eggs	½ teaspoon salt
1 teaspoon vanilla	1 cup milk

Cream butter and sugar and beat in eggs and vanilla. Sift together flour, baking powder, and salt. Add alternately with milk to creamed mixture. Beat well until light. Pour batter into 2 greased and floured 9" layer-cake pans. Bake at 350°F for 35 minutes. Cool, then spread with White Frosting (see below).

White Frosting

1 cup sugar	2 teaspoons vanilla
½ cup white corn syrup	4 egg whites, beaten stiff
¼ cup water	Grated coconut (optional)

In saucepan, combine sugar, corn syrup, and water and boil until a teaspoonful stays together in cold water. Remove from stove and add vanilla. Start beating egg whites again, and while beating, very slowly in a thin stream pour cooked syrup into egg whites. Keep beating until frosting is thick enough to spread. Spread frosting between layers, on top, and on sides of cake. If desired, sprinkle coconut between layers and on top and sides of cake.

Jeannette M. Miller, Morris Congregational Church, Morris, Connecticut

Broiler Cake

A great cake with an out-of-this-world topping. Serve warm.

Cake

3 eggs
1½ cups white sugar
1½ cups flour
1½ teaspoons baking powder

Pinch of salt
6 tablespoons butter
⅔ cup milk
1 teaspoon vanilla

Beat eggs and add sugar. Sift flour, baking powder, and salt together, and stir into egg mixture. Melt butter, add milk, and bring to boil. Add to flour and egg mixture along with vanilla. Bake in greased 9" × 13" pan at 325°F for 30 minutes. Make Topping (see below).

Topping

½ cup + 2 tablespoons butter, melted
1½ cups brown sugar
½ cup cream

1 cup chopped pecans
1 cup shredded coconut or crushed, drained pineapple

Beat together butter, brown sugar, and cream. Add pecans and coconut or pineapple. Spoon over hot cake and place under broiler until brown.

Marjorie M. Stultz, Concord Unitarian Church, Concord, New Hampshire

Red Velvet Cake

A subtly delicious cake that looks like its name; the frosting sets it off like white ruching.

½ cup shortening	½ teaspoon salt
1½ cups sugar	1 cup buttermilk
2 eggs, beaten	1 ounce red food coloring
2 cups flour	1 teaspoon baking soda
1 tablespoon cocoa	1 tablespoon vinegar

Cream shortening and sugar and add eggs. Sift flour, cocoa, and salt together, and mix buttermilk with coloring. Add dry ingredients alternately with liquid ingredients to creamed mixture. Beat well. Dissolve baking soda in vinegar and fold into batter. Grease and flour two 9" layer-cake pans. Bake at 350°F for 30–35 minutes. Remove from pans, cool, and spread with Vanilla Filling and Frosting (see below).

Vanilla Filling and Frosting

¼ cup flour	½ cup softened butter
1 cup milk	1 cup sugar
⅛ teaspoon salt	1 tablespoon vanilla
½ cup shortening	Grated coconut (optional)

In small saucepan, blend flour with milk and salt and cook over low heat, stirring, until of pudding consistency. Cool. In large mixer bowl, cream together shortening, butter, sugar, and vanilla. Add cooled flour mixture and beat until smooth. Spread between layers and over top and sides of cake. Sprinkle coconut on top, if desired. Refrigerate cake.

Winona Gilman, Old Brick Church, Claredon, Vermont

Extra-Rich Chocolate Cake

Baked in a tube pan or in 4 layers, this makes a nice high cake, easily sliced.
To make a 4-layer cake, divide the batter between 2 cake pans.
Cut each finished cake horizontally to make 4 layers.

2½ cups flour	2 cups + 2 tablespoons sugar
2 teaspoons baking soda	4 eggs, well-beaten
¾ cup cocoa	1 cup soured milk
½ teaspoon salt	1 teaspoon vanilla
1 cup butter	1 cup boiling water

Sift flour once; add baking soda, cocoa, and salt. Sift together 3 times. Cream butter; add sugar. Cream until light. Add eggs and beat. Add flour and sour milk alternately. Add vanilla and boiling water and beat. Bake in greased 10" tube pan at 375°F for about 45 minutes. Frost as desired.

Peg Rodenhiser, The Congregational Church, New Ipswich, New Hampshire

Fruit Cocktail Cake

Serve warm or cold for festive occasions.

1 cup flour	1 teaspoon vanilla
1 cup sugar	2 cups fruit cocktail, drained,
1 teaspoon baking soda	with ½ cup syrup reserved
¼ teaspoon salt	¾ cup brown sugar
1 egg, beaten	½ cup chopped nuts (any kind)

Combine flour, sugar, baking soda, and salt. Add egg, vanilla, fruit cocktail, and syrup. Beat well. Put in greased 9" × 13" pan and spread brown sugar and nuts on top of batter. Bake for 1 hour at 350°F (325°F if using glass pan). Top with ice cream or whipped cream.

Mildred G. Quayle, Good Shepherd Episcopal Church, Houlton, Maine

Satin's Velvet Robe Cake

High-rising and delicious; belongs in everyone's chocolate cake collection.

1½ teaspoons baking soda	1 teaspoon vanilla
1⅔ cups cold water	½ cup cocoa
½ cup butter	2½ cups sifted flour
1¾ cups sugar	3 egg whites
1 teaspoon salt	

Combine baking soda and ⅓ cup cold water; stir to dissolve and set aside. Cream butter. Gradually add 1 cup sugar and cream until fluffy. Blend in salt and vanilla. Mix cocoa with another ⅓ cup cold water. Beat into creamed mixture. Add flour alternately with remaining 1 cup cold water. Beat egg whites until soft peaks form, then beat in remaining ¾ cup sugar. Fold into batter. Add baking soda and water mixture; mix well. Pour into two 9" layer pans or one 9" × 13" pan, greased. Bake at 350°F for 30 minutes. Cool on racks and frost with Cocoa Frosting (see below).

Cocoa Frosting

¼ cup butter	½ cup cocoa
3½ cups confectioners' sugar	¼ teaspoon salt
1½ teaspoons vanilla	⅓ cup milk

Combine butter, sugar, vanilla, cocoa, salt, and milk. Beat together until well-blended.

Peg Rodenhiser, The Congregational Church, New Ipswich, New Hampshire

Chocolate Roll

Airy and light as a feather, it literally melts in your mouth.

5 egg whites
1 cup sifted confectioners' sugar
3 tablespoons cocoa

5 egg yolks, beaten
½ pint heavy cream, whipped and flavored with sugar and vanilla

Beat egg whites till frothier; add sugar and beat until stiff. Add cocoa, mix well. Fold in egg yolks. Grease jelly-roll (10" × 15") pan. Cut wax paper to fit. Grease and flour wax paper–lined pan. Spread mixture in pan and bake at 375°F for 20 minutes. Turn out on dish towel sprinkled with confectioners' sugar. Cover with damp towel until cool. Spread with whipped cream. Roll up (using dish towel to help) on long side. Cut in half and frost with Chocolate-Roll Icing (see below).

Chocolate-Roll Icing

2–3 tablespoons milk
1 cup sifted confectioners' sugar

1 tablespoon cocoa

Combine milk, sugar, and cocoa, and mix until smooth.

Arlene Foulds, Center Congregational Church, Torrington, Connecticut

Bohemian Coffee Cake

Despite its name, in America, this is definitely a dessert cake—
but also a sweet treat served with coffee. A handsome item for any occasion.

2½ cups flour
1 cup brown sugar
1 cup sugar
1 teaspoon salt
1 teaspoon cinnamon
1 teaspoon nutmeg
1 teaspoon baking soda

2 eggs
1 cup cooking oil
1 teaspoon vanilla
1 cup buttermilk
1 cup chopped nuts (any kind)
1 cup grated coconut

Combine flour with brown sugar, sugar, salt, cinnamon, nutmeg, and baking soda. Mix well. In separate bowl, beat eggs well, then beat in oil, vanilla, and buttermilk. Stir into dry ingredients until well-blended. Add ¾ cup nuts and coconut. Grease and flour a 10" tube pan. Turn batter into tube pan and bake at 350°F for 1 hour. Remove from pan and cool on rack. Spread with Cream Cheese Frosting (see below) and sprinkle with remaining ¼ cup nuts.

Cream Cheese Frosting

1 package (3 ounces) cream
   cheese, softened
½ teaspoon vanilla

½ box confectioners' sugar
2 tablespoons butter

Blend cream cheese, vanilla, sugar, and butter together, and beat until of spreadable consistency.

Marcia Fletcher, St. Anne's Episcopal Church, Calais, Maine

Cottage Pudding

Children usually love this old favorite, which is not a pudding at all but a mild cake served with different sauces. Use vanilla instead of lemon extract to flavor cake if you elect to serve it with a vanilla or chocolate sauce.

Cake

¼ cup shortening	1¾ cups flour
1 cup sugar	2½ teaspoons baking powder
1 egg	½ teaspoon salt
¼ teaspoon lemon extract, or ½ teaspoon vanilla	⅔ cup milk

Cream shortening and sugar. Add egg and lemon extract or vanilla and beat well. Sift flour together with baking powder and salt. Add to creamed mixture alternately with milk, beating after each addition. Bake in greased 8" × 8" or 9" × 9" pan at 350°F for 35 minutes, or until done. Cut into squares and serve with Lemon Nutmeg Sauce (see below).

Lemon Nutmeg Sauce

½ cup sugar	3 tablespoons butter
1 tablespoon cornstarch, dissolved in ¼ cup cold water	1 teaspoon grated lemon rind
⅛ teaspoon salt	2 tablespoons lemon juice
1¼ cups boiling water	½ teaspoon nutmeg

Mix sugar, cornstarch, and salt in saucepan. Gradually add boiling water, stirring constantly. Bring mixture to boil while continuing to stir. Turn down heat and simmer 5 minutes. Blend in butter, lemon rind and juice, and nutmeg. Pour hot sauce over each cake square.

Gladys Priest, Foxon Congregational Church, East Haven, Connecticut

Fruit Torte

Taking advantage of American packaged foods,
this is super quick and easy to prepare but tasty, too.

1 can (16 ounces) apple pie
  filling
1 can (16 ounces) crushed
  pineapple

1 package (15 ounces) lemon
  cake mix
½ cup butter
  Whipped cream

In a greased 10" × 15" pan, layer apple pie filling and pineapple (with juice). Sprinkle cake mix over fruit. Cut butter into bits and dot over top. Bake at 375°F for 45 minutes, or until golden brown. Top with whipped cream and cut into squares.

Elvira Howe, The Congregational Church, Laconia, New Hampshire

Key Lime Cake

A lovely cake for spring or summer—to make in a flat or tube pan.

1 package (3 ounces) lime gelatin
1½ cups sugar
2 cups flour, sifted
⅔ teaspoon salt
1 teaspoon baking powder
½ teaspoon baking soda
5 eggs
1⅓ cups cooking oil
¾ cup orange juice

½ teaspoon vanilla
1 teaspoon lemon extract
⅓ cup lime juice and ⅓ cup sifted
  confectioners' sugar (optional)
1 cup whipping cream,
  ⅛–¼ teaspoon green food
  coloring, and fresh lime slices
  (optional)

Soak gelatin in a little bit of cold water for 3–5 minutes. Combine sugar, flour, salt, baking powder, baking soda, and gelatin in mixing bowl. Add eggs, oil, orange juice, vanilla, and lemon extract. Beat until well-blended. Now, depending on the type of cake you wish:

1. Pour batter into greased 9" × 13" pan and bake at 350°F for 25–30 minutes. Let cool in pan for 15 minutes. Prick cake all over with fork. Drizzle well with lime juice mixed with confectioners' sugar.

2. Pour batter into greased 10" tube cake pan and bake at 350°F for 45–50 minutes. Cool. Whip cream and tint green. Use whipped cream to completely frost cake. Garnish with fresh lime slices (and a violet or two, if they are out!).

Ruth A. Palmer, St. John's Episcopal Church, Bethesda, Maryland

Mayonnaise Cake

Moist and light cocoa-colored, with an unexpected zing.

2 cups sifted flour	¼ cup cocoa
1 cup sugar	1 cup cold water
1½ teaspoons baking soda	1 cup mayonnaise

Mix together flour, sugar, baking soda, and cocoa. Beat cold water and mayonnaise together. Add to dry ingredients and mix well. Pour into greased pans (two 8" layer-cake pans or one 8" × 12" sheet-cake pan). Bake at 350°F for 45 minutes, or until cake springs back in center.

Dianne Johnson, Dublin Community Church, Dublin, New Hampshire

Molasses Cake

Similar to gingerbread but lighter in texture.
Cake can be frosted or served with lemon sauce or whipped cream.

1 cup butter	¾ teaspoon salt
1½ cups sugar	2 teaspoons cinnamon
3 eggs	1 teaspoon cloves
¾ cup molasses	1 teaspoon ginger
3¾ cups sifted flour	¾ cup milk
¾ teaspoon baking soda	

Cream butter and sugar. Add eggs and beat until fluffy. Add molasses and blend well. Sift flour, baking soda, salt, cinnamon, cloves, and ginger together. Add to mixture alternately with milk. Turn into buttered 9" × 13" pan. Bake at 350°F for about 35 minutes, or until toothpick inserted in center comes out clean.

Naomi Crook, Chocorua Community Church, Chocorua, New Hampshire

Mother's Hot Weather Cake

A quick, easy, and quite impressive spice cake.

½ cup shortening	½ teaspoon baking soda
1 cup brown sugar	½ teaspoon baking powder
1 egg	½ teaspoon cloves
1 egg yolk	½ teaspoon cinnamon
1⅓ cups cake flour	½ cup soured milk
½ teaspoon salt	

Topping

1 egg white	¼ cup chopped nuts (any kind)
½ cup brown sugar	

Cream shortening with brown sugar. Beat egg with egg yolk, and add to creamed mixture. Sift together cake flour, salt, baking soda, baking powder, cloves, and cinnamon. Add to creamed mixture alternately with milk. Grease and flour an 8" × 8" or 9" × 9" pan and line with waxed paper well up on sides of pan. Turn batter into pan. Make topping by beating egg white until stiff, then beating in brown sugar, adding a little at a time while beating. Spread over cake batter. Sprinkle nuts over top. Bake at 350°F for 40 minutes, or until done.

Marianne Jewell, United Methodist Church of the Hamptons, Hampton, New Hampshire

Fresh Pear Cake

Both light and moist, spicy yet pear-y, and altogether remarkable. Keeps well, too—
though there is usually little left to keep.

2 cups sugar	1 teaspoon salt
3 eggs, well-beaten	1 teaspoon vanilla
1½ cups cooking oil	2 teaspoons cinnamon
3 cups flour	3 cups thinly sliced pears, cored
1 teaspoon baking soda	and peeled

Combine sugar, eggs, and oil. Beat well. Combine flour, baking soda, and salt. Add to sugar mixture, 1 cup at a time, mixing well after each addition. Stir in vanilla, cinnamon, and pears. Turn into well-greased 10" Bundt or tube pan. Bake at 350°F for 1 hour. Remove from pan and allow to cool. Pour Confectioners' Sugar Glaze on top (see below).

Confectioners' Sugar Glaze

1¼ cups sifted confectioners' sugar   2–4 tablespoons milk

Combine sugar and milk, blending until smooth.

Joan Young, The Unitarian Church, Franklin, New Hampshire

Sauerkraut Surprise Cake

A novelty cake well worth serving to both delight and mystify your friends.
Most will guess the secret ingredient to be coconut!
The frosting is tart-sweet and very important to the cake.

½ cup butter
1½ cups sugar
3 eggs
1 teaspoon vanilla
2 cups sifted flour
1 teaspoon baking powder
1 teaspoon baking soda

¼ teaspoon salt
½ cup cocoa
1 cup water
1 can (8 ounces) sauerkraut,
    drained, rinsed, and finely
    snipped

In large mixing bowl, cream butter and sugar until light. Beat in eggs one at a time; add vanilla. Sift together flour, baking powder, baking soda, salt, and cocoa. Add to creamed mixture alternately with water, beating after each addition. Stir in sauerkraut. Turn into greased and floured 9" × 13" baking pan. Bake at 350°F for 35–40 minutes. Cool in pan. Frost with Sour Cream Chocolate Frosting (see below).

Sour Cream Chocolate Frosting

1 package (6 ounces) semisweet
    chocolate pieces
4 tablespoons butter
½ cup sour cream

1 teaspoon vanilla
¼ teaspoon salt
2½–2¾ cups confectioners' sugar,
    sifted

Melt chocolate and butter. Blend in sour cream, vanilla, and salt. Gradually add confectioners' sugar until frosting is of spreading consistency. Beat well.

Marcia Gehrke, United Methodist Church of the Hamptons, Hampton, New Hampshire

Pineapple Nut Cake

A very moist cake with a delicious frosting.

2 cups flour
2 cups crushed pineapple, drained
2 cups sugar

2 teaspoons baking soda
2 eggs
1 cup walnuts

Grease and flour 9" × 13" pan. Combine flour, pineapple, sugar, baking soda, eggs, and walnuts, and pour into pan. Bake at 350°F for about 40 minutes. Cool and frost cake with Vanilla Frosting (see below).

Vanilla Frosting

1 package (8 ounces) cream cheese
½ cup butter

1 tablespoon vanilla
1½–2 cups confectioners' sugar

Whip cream cheese and butter together. Then add vanilla and enough sugar to make icing spreadable.

Avis M. Ayotte, St. Mark's Church, Augusta, Maine

Pineapple Upside-Down Cake

A fluffy white cake with a caramelized pineapple topping.

3 tablespoons butter
½ cup brown sugar
6 or 9 slices pineapple (depending on size of pan)
6 or 9 cherries
1 egg
½ cup sugar

¼ cup milk
1 cup flour
1 teaspoon baking powder
⅛ teaspoon salt
1 tablespoon melted shortening
1 teaspoon vanilla

Melt butter in large ovenproof skillet. Add brown sugar. Stir until melted. Cover with pineapple slices. Place cherries in holes of pineapple slices. Set aside.

Beat egg lightly and add sugar. Beat well. Sift flour together with baking powder and salt. Add milk alternately with flour mixture. Beat well; add shortening and vanilla. Pour over pineapple. Cover and bake at 350°F for 30 minutes. Turn out upside down on plate and serve with whipped cream.

Dianne Johnson, Dublin Community Church, Dublin, New Hampshire

Poppy Seed Cake

A superb cake far easier to make than most of its ilk.

1 box (18½ ounces) yellow cake mix
1 package (3½ ounces) instant vanilla pudding
½ cup cooking oil
½ cup sherry

1 cup sour cream
¼ cup poppy seeds
4 eggs, separated
1 teaspoon cream of tartar
½ cup chopped walnuts

Stir together cake mix, pudding, oil, sherry, sour cream, and poppy seeds. Add egg yolks and beat 2 minutes. Beat egg whites with cream of tartar until stiff and fold into first mixture. Fold in walnuts. Bake in 10" Bundt or tube pan at 350°F for 40–50 minutes.

Gladys Priest, Foxon Congregational Church, East Haven, Connecticut

Pound Cake

Makes a nice sound pound cake. Freezes well, too.

1¼ cups sugar	2 cups flour
⅔ cup shortening	½ teaspoon baking powder
3 eggs	1 teaspoon salt
⅔ cup milk	
1 teaspoon lemon or vanilla extract	

Cream sugar and shortening. Beat in eggs. Add milk and extract. Combine flour with baking powder and salt and stir into batter. Mix well. Pour into greased and floured large loaf pan (or use 2 small ones). Bake at 300°F for 1 hour and 25 minutes.

Jeannette M. Miller, Morris Congregational Church, Morris, Connecticut

Pumpkin Cake

Good frosted or simply served with whipped cream.

½ cup butter
1¼ cups sugar
2 eggs
1 cup solid-pack canned
  pumpkin
2 cups flour
½ teaspoon cinnamon

½ teaspoon ginger
½ teaspoon nutmeg
½ teaspoon salt
3 teaspoons baking powder
¾ cup milk
½ cup chopped nuts (any kind)
½ teaspoon baking soda

Cream butter and sugar, add eggs, and beat. Stir in pumpkin. Sift together flour, cinnamon, ginger, nutmeg, salt, and baking powder. Add dry ingredients alternately with milk to pumpkin mixture. Then add nuts and baking soda; mix until well-blended and pour into greased and floured 10" × 10" pan. Bake at 350°F for 35 minutes. Cool and frost with Orange Frosting (see below).

Orange Frosting

1 pound confectioners' sugar
1 package (8 ounces) cream
  cheese

2 teaspoons vanilla
  Orange juice

Combine sugar, cream cheese, and vanilla with enough orange juice to make spreadable.

Donna Riley, United Church of Christ, Littleton, New Hampshire

Oatmeal Cake

A moist and spicy dessert cake with a coconut-nut topping

1¼ cups boiling water	1⅓ cups flour
1 cup quick rolled oats	¼ teaspoon salt
½ cup butter	1 teaspoon baking soda
1 cup sugar	Scant teaspoon cinnamon
1 cup brown sugar	1 teaspoon vanilla
2 eggs	

Pour boiling water over oats. Set aside to cool. Cream butter with sugar and brown sugar and beat in eggs. Mix in cooled oats. Add flour, salt, baking soda, cinnamon, and vanilla. Mix well. Pour into greased 7" × 11" pan, and bake at 350°F for 40 minutes, or until done. Cool and cover with Coco-Nut Topping (see below).

Coco-Nut Topping

4 tablespoons butter	2 tablespoons cream
1 cup brown sugar	½ cup grated coconut
½ teaspoon vanilla	½ cup chopped nuts (any kind)

Place butter, brown sugar, vanilla, cream, coconut, and nuts in saucepan and stir together until butter melts. Spread over cool Oatmeal Cake.

Pauline Hammond, Free Will Baptist Church, Northwood, New Hampshire

Scripture Cake

Certainly a must for a Church Supper Cookbook!
(But in this case, the Bible does not tell you everything.)

1 cup Judges 5:25 last clause (butter)

1 cup Jeremiah 6:20 (sugar)

1 tablespoon I Samuel 14:25 (honey)

3 Jeremiah 17:11 (eggs)

1 cup I Samuel 30:12 second food (raisins)

1 cup Nahum 3:12 (figs), chopped

¼ cup Numbers 17:8 (almonds), blanched and chopped

2 cups I Kings 4:22 (flour)

II Chronicles 9:9 (spices, such as cinnamon and nutmeg)

Pinch of Leviticus 2:13 (salt)

1 teaspoon Amos 4:5 (leavener, such as baking soda)

3 tablespoons Judges 4:19 last sentence (milk)

Cream Judges (butter), Jeremiah (sugar), and I Samuel (honey). Beat in the 3 Jeremiahs (eggs), one at a time. Add I Samuel (raisins), Nahum (figs), and Numbers (almonds), and beat again. Sift together I Kings (flour), II Chronicles (spices), Leviticus (salt), and Amos (leavener, or baking soda). Add to first mixture. Lastly, add Judges (milk). Bake at 325°F for 1½ hours, or until done.

French Onion Soup, page 142

Molded Beet Salad, page 144

24-Hour Layered Salad, page 146

Salad Excelsior, page 150

Danish Potato Salad, page 154

Astoria Salad, page 157

Dill Bread, page 182

Deli-Cakes, page 163

Orange Bow Knots, page 188

Tempting Bishop's Cake, page 193

Clockwise from bottom right: Apricot Coconut Squares, page 236; Chocolate Layer Bars, page 239;
Easiest Peanut Butter Cookies Ever, page 244; and Double-Chocolate Chip Pecan Cookies, page 309

Brownies, page 238

Key Lime Pie, page 263

Kentucky Bourbon Pumpkin Pie, page 266

Mile-High Strawberry Pie, page 271

Old-Fashioned Biscuits, page 291

Sponge Cake with Orange Sauce

A nice high sponge cake happily set off by the sauce and whipped cream.

4 large or 5 medium eggs, separated	1 teaspoon lemon extract
2 cups sugar	2½ cups sifted cake flour
1 cup boiling water	1½ teaspoons baking powder
1 teaspoon vanilla	½ teaspoon salt
	1 cup heavy cream

Beat egg whites until foamy. Still beating, gradually add ¼ cup sugar and continue beating until stiff. Beat egg yolks until thick and lemon-colored. Gradually add boiling water in thin stream to yolks, beating constantly until mixture is foamy and nearly fills large mixing bowl. Add remaining 1¾ cups sugar gradually, beating all the while until thick. Beat in vanilla and lemon extract. Sift together flour, baking powder, and salt, and carefully add to yolk mixture, beating slowly until well-blended. Fold in egg whites. Turn into ungreased 10" tube pan and bake at 325°F for 45–60 minutes. Whip cream and set aside.

Orange Sauce

1 cup sugar	2 tablespoons grated orange rind
½ teaspoon salt	1½ tablespoons lemon juice
2 tablespoons cornstarch	2 tablespoons butter
1 cup orange juice	

Mix sugar in saucepan with salt, cornstarch, and orange juice. Cook over medium-high heat, stirring constantly until thickened. Let boil 1 minute, stirring. Remove from heat and add orange rind, lemon juice, and butter. Keep warm.

When cake is done, impale pan upside down on spout of inverted funnel and let cool. Remove from pan when cool and cut into wedges. Serve with warm Orange Sauce and whipped cream.

Cheryl Tutt, Ascutney Union Church, Ascutney, Vermont

White Cake

Frost this 2-egg cake as you wish, or top when cool with hot lemon pie filling.
Makes good cupcakes, too.

2 cups + 2 tablespoons flour
1½ cups sugar
1 tablespoon baking powder
½ teaspoon salt

½ cup shortening
1 teaspoon vanilla
1 cup milk
2 large eggs

Sift flour, sugar, baking powder, and salt together. Add shortening, vanilla, milk, and eggs. Then beat by hand or with electric mixer for 3 minutes. Grease and flour two 8" layer-cake pans or one 8" × 12" pan. Turn batter into pans or pan and bake at 350°F for 35–40 minutes. For cupcakes, put paper liners in muffin pans, fill halfway, and bake at 400°F for 18–20 minutes.

Gladys Congdon, Old Brick Church, Claredon, Vermont

Yogurt Cake Dessert

An interesting variation on the Cottage Pudding (page 177) theme.

Syrup

1¼ cups sugar
2 cups water

1 tablespoon lemon juice
1 tablespoon grated orange rind

Mix sugar and water in saucepan and heat, stirring, until sugar is dissolved. Boil briskly without stirring for 10–15 minutes. Add lemon juice and orange rind. Boil 2 more minutes and set aside to cool.

Cake

¾ cup sugar
3 eggs
1 cup flour
1 cup yogurt

1 teaspoon baking powder
Whipped cream (optional)
Sliced almonds or coconut for
garnish

Beat sugar into eggs until dissolved. Combine flour with yogurt and baking powder and fold into egg mixture. Pour into greased 8" × 8" or 9" × 9" pan and bake at 350°F for 45 minutes, or until slightly browned and toothpick inserted in center comes out clean.

While cake is still hot, cut into diamonds or squares. Pour cooled syrup over cake pieces. When syrup is absorbed, serve cake with whipped cream, if desired, garnished with almonds or coconut.

Belkis H. Vassaf, Concord Unitarian Church, Concord, New Hampshire

Upside-Down Gingerbread

A novel idea that makes a handsome church supper dessert.

2 tablespoons butter
1½ cups molasses
6 slices canned pineapple
¼ cup raisins
¼ cup chopped nuts (any kind)
2 tablespoons sugar
½ cup shortening
1 egg

2¼ cups flour
¼ teaspoon salt
1 teaspoon baking soda
1 teaspoon ginger
1 teaspoon cinnamon
½ teaspoon cloves
¾ cup hot water

Melt butter in 10"–11" ovenproof frying pan or deep round cake pan. Pour in ½ cup molasses. Arrange pineapple slices in pan, filling in spaces with raisins and nuts. Set in warm place. Cream sugar, shortening, remaining 1 cup molasses, and egg. Sift flour with salt, baking soda, ginger, cinnamon, and cloves, and stir into sugar mixture. Add hot water and pour mixture over fruit. Bake at 350°F for 45–60 minutes. Serve hot with whipped cream.

Wacky Cake

This eggless brownie-like cake takes only about 10 minutes to make.
You don't even have to grease the pan!

1½ cups flour
1 cup sugar
3 tablespoons cocoa
1 teaspoon baking soda
1 teaspoon salt

5 tablespoons cooking oil
1 teaspoon vanilla
1 teaspoon vinegar
1 cup cold water

Combine flour, sugar, cocoa, baking soda, and salt in bowl, and turn into ungreased 9" × 13" baking pan. Make 3 holes, or wells, in dry ingredients. Pour oil into one, vanilla into another, and vinegar into the third. Pour cold water over all and stir to mix well. Bake at 350°F for about 40 minutes, or until center is firm.

Thomas A. Nerbonne, United Baptist Church, Concord, New Hampshire

Walnut Cake

A beige cake with a gingerbready texture that tastes wonderfully of walnuts.

1 cup walnuts, broken	½ teaspoon salt
Boiling water	1 tablespoon baking powder
½ cup butter	½ teaspoon cinnamon
2 cups brown sugar	½ teaspoon nutmeg
3 eggs, separated	½ teaspoon cloves
3 cups sifted flour	¾ cup milk

Cover broken walnuts with boiling water for a few minutes and drain. Set aside. Cream butter and brown sugar together and add well-beaten egg yolks. Beat egg whites until stiff and set aside. Sift together flour, salt, baking powder, cinnamon, nutmeg, and cloves. Add to creamed mixture alternately with milk. Add walnuts. Fold in egg whites. Bake in 3 greased 8" layer pans at 350°F for 20 minutes, or until lightly brown. Cool and frost with Butter Cream Frosting (see below).

Butter Cream Frosting

1 cup butter	6 tablespoons cream
3 cups confectioners' sugar	1 tablespoon vanilla

Cream together butter and sugar, then beat in cream and vanilla.

Dianne Johnson, Dublin Community Church, Dublin, New Hampshire

Cookies and Bars

Do you suppose there exists a person who doesn't like cookies? Surely one of the handiest and dandiest of all goodies, cookies and bars tuck neatly into pockets or lunch boxes, preside with delicate grace over the tea table, are the perfect after-school snack, and, of course, make wonderful Christmas or anytime gifts.

Almond Butter Balls

A wonderful old-fashioned butter cookie.

¾ cup butter
1 cup brown sugar
1 egg, lightly beaten
1 teaspoon vanilla
2 cups flour

1½ teaspoons baking powder
½ teaspoon salt
½ cup sugar
1½ cups whole almonds

Cream butter and brown sugar. Add egg and vanilla. Sift flour, baking powder, and salt, and add to mixture. Beat well. Form into balls, 1 teaspoon at a time. Roll in sugar. Place on greased cookie sheet. Press whole almond in center of each. Bake at 400°F for 12 minutes. ***Makes about 5 dozen.***

Marion Sarsfield, Woodmont United Church of Christ, Milford, Connecticut

Almond Spice Cookies

Can be made way ahead and kept frozen until wanted. No need to thaw dough before baking.

1 cup butter
⅓ cup molasses
1 cup sugar
2 egg yolks
3 tablespoons crystalline ginger, cut up fine

1 tablespoon cinnamon
2 teaspoons cloves
1 teaspoon baking soda
2 cups flour
1 cup slivered almonds

Beat together butter, molasses, sugar, and egg yolks. Stir in ginger. Sift together cinnamon, cloves, baking soda, and flour. Add almonds. Stir into first mixture. Mix well. Pat dough into 2 long rolls about 1½" in diameter. Cover with plastic wrap and freeze. When ready to bake, slice frozen dough into ¼" rounds; place 1" apart on ungreased cookie sheet and bake at 350°F for 8–10 minutes, or until brown and crisp. Cool on racks. ***Makes about 6 dozen.***

Real Almond Macaroons

No flour, no baking powder, no coconut—*real* macaroons.
A treat for any occasion. They will keep well packed in an airtight container.

1 package (7 to 8 ounces) almond
    paste
2 egg whites

1 cup + 2 tablespoons sugar
1 teaspoon vanilla

Put almond paste in bowl and break up into small pieces. Pour egg whites on top of paste. Let stand, covered, in refrigerator 12–24 hours, turning and stirring from time to time. (Egg whites will liquefy almond paste.) Blend whites and almond paste together into smooth paste, and add sugar and vanilla, mixing all well together to form smooth but sticky dough. Line cookie sheet or sheets with aluminum foil. Lightly oil foil. Shape dough into balls the size of large marbles and place on foil 2" apart. Bake at 325°F for 15–20 minutes, or until lightly browned around edges and center is firm. Remove cookie sheet from oven. Transfer foil in one piece with cookies still on it to cooling rack. Re-line cookie sheet with new oiled foil and put in another batch to bake. When first batch of cookies is completely cool, peel macaroons carefully off foil; discard used sheets of foil. (If you try to take macaroons off foil before completely cool, their chewy centers will stick to foil and fragment the cookies.) ***Makes about 3 dozen.***

O. P. Valhalla, St. Matthew's Church, Bedford, New York

Apricot-Coconut Squares

Serve warm to have these at their melt-in-the-mouth best.

1 cup sugar
2 cups flour
¾ cup butter
1 cup grated coconut
½ cup chopped nuts (optional)
1 egg

¼ teaspoon salt
1 teaspoon vanilla
1 jar (10 ounces) apricot jam
    (or substitute your favorite
    fruit jam)

With a fork, mix together sugar, flour, butter, coconut, nuts, if using, egg, salt, and vanilla. Press three-fourths of batter in bottom of greased 9" × 13" pan. Spread jam over top. Spread rest of batter over jam with fork, letting some of jam show through. Bake at 350°F for 25–30 minutes, or until light golden brown. Cool. ***Makes 12–20 bars, depending on size.***

Mrs. James W. Snow, Jr., Wapping Community Church, South Windsor, Connecticut

Chocolate Brownies

Very rich, very sweet, very fudgy, and unsurpassed for those
who like their brownies like that.

1 cup butter	5 eggs
1 package (6 ounces) chocolate bits	1 tablespoon vanilla
	1½ cups flour
3 cups sugar	½ cup chopped walnuts (optional)

Melt together butter and chocolate bits. Remove from heat and add sugar. Beat in eggs, one at a time, and vanilla. Add flour and walnuts, if using, and stir well. Spread on ungreased jelly-roll pan (10" × 15") and bake at 350°F for 25–30 minutes. Do not overbake—they should be fudgy when done. Cool and cut—small, because they *are* rich. ***Makes 32.***

Diana G. Mac Veagh, Church of the Heavenly Rest, New York City, New York

Brownies

Chocolate treats not quite as rich and sweet as those in preceding recipe,
but perfect for those who like *their* brownies like *that*.

½ cup butter
4 ounces unsweetened chocolate
4 eggs
2 cups sugar
¼ teaspoon salt

1 teaspoon vanilla
1 cup flour
½ cup semi-sweet chocolate chips
¾ cup chopped nuts (any kind),
    optional

Melt together butter and chocolate. Beat eggs and add sugar, salt, and vanilla. Beat in chocolate mixture. Stir in flour, chocolate chips, and nuts, if using. Pour into greased 9" × 9" pan and bake at 325°F for 25–30 minutes, or until center is done. Cool and cut into squares. *Makes 18.*

Inge Schermerhorn, United Church of Christ, North Hampton, New Hampshire

Ever-So-Good Golden Brownies

A nice change from chocolate brownies. Rich, fudgy, and butterscotchy-sweet.

½ cup butter
2 cups brown sugar
2 teaspoons vanilla
2 eggs, well-beaten

1½ cups flour
2 teaspoons baking powder
½ teaspoon salt
½ cup chopped nuts (any kind)

Melt butter. Remove from stove and add brown sugar and vanilla. Beat in eggs. Sift together flour, baking powder, and salt, and add to egg mixture. Stir in nuts. Pour into lightly greased 9" × 9" pan. Bake at 350°F for 25–30 minutes. *Makes 18.*

Mildred Cutter, United Church of Jaffrey, Jaffrey, New Hampshire

Chocolate Layer Bars

These rich chocolate treats are doubly delectable.
The moist fudgy center is encased in a crisp cookie shell.

2 cups flour
1 teaspoon baking soda
½ teaspoon baking powder
1 cup butter or margarine, softened
1 cup granulated sugar
1 cup packed light brown sugar
2 eggs, beaten

1 teaspoon vanilla
1 cup walnuts, chopped
1 bag (12 ounces) semi-sweet or
   bittersweet chocolate chips
½ cup butter or margarine
1 can (14 ounces) sweetened
   condensed milk

Line 13" × 9" baking pan with sheet of aluminum foil long enough for lifting flaps after baking; grease foil. In bowl, whisk flour, baking soda, and baking powder; set aside. In mixing bowl, beat butter or margarine until smooth. Add granulated and brown sugars. Beat until smooth. Add eggs and vanilla; mix well. Stir in flour mixture until blended. Stir in walnuts. Spread half of dough into prepared pan; set aside.

In saucepan, melt chocolate and butter or margarine over low heat. Stir in milk until smooth. Pour into pan. Dollop remaining dough over filling, spreading to cover as well as possible (chocolate filling may be visible in some spots). Bake at 375°F for 30 minutes or until topping is browned (filling will still be jiggly). Remove to cool about 1 hour. Using foil flaps, lift entire sheet of cookies out of pan. Cut into 24 bars. Refrigerate in airtight container. *Makes 24.*

Nancy Eichler, Roswell Presbyterian Church, Roswell, Georgia

No-Bake Oatmeal Fudgies

Very easy and very good.

½ cup milk
½ cup cocoa
1½ cups sugar
½ cup butter

½ cup peanut butter
1 teaspoon vanilla
2½ cups quick-cooking oats

In 2-quart saucepan over medium-high heat, mix milk, cocoa, sugar, and butter. Bring to boil and boil for 2 minutes. Remove from heat and stir in peanut butter and vanilla. Then beat in oats. When dough is well-blended, put into greased 8" × 8" pan and cut into bars, or drop by teaspoonsful on waxed paper. Let cool. ***Makes about 32 bars or 40 cookies.***

Carol Jensen, The United Church of Hardwick, Hardwick, Vermont

No-Bake Carob Oatmeal Bars

Similar to preceding recipe, but with the taste of carob rather than chocolate.

⅓ cup milk
¾ cup honey
½ cup carob powder
½ cup butter

1 teaspoon vanilla
½ cup peanut butter
3 cups quick-cooking oats

In 2-quart saucepan over medium-high heat, mix milk, honey, carob powder, and butter. Bring to full boil for 3 minutes, stirring constantly. Remove from heat and add vanilla and peanut butter. Mix well, then stir in oats and blend well. Put into greased 8" × 8" pan and refrigerate. ***Makes 32.***

Carol Jensen, The United Church of Hardwick, Hardwick, Vermont

Oatmeal-Cranberry Bar Cookies

These chewy bars can be adapted with different fruit fillings.
Try dried apricots or raisins in place of cranberries.

2 navel oranges
Water
3½ cups (1 pound) dried
    sweetened cranberries
¼ cup granulated sugar
Salt
2 cups flour
2 cups rolled oats

1 cup chopped walnuts
1½ teaspoons baking powder
1 teaspoon cinnamon
1 cup butter, softened
2 cups packed light brown sugar
2 eggs, beaten
1 teaspoon vanilla

Grate rind from oranges. Squeeze juice into measuring cup; add enough water to make 1 cup. Place rind, juice-water, cranberries, granulated sugar, and a pinch of salt in medium saucepan. Cook over medium-high heat until boiling. Reduce heat and simmer, stirring occasionally, for 4 minutes or until syrupy. Remove to cool slightly.

    In bowl, combine flour, oats, walnuts, baking powder, cinnamon, and pinch of salt. In another bowl, beat butter. Gradually add brown sugar, beating until smooth. Beat in eggs and vanilla until smooth. In three additions, stir in dry ingredients until no flour is visible. Dollop half of batter in greased 13" × 9" pan. With clean, wet hand, spread dough evenly. Cover evenly with cranberry mixture. Dollop remaining dough in tablespoonfuls over cranberries. With clean, wet hand, spread dough evenly. Bake at 350°F for 30 minutes or until puffed and browned. Remove to cool completely before cutting. ***Makes 48 bars.***

Macadamia Rum Balls

These tropical no-bake cookies develop even more flavor after a few days in the refrigerator. They're ideal for advance preparation.

2 cups sifted graham cracker crumbs, sifted
1 cup sifted confectioners' sugar
2 tablespoons sifted cocoa
1 cup finely chopped macadamia nuts

⅛ teaspoon salt
3 tablespoons honey
2 teaspoons rum extract
4–5 tablespoons cold water
1 cup sweetened, flaked coconut

In bowl, combine crumbs, sugar, cocoa, macadamias, and salt. In small measuring cup, whisk honey, rum extract, and 4 tablespoons water until thoroughly mixed. Add to dry ingredients. Stir until moist enough to clump together. Gradually add up to 1 additional tablespoon water, if needed, to make mixture moist enough to stick together but not so moist that it falls apart. With hands, roll into 1" balls. Roll balls in coconut to coat. Chill in airtight container for 12 hours to firm up. *Makes about 2½ dozen.*

Li-hwa Ong, Kilohana United Methodist Church, Honolulu, Hawaii

Easy Filled Drops
Drop cookies with a date-nut filling

Filling

2 cups chopped dates
¾ cup sugar

¾ cup water
½ cup chopped nuts (any kind)

Combine dates, sugar, and water in saucepan and cook, stirring constantly, until thick. Remove from stove, stir in nuts, and allow to cool.

Cookies

3½ cups flour
⅛ teaspoon cinnamon
1 teaspoon salt
1 teaspoon baking soda
1 cup shortening

2 cups brown sugar
2 eggs, beaten
½ cup soured milk or buttermilk
1 teaspoon vanilla

Sift together flour, cinnamon, salt, and baking soda. Cream shortening and brown sugar. Add eggs, milk, and vanilla; stir in dry ingredients and mix well. Drop most of dough by teaspoonfuls on ungreased cookie sheet.

Flatten cookies a little and place ½ teaspoon date filling on top of each. Cover filling with ½ teaspoon more cookie dough. Bake at 350°F for 15 minutes. *Makes 3½ dozen.*

Bob Gates, Advent Christian Church, Pittsfield, New Hampshire

Forgotten Cookies

Don't forget and turn on the oven to cook something else
while these meringuey treats are in residence.

2 egg whites
½ cup sugar
Dash of salt

½ teaspoon vanilla
½ cup semisweet chocolate bits
½ cup chopped walnuts

Preheat oven to 350°F. Beat egg whites until foamy and gradually add sugar, salt, and vanilla, still beating. Beat until stiff. Fold in chocolate bits and walnuts. Place by tablespoonsful on greased cookie sheet. Turn off oven and put cookies in. Leave in oven overnight. *Makes 24.*

Laura Goodenough, The Congregational Church, Winchester Center, Connecticut

Easiest Peanut Butter Cookies Ever

People are always surprised to hear there's no flour in this peanut butter cookie.
It's a sure-fire hit with children and adults alike.

1 jar (8 ounces) creamy peanut
  butter
2 cups sugar

2 eggs, beaten
2 teaspoons vanilla

In mixing bowl, combine peanut butter and sugar with fork. Add eggs and vanilla. Beat until smooth. Roll into 1½" balls and place 2" apart on greased cookie sheet. Press cookies with fork in crisscross pattern. Bake at 375°F for 8 minutes or until edges start to color. Remove and allow cookies to cool 5 minutes on sheet before transferring to rack. Continue in batches until all dough is baked. *Makes 3½ dozen.*

Gayla Magnus, Evangelical Lutheran Church, Frederick, Maryland

Great-Great-Grandma's Old-Fashioned Gingersnaps

The thin, crispy kind of ginger cookie, today more usually called ginger wafers.

1 cup molasses
½ cup butter
1 tablespoon ginger

1 rounded teaspoon baking soda
3 cups flour

Boil together molasses and butter. Cool. Add ginger, baking soda, and flour. Roll dough thin on floured board and cut with cookie cutters. Bake on ungreased cookie sheet at 350°F for 8–10 minutes. *Makes 4–6 dozen.*

Helen E. Goodwin, Our Savior Lutheran Church, Hanover, New Hampshire

Vermont Ginger Cookies

A cakier cookie covered with sugar grains
and pressed down with a fork like peanut butter cookies.

⅔ cup cooking oil
1½ cups sugar
1 egg
¼ cup molasses
2 cups flour

2 teaspoons baking soda
½ teaspoon salt
1 teaspoon cinnamon
1 teaspoon ginger

In large bowl, mix oil, 1 cup sugar, egg, molasses, flour, baking soda, salt, cinnamon, and ginger. Drop dough by teaspoonsful into dish of remaining ½ cup sugar to coat each cookie. Place on greased cookie sheet and press flat with fork. Bake at 350°F for 8–10 minutes. ***Makes 4 dozen.***

Mildred D. Chamberlain, The Congregational Church, South Hero, Vermont

Foxon Ginger Cookies

These crisp cookies are more like what we think of today as gingersnaps.
You can make a fine Icebox Cake by stacking layers of whipped cream
between the cookies and chilling for several hours.

1 cup shortening
1 cup sugar
1 egg
1 cup molasses

4 cups flour
1 teaspoon baking soda
½ teaspoon salt
1 teaspoon ginger

Cream shortening and sugar. Add egg and mix well. Beat in molasses. Then combine flour, baking soda, salt, and ginger, and stir into molasses mixture. Roll thin, cut out, and bake on ungreased cookie sheet at 350°F for 10 minutes. ***Makes 6–7 dozen.***

Elizabeth K. Watrous, Foxon Congregational Church, East Haven, Connecticut

Molasses Cookies

A *very* good soft molasses cookie with just the right amount of spice.
Is the heated cookie sheet the secret?

3½	cups flour	1	teaspoon ginger
1	teaspoon baking soda	½	cup butter
½	teaspoon salt	1	cup sugar
1½	teaspoons cinnamon	2	eggs, beaten
1	teaspoon cloves	1	cup molasses

Sift flour, baking soda, salt, cinnamon, cloves, and ginger together. Cream butter and sugar. Beat in eggs and molasses. Add flour mixture and stir well. Have all ingredients at room temperature and cookie sheets *hot*. Drop by teaspoonful on ungreased sheets and bake at 350°F for 10 minutes or less. ***Makes 4 dozen.***

Eva Day, The Unitarian Church, Peterborough, New Hampshire

Pineapple Cookies

Light, pretty, and absolutely scrumptious.

1⅔	cups sugar	2⅔	cups flour
⅔	cup butter	½	teaspoon baking soda
2	eggs	½	teaspoon salt
½	cup crushed pineapple (canned in syrup or fresh in natural juice)	2	teaspoons lemon extract

Mix sugar, butter, eggs, pineapple (with juice), flour, baking soda, salt, and lemon extract. Drop by teaspoonful on greased baking sheet. Bake at 350°F for 12–15 minutes, or until lightly brown. Let stand a few seconds before removing to cooling racks. ***Makes approximately 6 dozen.***

Regina Stanhope, Our Savior Lutheran Church, Hanover, New Hampshire

Potato Chip Cookies

Hard to tell from the title, but this recipe makes a superb sugar cookie.

1 cup sugar	1 teaspoon baking soda
1 cup light brown sugar	2 teaspoon vanilla
1 cup butter	1 cup potato chips, finely crushed
2 eggs, well-beaten	¾ cup chopped nuts (any kind),
2 cups flour	optional

Combine sugar and brown sugar and cream with butter. Beat in eggs. Sift flour and baking soda together and add to creamed mixture. Stir in vanilla, potato chips, and nuts, if using. Drop by teaspoonsful 3" apart on ungreased baking sheet. Bake at 350°F for 10–12 minutes. *Makes 5 dozen.*

Marion R. Andrew, United Church of Christ, Keene, New Hampshire

Rich Cookies

Wonderful thin tea cookies. Before baking, decorate with nuts, candied fruit, raisins, or coconut; after baking, decorate when cool with a chocolate cream frosting.

1 cup butter	1½ cups flour
⅔ cup sugar	1 teaspoon vanilla
2 eggs, well-beaten	

Cream butter and add sugar gradually, then eggs, flour, and vanilla. Drop from tip of spoon in small portions on greased baking sheets, 2" apart. Spread thin with knife dipped in cold water and bake at 375°F for about 5 minutes. *Makes 3–3½ dozen.*

Margaret Michaelsen, North Bennington Congregational Church, North Bennington, Vermont

Sour Cream Cookies

The old-fashioned kind, with raisins.

2 cups sugar	½ teaspoon salt
1 cup butter	1 teaspoon nutmeg
2 eggs	1 cup sour cream
3 cups flour	1½ cups raisins
1 teaspoon baking soda	

Cream sugar and butter. Add eggs and beat well. Sift together flour, baking soda, salt, and nutmeg, and add alternately with sour cream to creamed mixture. Add raisins. Drop by teaspoonsful on ungreased cookie sheet and bake at 375°F for 7 minutes. *Makes 5 dozen.*

Lillian Farrar, United Church of Christ, Keene, New Hampshire

Saucy Bars

Similar in taste and consistency to a carrot cake.
Would also be good with Cream Cheese Frosting (page 176).

½ cup butter	½ teaspoon salt
1 cup sugar	½ teaspoon cloves
1 cup applesauce	1 teaspoon cinnamon
1 teaspoon vanilla	1 teaspoon nutmeg
2 cups flour	¾ cup raisins
1 teaspoon baking soda	½ cup chopped nuts (any kind)

Cream butter and sugar. Add applesauce and vanilla. Sift together flour, baking soda, salt, cloves, cinnamon, and nutmeg, and add to applesauce mixture. Mix well. Stir in raisins and nuts. Spread in greased 9" × 13" baking pan. Bake at 350°F for 35–40 minutes. Frost while warm. *Makes 2 dozen.*

Frosting

¼ cup melted butter	1¾ cups confectioners' sugar
¼ cup cream	½ teaspoon vanilla

Beat together butter, cream, sugar, and vanilla.

Margaret Wister, North Congregational Church, Concord, New Hampshire

Thumb Cookies

A dainty and altogether fetching confection. Keep them small.

1 cup butter
½ cup sugar
2 egg yolks, beaten
½ teaspoon vanilla

1½ cups flour
Pinch of salt
¼ cup raspberry or apricot jam

Cream butter and sugar. Add egg yolks and vanilla and beat well. Mix in flour and salt. Form into balls just big enough to hold thumbprint. Place on ungreased cookie sheet 1½" apart. Press thumb into center of each cookie to make indentation. Fill indentation with dab (about ¼ teaspoon) of jam. Bake at 350°F for about 15 minutes. They should still be very pale when baked. *Makes about 40.*

Diana Boulet, The Oratory Chapel, East Burnham, New Hampshire

Date Balls

Easy to make but special enough for holidays.

2 eggs, beaten
1 cup sugar
¼ cup soft butter
1 cup (8 ounces) dates, finely chopped

½ cup chopped walnuts
1 teaspoon vanilla
2 cups crispy rice cereal
1½ cups grated coconut or 2 cups confectioners' sugar (optional)

Combine eggs, sugar, butter, dates, walnuts, and vanilla in bowl and blend well. Turn into heavy skillet and cook over medium heat for 5 minutes, stirring constantly. Remove from heat and add cereal. Mix well. Cool. Shape into small balls by rolling dough in buttered hands. Roll each cookie to coat in coconut or confectioners' sugar, if desired. Let set for 24 hours on wax paper for best flavor. *Makes 24.*

Edna Foss, Suncook United Methodist Church, Suncook, New Hampshire

Frosted Orange Cookies

Passed down through several generations of a Kansas family,
these tender cookies are really good keepers.

3 cups flour
2 teaspoons baking powder
½ teaspoon baking soda
⅛ teaspoon salt
1 orange
3/4 cup solid vegetable shortening
1½ cups light brown sugar

2 eggs, beaten
½ cup buttermilk
1 teaspoon orange extract or vanilla
2 cups confectioners' sugar
3 tablespoons butter, softened

On a sheet of waxed paper, combine flour, baking powder, baking soda, and salt; set aside. Grate orange rind; set aside. Squeeze 3 tablespoons of orange juice into small bowl; set aside.

In a mixing bowl, beat shortening and sugar until smooth. Add eggs, buttermilk, orange extract or vanilla, and all but 1 teaspoon orange rind. Beat until smooth. Add dry ingredients, one-third at a time, stirring until blended. Drop by teaspoonfuls on ungreased cookie sheets. Bake at 350°F about 10 minutes or until tops spring back when pressed. Remove to rack. Meanwhile, in mixing bowl, whisk confectioners' sugar, butter, reserved orange juice, and remaining 1 teaspoon orange rind until smooth. Frost cookies. *Makes 4½ dozen.*

Angie Johnston, Crossroads Christian Church, Shawnee, Kansas

Pies, Pies, and More Pies

Few homemakers will undertake to bake a pie for public consumption unless they are very sure of its success. For some reason, perhaps stemming from the "Home, Mother, and Apple Pie" ideal, makers of memorable pies are elevated to a high culinary pedestal in America and remembered when other cooks and their creations are forgotten. All the pies in this chapter have been tested by the ultimate critic: time. They have been enjoyed and admired year after year by families and communities across the country.

Classic Apple Pie

Need we say more . . .

Crust

2⅔ cup flour
1 teaspoon salt

1 cup shortening
½ cup (approximately) cold water

Mix flour, salt, and shortening (I use margarine) until consistency of cornmeal. Add water until dough sticks together and you can form it into a ball. Divide dough in 2 halves. Roll out 1 half to fit 10" pie plate. Line plate with pastry.

Filling

12 cups apples, peeled, cored, and sliced (10–12 large apples)
¾ cup sugar
1 tablespoon lemon juice

1 teaspoon nutmeg
1 teaspoon cinnamon
1 tablespoon butter

Slice apples into 10" pie plate until heaping full. Then turn apples into bowl along with sugar, lemon juice, nutmeg, and cinnamon. Mix well. Return apple mixture to pie plate, pressing apples firmly as you do. Dot with butter. Roll out second half of pastry and place on top of pie, sealing edges firmly. Slash the letter *A* in top to let steam out. Bake at 425°F for 20 minutes, reduce heat to 400°F, and bake another 20 minutes. Then reduce heat again to 375°F for 20 minutes more, or until crust is nicely browned and apples feel done when you put knife through slashed *A*. If you use McIntosh apples, this may not take whole hour. ***Serves 12.***

Moira Burnham, Church of the Epiphany, New York, New York

Apples and Cream Pie

Apple pie with an attractive difference.

4 medium apples, peeled, cored,
   and sliced
1 unbaked 9" pie shell
1 cup whipping cream
3 tablespoons flour
1 teaspoon cinnamon

¼ teaspoon nutmeg
1 cup sugar
1 egg, beaten
1 teaspoon vanilla
⅛ teaspoon salt
¾ cup coarsely chopped walnuts

Arrange apples in pie shell. Mix together cream, flour, cinnamon, nutmeg, sugar, egg, vanilla, and salt until well-blended. Pour over apples. Sprinkle with walnuts. Bake at 450°F for 10 minutes, then reduce heat to 350°F and bake until apples are tender, 35–40 minutes. *Makes one 9" pie.*

Evelyn H. Chase, Concord Unitarian Church, New Hampshire

Swedish Apple Pie

Apples with a crunchy topping instead of a pie crust.

7 medium apples, peeled, cored,
   and sliced
1 tablespoon + 1 cup sugar
1 tablespoon cinnamon
¾ cup melted butter

1 cup flour
1 egg, beaten
1½ cups chopped nuts (any kind)
   Pinch of salt

Fill 9" pie pan two-thirds full of apple slices. Sprinkle with 1 tablespoon sugar and cinnamon. In medium bowl, combine butter, remaining 1 cup sugar, flour, egg, nuts, and salt. Spread over apples in pan to cover. Bake at 350°F for 45 minutes, or until golden brown. *Serves 6–8.*

Eldora Hager, United Church of Christ, Keene, New Hampshire

Wild Blueberry Pie

The lemon and spices make this blueberry pie something really special.
Cultivated berries may be substituted for the wild ones.

¾ cup sugar
3½ tablespoons quick-cooking
   tapioca
¼ teaspoon salt
½ teaspoon cinnamon
¼ teaspoon cloves
1 tablespoon lemon juice

4 cups fresh wild blueberries, or
   frozen berries, thawed
1 unbaked 9" pastry shell, and
   pastry for lattice crust
1 tablespoon butter + 2
   tablespoons melted butter
2 tablespoons sugar

Combine sugar, tapioca, salt, cinnamon, and cloves. Mix with lemon juice and blueberries. Turn into unbaked pastry shell. Dot with 1 tablespoon butter. Top with lattice crust. Brush with melted butter and sprinkle with sugar. Cover edges with foil to prevent burning and bake at 425°F for 30 minutes. Remove foil and bake 10 more minutes, or until crust is browned. *Serves 8.*

Carol Jensen, The United Church, Hardwick, Vermont

Crustless Coconut Pie

Though there is no crust, the dessert bakes into a pie and cuts like one.

4 eggs
¼ cup butter
1 cup sugar
¼ cup flour
½ teaspoon baking powder

2 cups milk
1 teaspoon vanilla
¼ teaspoon salt
1 cup coconut

In blender, combine eggs, butter, sugar, flour, baking powder, milk, vanilla, salt, and coconut. Blend until smooth. Pour into greased 10" pie pan. Bake at 350°F for 1 hour. *Serves 8.*

Pauline Hammond, Free Will Baptist Church, Northwood, New Hampshire

Blueberry-Yogurt Pie

Creamy and smooth, this dessert is very rich in a graham cracker crust.

1 envelope (1 tablespoon)
  unflavored gelatin
½ cup sugar
½ teaspoon salt
¼ cup water
2 slightly beaten egg yolks
1 cup cottage cheese

1 cup blueberry yogurt
2 egg whites
½ cup fresh (or canned, drained)
  blueberries
1 baked 9" pastry or graham
  cracker shell
  Whipped cream

Soak gelatin in a little bit of cold water for 3–5 minutes. In saucepan, combine ¼ cup sugar, gelatin, and salt; add water and egg yolks. Cook and stir over low heat until gelatin is dissolved and mixture begins to thicken. Cool. Sieve cottage cheese; stir in egg-gelatin mixture. Add yogurt and beat until well-blended. Beat egg whites to soft peaks. Gradually add remaining ¼ cup sugar, beating to stiff peaks. Fold yogurt mixture and blueberries into egg whites. Turn into pie shell. Chill 6 hours till firm. Garnish with whipped cream. *Serves 6.*

Don Wyant, Woodmont United Church of Christ, Milford, Connecticut

Butterscotch Chiffon Pie

Tastes good, like butterscotch chiffon should.

1 envelope plain gelatin
¼ cup cold water
3 eggs, separated
1 cup light brown sugar
1 cup scalded milk
2 tablespoons butter

¼ teaspoon salt
½ teaspoon vanilla
¼ cup sugar
1 baked 10" pie shell
  Whipped cream

Soak gelatin in cold water 5 minutes. Beat egg yolks. Gradually beat in brown sugar, then beat in milk gradually. Add butter and salt and cook in double boiler, stirring until custardlike, about 10 minutes. Stir in gelatin. Cool, then add vanilla. Beat egg whites with sugar until stiff. Fold into mixture. Pour into pie shell. Cool and top with whipped cream. *Serves 6–8.*

Louise Coleman, First Congregational Church, Littleton, New Hampshire

Cheesecake Pie

Easy to make, good to eat, and looks great. Serve with thawed frozen strawberries.

2 packages (8 ounces each) cream cheese	**⅔ cup sugar**
3 eggs	**½ teaspoon almond extract**
	Pinch of salt

Topping

2 cups sour cream	**1 teaspoon vanilla**
3 tablespoons sugar	**Pinch of salt**

Beat cream cheese until smooth. Beat in eggs. Add sugar, almond extract, and salt. Pour into greased 9" pie pan. (There is *no* crust in this recipe.) Bake at 325°F for 50 minutes. Cool for 20 minutes. Combine sour cream, sugar, vanilla, and salt. Pour over pie, return to oven, and bake at 325°F for 15 minutes more. *Serves 8.*

Marcia Fletcher, St. Anne's Episcopal Church, Calais, Maine

Cherry Breeze

No-cook filling. No-bake crust. Just blend and chill.

1 cup crushed cornflakes
⅓ cup butter, melted
1 package (8 ounces) cream cheese, softened
1 can (15 ounces) sweetened condensed milk
½ cup lemon juice
1 teaspoon vanilla
1 can (21 ounces) chilled cherry pie filling

Mix cornflake crumbs and butter thoroughly in 9" pan. Press firmly and evenly over bottom and sides of pan to form crust. Chill. Beat cream cheese until light and fluffy. Add condensed milk and blend thoroughly. Stir in lemon juice and vanilla. Turn into crust. Refrigerate 3–4 hours, or until firm. (Do not freeze.) Top with filling just before serving. *Serves 8.*

Woodmont United Church of Christ, Milford, Connecticut

Coconut Pie

The coconut rises to the top over a rich, puddinglike layer.

3 beaten eggs
1½ cups sugar
½ cup melted butter
4 teaspoons lemon juice
1 teaspoon vanilla
1⅓ cups coconut
1 unbaked 9" pie shell
Whipped cream

Combine eggs, sugar, butter, lemon juice, and vanilla. Stir in coconut and pour mixture into pie shell. Bake at 350°F for 40–45 minutes until coconut is browned and pie has begun to set. Cool thoroughly. Pie will become firmer as it cools. Serve with whipped cream. *Serves 8.*

Marcia Fletcher, St. Anne's Episcopal Church, Calais, Maine

Chocolate Angel Pie

Serve this heavenly food in small portions—a little goes a long way.

2 egg whites
⅛ teaspoon salt
⅛ teaspoon cream of tartar
½ cup sugar
½ cup chopped nuts (any kind)
1½ teaspoons vanilla

1 package (4 ounces) Baker's German Chocolate
3 tablespoons water
1 cup sweetened whipped cream
1 Heath candy bar (1.4 ounces)

Beat egg whites with salt and cream of tartar until foamy. Add sugar gradually, beating until stiff peaks hold. Fold in nuts and ½ teaspoon vanilla. Spread in 8" pan, building up sides. Bake at 300°F for 50 minutes. Cool.

Melt chocolate in water over low heat, stirring constantly. Cool until thickened. Add remaining 1 teaspoon vanilla. Fold in half of whipped cream. Pile into meringue shell. Chill 3 hours. Put rest of whipped cream on top. Grate candy bar on top. *Serves 8.*

Barbara Lockhart, United Church of Christ, Keene, New Hampshire

Cottage Cheese Pie

Use of the blender is necessary to the texture of this superb pie.

4 eggs, separated
16 ounces cottage cheese
1½ cups sugar

Juice and grated rind of
1 lemon
1 baked 10" pie shell

Put yolks, cottage cheese, sugar, and lemon juice and rind into blender and blend at medium speed. Beat egg whites until stiff and fold into blended mixture. Turn into pie shell and bake at 375°F for 35–40 minutes, or until set. *Serves 8.*

Jeannette M. Miller, Morris Congregational Church, Morris, Connecticut

Cranberry Parfait Pie

A festive note for Thanksgiving.

1 package (3 ounces) lemon
  gelatin
1 cup cranberry juice cocktail
1 pint vanilla ice cream
1 can (16 ounces) whole-berry
  cranberry sauce

3 tablespoons lemon juice
1 teaspoon grated lemon rind
1 baked 9" pastry shell
Whipped cream
Whole cranberries

Soak gelatin in a little bit of cold water for 3–5 minutes. Heat cranberry juice in 2-quart saucepan. Remove from heat and add gelatin, stirring until dissolved. Stir in ice cream until melted. Chill mixture until it begins to thicken. Fold in cranberry sauce, lemon juice, and rind. Pour into cooled pastry shell. Garnish with whipped cream and whole cranberries. *Serves 6–8.*

Custard Pie

Baked egg custard in a shell. Be sure pie shell is well-chilled.

4 eggs
½ cup sugar
1 teaspoon vanilla
½ teaspoon + ⅛ teaspoon nutmeg

Pinch of salt
2½ cups warm milk
1 unbaked 9" pie shell, chilled

Beat eggs lightly and add sugar, vanilla, ½ teaspoon nutmeg, and salt. Stir in milk and pour into pie shell. Sprinkle with remaining ⅛ teaspoon nutmeg. Bake at 425°F for 10–15 minutes, or until pie begins to brown. Then reduce heat to 300°F and bake about 30 minutes longer, or until knife inserted in center comes out clean. *Serves 6–8.*

Barbara Lockhart, United Church of Christ, Keene, New Hampshire

Lemon Meringue Pie

Famous among all those lucky enough to have tasted it.

1¼ cups sugar
⅛ teaspoon salt
6 tablespoons cornstarch
2 cups boiling water
Grated rind of 1 lemon

4 tablespoons butter
3 egg yolks
½ cup lemon juice
1 baked 9" pie shell

Mix sugar, salt, and cornstarch. Add water and lemon rind. Cook gently, stirring until thickened; simmer for 10 minutes. Add butter but do not stir. Mix egg yolks with lemon juice and stir into hot sugar mixture. When thoroughly blended, put into lightly browned pastry shell and bake at 400°F for 10 minutes. Top with Meringue (see below) and continue baking at 350°F until lightly browned. *Serves 6–8.*

Meringue

3 egg whites
Pinch of salt

1 teaspoon lemon juice or vanilla
6 tablespoons sugar

Beat egg whites and salt until soft peaks form. Add lemon juice or vanilla and beat in sugar gradually until meringue is stiff.

Blanche Burnett, Dublin Community Church, Dublin, New Hampshire

Frozen Lemon Pie

Icy-cold summer delight to serve during the "dog days."

3 eggs, separated
½ cup sugar
¼ cup lemon juice
Rind of ½ lemon, cut into
strips, with white part removed

1 cup whipped cream
½ cup vanilla-wafer crumbs

Beat egg yolks well in top of double boiler; add all but 1 tablespoon of sugar, along with lemon juice and rind. Cook over rapidly boiling water for 10 minutes, or until thickened, stirring constantly. Remove rind and chill. Beat egg whites until stiff and dry. Add remaining sugar and beat until whites hold peaks. Fold in custard and whipped cream. Butter 9" pie pan; coat thoroughly with wafer crumbs. Pour lemon mixture over crumbs, and sprinkle more crumbs over top. Freeze until firm. *Serves 6.*

Lemon Sponge Pie

Custardy on the bottom, cakey on top.

1 cup sugar
2 tablespoons flour
1 egg, separated
Juice and grated rind of 1 lemon

1 tablespoon melted butter
1 cup milk
1 baked 8" pie shell

Mix together sugar, flour, egg yolk, lemon juice and rind, butter, and milk. Beat egg white until stiff and fold into lemon mixture. Fill pie crust and bake at 375°F for 30 minutes, or until top is brown. Reduce oven temperature to 350°F and bake for 30 minutes longer, or until firm. *Serves 6.*

Key Lime Pie

If a pie can be gorgeous, this one is—delicious, too.

2 eggs, separated
1 can (15 ounces) sweetened
  condensed milk
½ cup lime juice (6–8 limes)

2–3 drops green food coloring
  (optional)
1 8"–9" graham cracker pie shell
3 tablespoons sugar

Beat egg yolks and mix thoroughly with milk. Fold in lime juice and add food coloring, if desired. Pour into pie crust. Beat egg whites until soft peaks form, and beat in sugar gradually until stiff. Spread over pie and put under broiler until lightly browned. Refrigerate 3–4 hours before serving. *Serves 6.*

Mary Lewis, Christchurch Cathedral, Nassau, Bahamas

Pecan Pie

The whipped cream is a New England touch, but it is just as good without.

3 eggs
½ cup sugar
¼ teaspoon salt
1 cup light corn syrup
½ teaspoon vanilla

1 cup pecans, broken
1 unbaked 9" pie crust
1 cup heavy cream, whipped
  (optional)
  Pecan halves

Beat eggs slightly. Add sugar, salt, corn syrup, vanilla, and pecans. Mix well. Pour into pie shell and bake at 300°F for 50–55 minutes. Top with whipped cream, if desired, and garnish with pecan halves. *Serves 6–8.*

Barbara Lockhart, United Church of Christ, Keene, New Hampshire

Tiny Pecan Pies

Once you make these, there is no escape. You just have to go on making them!

1 package (3 ounces) cream
 cheese
½ cup + 1 tablespoon butter
1 cup sifted flour
1 egg

¾ cup brown sugar
1 teaspoon vanilla
 Pinch of salt
⅔ cup coarsely broken pecans

Let cream cheese and ½ cup butter soften to room temperature. Then blend. Stir in flour, and chill about 1 hour. Shape dough into twenty-four 1" balls. Press on bottom and sides of small cupcake pans.

Beat together egg, brown sugar, remaining 1 tablespoon butter, vanilla, and salt until smooth. Divide half the pecans among pastry-lined cups. Add egg mixture and top with remaining pecans. Bake at 325°F for 25 minutes, or until filling is set. Remove from pans. *Makes 24 tarts.*

Lucille Pineault, First Congregational Church, Littleton, New Hampshire

Raisin–Sour Cream Pie

Rich as rich—serve in small portions.

Pastry for 2-crust pie
1 cup raisins
¼ cup sugar
1 tablespoon flour

¼ teaspoon salt
1 egg, beaten
1 cup sour cream
 Vanilla ice cream

Line bottom of 9" pie plate with half of pastry. Set aside. Put raisins through food chopper. Add sugar, flour, salt, egg, and sour cream. Heat in top of double boiler. Pour hot filling into pastry-lined pie plate. Cover with top crust, seal, and flute edges. Cut slits in top crust. Cover edge of crust with 2"–3" strip of aluminum foil to prevent excessive browning. Remove foil for last 15 minutes of baking. Bat at 425°F for 30–40 minutes, or until crust is brown and juice begins to bubble through slits. Serve warm, topped with scoop of ice cream. *Serves 8.*

Glorious Pineapple Pie

Not only glorious but glamorous and wickedly rich. A real star.
Best served the same day it is made.

3 egg whites
1 cup + 1 tablespoon sugar
1 teaspoon vanilla
21 crushed Ritz or similar
   crackers
⅔ cup chopped nuts (any kind)
1 package (8 ounces) cream
   cheese, softened

¾ cup confectioners' sugar
1 cup heavy cream
1 can (8 ounces) crushed
   unsweetened pineapple,
   drained
   Chopped nuts for garnish

Beat egg whites until stiff, then beat in 1 cup sugar and vanilla gradually. Fold in cracker crumbs and nuts. Spread in nonstick or lightly greased 9" pie pan. Bake at 350°F for 30 minutes, then cool.

Blend cream cheese with confectioners' sugar and spread over baked crust. Beat cream with remaining 1 tablespoon sugar until stiff, and fold in pineapple. Spread over pie and refrigerate 2 hours or more. Decorate top with a few chopped nuts. *Serves 8.*

Mildred T. Melvin, Concord Unitarian Church, Concord, New Hampshire

Kentucky Bourbon Pumpkin Pie

Somehow, this makes one of the best pumpkin pies ever.
Maybe it is the bourbon, but you certainly don't taste it.

1 unbaked 9" pie shell	1 teaspoon ginger
1 tablespoon melted shortening	2 teaspoons cinnamon
2 large eggs	¼ tablespoon cloves
½ cup brown sugar	2 cups solid-pack canned pumpkin
2 tablespoons molasses	1½ cups light cream
½ teaspoon salt	1 tablespoon bourbon whiskey

Brush pie shell lightly with shortening. Preheat oven to 450°F. Beat eggs with brown sugar, molasses, salt, ginger, cinnamon, and cloves until well-blended. Add pumpkin, cream, and bourbon and mix well. Pour into pie shell and bake on lower shelf of oven for 10 minutes. Lower oven temperature to 400°F and bake about 30 minutes longer, or until knife inserted in center comes out clean. *Serves 6.*

Elizabeth Bauhan, All Saints Episcopal Church, Peterborough, New Hampshire

Pumpkin Ice Cream Pie

A frozen variation of good old pumpkin pie, this is both easy and delicious.

1 pint vanilla ice cream	½ teaspoon ginger
1 baked 9" pie shell	¼ teaspoon nutmeg
¾ cup sugar	1 cup solid-pack canned pumpkin
½ teaspoon salt	1 cup heavy cream, whipped
½ teaspoon cinnamon	

Spread softened ice cream in bottom of cooled pie shell. Put in freezer while mixing together sugar, salt, cinnamon, ginger, nutmeg, and pumpkin. Fold pumpkin mixture into whipped cream and spread over ice cream. Freeze. Set out 20–30 minutes before serving. *Serves 8.*

Martha Fountain, Center Congregational Church, Torrington, Connecticut

Impossible Pumpkin Pie

"Impossible" because the biscuit mix somehow
magically gets its act together to form a bottom crust!

2 eggs
1½ cups solid-pack canned pumpkin
¾ cup sugar
2 tablespoons butter, melted
½ cup biscuit mix
1 cup evaporated milk

1 cup water
½ teaspoon salt
1 teaspoon cinnamon
¼ teaspoon cloves
¼ teaspoon nutmeg
½ teaspoon ginger

In blender, combine eggs, pumpkin, sugar, butter, biscuit mix, milk, water, salt, cinnamon, cloves, nutmeg, and ginger. Blend on low for 2 minutes. Grease and flour 10" pie plate. Pour filling in and bake at 350°F for 45–50 minutes. *Serves 6–8.*

Mary Nichol, First Presbyterian Church, Monroe, New York

Pink Lady Pie

Raspberries, orange juice, marshmallows, and whipped cream—
delicate flavor and rich texture.

1½ cups finely crushed vanilla wafers
¼ cup softened butter
¼ cup sugar
¾ cup orange juice

12 ounces marshmallows
1½ cups heavy cream, whipped
1 package (10 ounces) frozen raspberries, thawed

Blend vanilla wafers, butter, and sugar together and press firmly into 9" pie plate. Bake at 375°F for 5 minutes. Cool and chill.

Heat orange juice in double boiler, add marshmallows, and stir until melted. Cool mixture and chill in refrigerator until partially set. Fold in whipped cream, then raspberries. Pour filling into crust. Top with extra whipped cream, if desired. *Serves 8.*

Raspberry Ribbon Pie

Light and delicious, with super eye appeal.

1 package (3 ounces) raspberry gelatin
¼ cup sugar
1¼ cups boiling water
1 package (10 ounces) frozen red raspberries
1 tablespoon lemon juice

1 package (3 ounces) cream cheese, softened
⅓ cup sifted confectioners' sugar
1 teaspoon vanilla
Dash of salt
1 cup cream, whipped, no sugar
1 baked 9" pie shell

Red Layers: Soak gelatin in a little bit of cold water for 3–5 minutes, dissolve gelatin and sugar in boiling water. Add berries and lemon juice. Stir until berries thaw. Chill until partially set.

White Layers: Blend cream cheese, confectioners' sugar, vanilla, and salt. Fold in small amount of whipped cream first, then fold in remainder.

Spread half of white cheese mixture on bottom of pie shell. Cove with half of red gelatin mixture. Repeat layers, ending with red layer on top. Chill until set. Garnish with more whipped cream on top, if desired. ***Serves 6–8.***

Barbara Lockhart, United Church of Christ, Keene, New Hampshire

Pastiera Di Grano (Wheat Pie)

The traditional Italian Easter dessert.

Sweet Pastry

3 cups sifted flour
Pinch of salt
¾ cup sugar

¾ cup butter
4 egg yolks
1½ tablespoons milk

Sift flour, salt, and sugar into bowl. Cut in butter evenly with fingertips, knives, or pastry blender. Stir in egg yolks one at a time, mixing with wooden spoon. Work dough with hands until it is manageable and clears the bowl. Add ½ tablespoon milk at a time as necessary to hold dough together. Form into 3 balls and chill for at least 30 minutes. Roll out 2 pastry balls and line two 9" pie plates, leaving ½" overhang. Roll out remaining ball and cut into strips to use as lattice.

Filling

1½ cups cooked soaked wheat,* tapioca, or rice	6 egg yolks, beaten
½ cup scalded milk	1 teaspoon vanilla
1 teaspoon salt (not necessary if cereal was cooked in salted water)	Dash of cinnamon Grated rind of 1 lemon
1 teaspoon + 1½ cups sugar	1–2 tablespoons orange flower water, or ½ tablespoon orange extract
¼ cup minced glacé citron†	
¼ cup orange peel	4 egg whites, beaten stiff
24 ounces ricotta cheese	Confectioners' sugar

To hot cooked wheat, tapioca, or rice, add milk, salt (if necessary), and 1 teaspoon sugar. Return to heat and simmer for 5 minutes. Remove from stove, stir in citron and orange peel, and let stand until cool.

Beat ricotta and remaining 1½ cups sugar together. Add beaten egg yolks, vanilla, cinnamon, lemon rind, and orange flower water or extract and blend well. Stir in cooled cereal and fold in egg whites. Turn filling into prepared pie shells. Arrange lattice strips crisscross over fillings to edge and, using overhang, flute heavily. Bake pies at 350°F for 1 hour, or until firm in center and crust is nicely browned. Turn off oven and leave pies in oven to cool. Serve sprinkled with confectioners' sugar. *Serves 16.*

Margharita Amoroso, St. Mary's Church, Marlboro, New York

*Wheat, dry or soaked, may be bought in health food stores. To make soaked wheat from dry, cover dry wheat with cold water and boil for 15 minutes, or until husks crack open. Remove husks and let wheat soak in water to cover for 24 hours. Drain soaked wheat and cook in salted boiling water in covered saucepan, stirring frequently to prevent sticking. When wheat thickens (as when making oatmeal), it is cooked.
†Glacé citron is a type of candied citrus. It is available in most supermarkets and in specialty shops.

Strawberry Crumb Pie

Serve this different sort of strawberry pie either warm or cool, with cream.

3 pints fresh strawberries, hulled
and halved
¼ cup sugar
¼ cup cornstarch
1⅓ cups sifted flour
½ teaspoon salt

½ cup shortening
2–3 tablespoons water
¼ cup brown sugar
½ teaspoon cinnamon
½ cup light cream (optional)

Combine strawberries, sugar, and cornstarch and let stand while you make pastry. Combine flour and salt in bowl. Cut in shortening until uniform but coarse. Set aside about ⅔ cup of mixture. Sprinkle water over remainder, toss with fork, and press into ball. On lightly floured surface, roll out pastry 1½" larger than inverted 9" pie plate. Fit into plate and trim ½" beyond plate edge. Fold under to make double thickness around edge, and flute so that edge is high. Fill pastry shell with strawberry mixture. Blend reserved flour mixture with brown sugar and cinnamon. Sprinkle crumbs over strawberries. Bake at 400°F on sheet of aluminum foil for 45 minutes, or until crust is nicely browned. Pass cream, if desired, with pie. *Serves 6–8.*

Strawberry Parfait Pie

A dainty strawberry treat that is oh, so easy to make.

1 package (3 ounces) strawberry
gelatin
1 package (16 ounces) frozen
strawberries, thawed
Water

1 pint vanilla ice cream
1 baked 9" pie shell, chilled
1 cup heavy cream, whipped
Few fresh strawberries for
garnish

Soak gelatin in a little bit of cold water for 3–5 minutes. Drain strawberries, reserving the juice, and set aside. Combine strawberry juice with enough water to make 1¼ cups liquid; heat liquid to boiling. Remove from heat and add gelatin, stirring until dissolved. Cut vanilla ice cream into chunks and add to hot mixture, stirring until melted. Fold in strawberries. Chill in refrigerator for 15–30 minutes, stirring occasionally. Spoon into pie shell. Chill for 30 minutes, or until firm. Top with whipped cream and fresh berries. *Serves 6–8.*

Lynette R. Tuttle, United Methodist Church of the Hamptons, Hampton, New Hampshire

Mile-High Strawberry Pie

A celestial way to beat the heat.

1 package (10 ounces) frozen strawberries, thawed to mushy state
2 egg whites
⅛ teaspoon salt
¾ cup sugar
1 tablespoon lemon juice
½ cup heavy cream
1 teaspoon vanilla
1 baked 9" pie shell

Chill large mixer bowl and beaters in refrigerator. (Make sure they are spotlessly clean, or egg whites will not beat up properly.) Turn strawberries into bowl and add egg whites, salt, sugar, and lemon juice. Beat at top speed of electric mixer until stiff (about 20–25 minutes). Whip cream and flavor with vanilla. Fold gently into strawberry mixture. (Large mixer bowl should be completely filled.) Turn into pie shell. Place pie in freezer. Serve frozen. Do not keep frozen more than 3–4 days. *Serves 6–8.*

Banana Split Pie

For a pretty garnish, use a vegetable peeler to shave chocolate curls from a 3½-ounce chocolate bar.

1 prepared 9" deep-dish pie crust, baked and cooled or 1 large (9-ounce) prepared graham cracker or cookie crumb crust
2 medium bananas, sliced
2 packages (3.4 ounces each) French Vanilla Pudding and Pie Mix
3 cups cold milk
2 cans (8-ounces each) pineapple chunks, drained, patted dry, finely chopped
1 pint strawberries, sliced
1 carton (8 ounces) whipped non-dairy topping
1 ounce semi-sweet chocolate shavings

Cover bottom and sides of prepared crust with bananas. In mixing bowl, beat pudding mix and milk with whisk for 2 minutes, until thickened. Pour one-third over bananas. Top with pineapple and half of remaining pudding. Cover with strawberries and remaining pudding. Refrigerate for at least 1 hour, until pudding is firm. Spread topping over pie, swirling to make peaks. Sprinkle with chocolate. Serve right away or refrigerate for several hours. *Makes 8 servings.*

Mel Stephenson, Estancia United Methodist Church, Estancia, New Mexico

Puddings, Crisps, and Such

Yummy, yummy, yummy may not always be the *best* thing for the tummy, but it is true that "a bit of sweet makes the meal complete"! Years ago, when we all had more time (and got more exercise), dessert was part of every meal. But no matter how time-pressed we are today, a good dessert still puts the seal on a meal. So take a little time to enjoy the pleasure of a well-made dessert. Just keep in mind that age-old maxim, still true today, which says that a rich dessert is best enjoyed with a light meal and vice versa.

Apple Cake

Despite its name, more strudel than cake.

2½ cups flour
1 tablespoon + 1 cup sugar
1 teaspoon salt
¼ cup shortening
1 egg yolk
Milk

¾ cup crushed cornflakes
6 cups apples, peeled, cored, and sliced
2 tablespoons quick tapioca
2 teaspoons cinnamon
¾ cup confectioners' sugar

Sift flour, 1 tablespoon sugar, and salt into mixing bowl. Cut in shortening. Drop egg yolk into measuring cup and add milk to make ⅔ cup. Stir well with fork, add to dry ingredients, and mix well. Chill pastry thoroughly. Divide in half on floured board and roll out one half to fit over bottom of jelly-roll pan. Place in pan and sprinkle with cornflakes. Mix apples with remaining 1 cup sugar, tapioca, and cinnamon, and lay on top of cornflakes. Roll out other half of pastry and cover as top crust (slit crust every 2"). Bake at 400°F for 30 minutes, or until golden brown. Glaze with confectioners' sugar thinned with a little water. *Serves 8–10.*

Opal Wilkinson, Killingworth Congregational Church, Killingworth, Connecticut

Apple Crumb–Crunch

Everybody likes apple crisp! Serve with hard sauce; plain, whipped, or ice cream; or as is.

4 cups apple slices
1 teaspoon cinnamon
½ teaspoon salt
¼ cup water

¾ cup flour
¾ cup sugar
⅓ cup butter

Grease 8" × 8" pan. Put apples in pan. Sprinkle cinnamon and salt over apples. Pour on water. Mix flour and sugar and cut in butter until it reaches coarse, crumblike consistency. Sprinkle over apples in pan. Bake at 350°F for 20 minutes. Cut into squares. *Serves 6.*

Lois W. White, First Congregational Church, Newbury, Vermont

Apple Roly-Poly

Flaky apple-filled pastry roll.

Pastry

1½ cups flour	½ cup shortening
1 teaspoon salt	5–8 tablespoons water

Sift flour with salt. Cut in shortening. Add enough water to make rollable pastry. Roll pastry into a 12" × 14" rectangle.

Filling

3 cups diced apples	1 tablespoon lemon juice
½ cup brown sugar	2 tablespoons butter, melted
1 teaspoon cinnamon or nutmeg	

Combine apples, brown sugar, cinnamon or nutmeg, lemon juice, and butter, and spread evenly over pastry. Roll up pastry (14" side) like jelly roll. Pinch edges together to seal. Cut 3 slits in top crust, or punch design of small holes with ice pick. Place on greased jelly-roll pan and bake at 425°F for about 40 minutes, or until tender. Serve warm with heavy cream or vanilla ice cream. *Serves 6.*

Flora C. Hammond, Unitarian Universalist Church, Keene, New Hampshire

Maple Apple Crunch

A whole cup of maple syrup makes this a super apple crisp.

8 baking apples (about
   2 pounds), peeled, cored,
   and sliced
2 tablespoons flour
¾ cup sugar
1 cup maple syrup
1 teaspoon cinnamon

1½ cups old-fashioned rolled oats
1½ cups flour
¾ cup brown sugar
¾ cup melted butter
1 teaspoon baking soda
1 teaspoon baking powder
½ cup chopped nuts (any kind)

Mix apples, flour, sugar, ½ cup maple syrup, and cinnamon, and put in ungreased 8" × 12" glass baking dish or 9" pie plate. Combine oats, flour, brown sugar, remaining ½ cup maple syrup, butter, baking soda, baking powder, and nuts. Spread on top of apple mixture. Bake at 350°F for 40 minutes. Good served warm with cream or ice cream. *Serves 12.*

Evelyn I. Johnson, Our Savior Lutheran Church, Hanover, New Hampshire

Cranberry Crunch

Though made in a jiffy, ver-y spiffy!

1 cup uncooked rolled oats
½ cup flour
1 cup brown sugar
½ cup butter

1 can (16 ounces) cranberry
   sauce (either whole-berry
   or jellied)

Mix oats, flour, and brown sugar. Cut in butter until crumbly. Place half the mixture in greased 8" × 8" pan and cover with cranberry sauce. Top with other half of crumb mixture. Bake at 350°F for 45 minutes. Serve hot or cold with whipped cream or ice cream. *Serves 6–8.*

Cheryl Tutt, Ascutney Union Church, Ascutney, Vermont

Pioneer Bread Pudding

Inspired version of an old-time favorite.

2 cups milk	½ teaspoon vanilla
3 tablespoons butter	¼ teaspoon nutmeg
¼ cup sugar	½ cup raisins
2 eggs	2 cups bread cubes
Pinch of salt	

Scald milk with butter and sugar. Beat eggs slightly. Add salt. Stir in warm milk and vanilla gradually. Add nutmeg and raisins and pour over bread cubes placed in greased casserole. Set baking dish in warm water up to level of pudding. Bake at 350°F for 1 hour. *Serves 6.*

Shirley T. Oladell, Harwinton Congregational Church, Harwinton, Connecticut

Steamed Chocolate Pudding

A truly luscious pudding with a cakelike texture.

3 tablespoons butter	¼ teaspoon salt
⅔ cup sugar	¾ cup milk
1 egg, beaten	2 squares chocolate, melted
2¼ cups flour	1 teaspoon vanilla
1½ tablespoons baking powder	

Cream butter and sugar and add egg. Sift flour, baking powder, and salt together and add alternately with milk to creamed mixture. Add melted chocolate and vanilla and beat thoroughly. Put in pudding mold.

Bring to boil about 5" of water in pot large enough to hold mold and be covered. Put pudding mold into pot and cover pot tightly. Cook, keeping water at simmer, for 1–1½ hours. Check water level often. Pudding is done when it springs back from touch. This is very easy to make and cooks well on woodstove. Serve with Hard Sauce. *Serves 8–10.*

Hard Sauce

¼ cup butter, softened
1 cup confectioners' sugar

¼ cup heavy cream, whipped
½ teaspoon vanilla

Cream butter and sugar. Add whipped cream and vanilla. *Makes about 1½ cups.*

Dianne Johnson, Dublin Community Church, Dublin, New Hampshire

Cranberry Goodin'-Puddin'

A baked cranberry pudding cake with a rich, foamy sauce.

1 cup cranberries
¾ cup sugar
¼ cup walnuts
1 egg

½ cup flour
¼ cup butter, melted
2 tablespoons melted shortening

Grease an 8" pie pan *well*. Spread cranberries over bottom. Sprinkle with ¼ cup sugar and walnuts. Beat egg well. Add remaining ½ cup sugar, then flour, butter, and shortening to egg and beat well. Pour batter over cranberries. Bake at 325°F for 45 minutes, or until crust browns. Serve with either vanilla ice cream or Sterling Sauce (see below). *Serves 6.*

Sterling Sauce

½ cup butter
1 cup brown sugar

1 teaspoon vanilla
¼ cup hot milk

Mix butter and brown sugar until fluffy. Put vanilla in hot milk and dribble into butter mixture while beating in mixing bowl.

Ruth Howes Oleskey, Concord Unitarian Church, Concord, New Hampshire

Steamed Cranberry Pudding

A great-tasting and great-looking holiday pudding. Needs its sauce.

2 cups whole cranberries
1⅓ cups flour
½ teaspoon salt

2 teaspoons baking soda
⅓ cup boiling water
½ cup molasses

Wash and drain cranberries. Sift flour and salt over them and dredge well. Dissolve baking soda in water and add molasses, then stir into cranberry mixture. Mix well and turn into greased and floured 1-quart pudding mold with tight-fitting cover. Place covered mold on rack in pot filled with boiling water halfway up to depth of mold. Cover pot tightly. Cook, keeping water at simmer, for 1–1½ hours. Check water level often. Pudding is done when it springs back from touch. Unmold pudding and serve with Sauce (see below) in separate bowl. *Serves 6.*

Sauce

1 cup sugar
1 cup butter

1 cup cream
1 teaspoon vanilla

Mix together sugar, butter, cream, and vanilla. Cook until slightly thickened, stirring frequently.

Laverna E. Murphy, Durham Evangelical Church, Durham, New Hampshire

Cream Puffs

Easy to make, but always impressive—a wonderful finishing touch.

1 cup water
½ cup cooking oil
½ teaspoon salt

1 cup flour
4 eggs

Bring water to boil in saucepan. Add oil and salt. Then add flour all at once and beat rapidly over low heat until mixture leaves sides of pan and forms smooth, compact ball. Remove from heat. Add unbeaten eggs, one at a time, beating *hard* after each addition, until mixture is shiny. Drop by tablespoonfuls onto greased baking sheet 2" apart. Bake at 450°F for 20 minutes. Reduce heat to 350°F and bake 20 minutes longer. Let cool. Slice off tops, scoop out filaments, and fill (see below). Top with Chocolate-Roll Icing (page 175) or Confectioners' Sugar Glaze (page 181). ***Makes 12 puffs.***

Custard Filling

½ cup sugar	4 egg yolks, beaten
⅓ cup flour	2 teaspoons vanilla, or
½ teaspoon salt	1 teaspoon almond extract and
2 cups milk	1 teaspoon vanilla

Mix sugar, flour, and salt in saucepan. Stir in milk. Cook over medium heat, stirring until it boils. Boil 1 minute; remove from heat. Stir about one-third of mixture into egg yolks. Blend back into hot mixture in saucepan. Bring just to boil, then remove from heat, cool, and blend in vanilla or almond extract with vanilla. Fill cream puffs.

Caramel Fluffy Filling

2 cups heavy cream	1 teaspoon vanilla
¾ cup brown sugar	

Combine cream, brown sugar, and vanilla. Chill 1 hour. Whip until stiff. Fill cream puffs.

Fruity Filling

1 cup heavy cream	1 cup fruit cocktail, drained, or
	1 cup mincemeat

Chill deep bowl and beaters. Whip cream until stiff. Blend in fruit cocktail or mincemeat. Fill cream puffs.

Mary Wakefield, First Congregational Church, Rindge, New Hampshire

Puddings, Crisps, and Such   279

Strawberry Cheesecake

One of the very best! The tester, whose own cheesecake recipe is famous, discarded hers for this one. Lucky enough to have tasted it, we agree—superlative! If fresh berries are in season, you could skip the topping and decorate the top with fresh strawberries, blueberries, or your favorite berries.

Crust

16 double graham crackers, crushed (about 2 cups)
½ cup butter, melted

¼ cup sugar
Dash of cinnamon

Cheesecake

2 packages (8 ounces each) cream cheese
½ cup + ⅓ cup sugar

2 eggs
½ teaspoon vanilla
1 pint sour cream

Topping

1½ pounds frozen sliced strawberries (about 3 cups)
1½ teaspoons cornstarch

1½ tablespoons sugar
Juice of ½ lemon

Mix graham crackers, butter, sugar, and cinnamon. Line 9" springform pan with mixture, going up 1" along sides. Mix cream cheese, ½ cup sugar, eggs, and vanilla until smooth and pour into pan. Bake at 350°F for 20 minutes. Mix sour cream with remaining ⅓ cup sugar. Pour over baked mixture and return to 350°F oven for 20 minutes. Let cool. For topping, thaw and drain strawberries, reserving liquid. Return berries to refrigerator. Stir together cornstarch, sugar, and lemon juice; add to reserved strawberry juice and bring to boil in 1½-quart saucepan, stirring constantly. Boil and stir until thick and clear. Cool, then add to berries. Spread on top of cheesecake. Refrigerate 3–4 hours. *Serves 10–12.*

Lyn Matzke, Our Savior Lutheran Church, Hanover, New Hampshire

Aunt Vi's Grape-Nuts Custard

A different sort of custard dessert.

1 cup Grape-Nuts cereal
1 quart milk
1 cup sugar

2 beaten eggs
1 teaspoon vanilla

Combine cereal, milk, sugar, eggs, and vanilla, and pour into greased 2-quart casserole dish. Set dish in another pan of hot water and bake at 350°F for 1 hour, or until custard is set and silver knife inserted into center comes out clean. Stir twice during first half-hour of baking time. *Serves 8.*

Mark Jeffreys, Elmwood Community Church, West Hartford, Connecticut

Indian Pudding

A recipe that has been brought to church suppers by
three generations of Mrs. Slipp's family, especially in fall and winter.

½ cup yellow cornmeal
5 cups milk
½ teaspoon salt
2 tablespoons butter
2 eggs, beaten

½ cup brown sugar
¾ cup molasses
1 teaspoon cinnamon
½ teaspoon ginger
1 cup raisins

In 2-quart saucepan, combine cornmeal, 3 cups milk, salt, and 1 tablespoon butter. Heat slowly to boil, stirring constantly. Remove from heat. Combine eggs, brown sugar, molasses, remaining 1 tablespoon butter, cinnamon, and ginger. Add to cornmeal mixture with raisins and 1 cup milk. Pour into greased 2-quart baking dish. Bake at 300°F, stirring every 20 minutes, for 2 hours. Stir in 1 more cup milk halfway through baking time.

At end of 2 hours, stop stirring, turn off oven, and let pudding set for about 30 minutes. Serve warm, topped with whipped cream or ice cream. *Serves 6–8.*

Leeda H. Slipp, Killingworth Congregational Church, Killingworth, Connecticut

Jewel Dessert

Takes time to make, but a tasty and very decorative holiday dessert. Use red and green gelatins for Christmastime, orange and yellow for Thanksgiving or Halloween.

4 packages (3 ounces each) gelatin dessert, of which one must be lemon
3 cups boiling water

1½ cups cold water
2 cups whipping cream
¼ cup sugar
1 cup pineapple juice

Soak each package of gelatin separately in a little bit of cold water for 3–5 minutes. Reserving lemon gelatin, dissolve each of the other 3 in separate bowls each containing 1 cup boiling water. Then add ½ cup cold water to each bowl and stir. Pour into separate shallow pans (cake pans are fine) and refrigerate to set. Meanwhile, whip cream. Combine sugar with pineapple juice in saucepan and bring to boil. Then add lemon gelatin and cool to syrupy stage. Cut 3 cake pans of gelatin into cubes. Fold lemon-pineapple mixture into whipped cream, then gelatin cubes. Pour over Graham Cracker Crust (see below) and refrigerate at least 4 hours. *Serves 15–18.*

Graham Cracker Crust

20 double graham crackers
¼ pound butter, softened

¼ cup sugar

Roll crackers to fine crumbs. Mix with butter and sugar and press firmly into 9" × 13" pan to form crust.

Vera MacLeay, Plainfield Community Church, Plainfield, New Hampshire

Pineapple Delight

Unusual and delightful whether served as a dessert or as a side dish with baked ham.

½ cup butter
¾ cup sugar
3 eggs

1 can (16 ounces) crushed pineapple
5 slices white bread, cubed and crusts removed

Cream butter and sugar. Add eggs and beat well. Stir in pineapple (with juice) and bread cubes. Bake in 8" × 8" greased pan at 325°F for 40–50 minutes. *Serves 6.*

Doree McCauley, Seventh Day Adventist Church, Concord, New Hampshire

Judge Peter's Pudding

Fruited gelatin made from scratch, this well-traveled recipe originated in New Hampshire during the 19th century but was picked up by its Vermont contributor on Cape Cod. Dried fruits should not be cut up too fine.

3 tablespoons plain gelatin
1 cup cold water
2 cups boiling water
¼ cup lemon juice
Juice of 2 oranges
⅛–¼ teaspoon food coloring (optional)

1¾ cups sugar
6 dried figs, cut up
9 dates, cut up
2 bananas, sliced
2 oranges, sectioned
½ cup walnut meats, broken up

In 3- or 4-quart bowl, dissolve gelatin in cold water, then add boiling water. Add lemon and orange juices, food coloring, if using, and sugar. Refrigerate until thickened to syrupy stage. Add cut-up figs, dates, bananas, oranges, and walnuts. Stir only enough to mix through gelatin. Return to refrigerator until set. *Serves 12.*

Elizabeth Hughes, Old Brick Church, Clarendon, Vermont

Frosted Strawberry Squares

Light-'n'-easy summer dessert. Serve with a dollop of whipped cream atop each square.
Count on 6-hour freezing time.

1 cup flour
½ cup chopped nuts (any kind)
¼ cup brown sugar
½ cup butter, melted
2 egg whites
⅔ cup sugar

2 cups sliced fresh strawberries
   or 1 package (10 ounces)
   frozen strawberries, thawed
2 tablespoons lemon juice
1 cup heavy cream, whipped

Mix together flour, nuts, brown sugar, and butter, and spread evenly over bottom of jelly-roll pan or cookie sheet. Bake at 350°F for 20 minutes. Stir occasionally. Sprinkle two-thirds of these crumbs in 9" × 13" pan.

Combine egg whites, sugar, strawberries, and lemon juice in large bowl. Beat at high speed until stiff peaks form. Fold in whipped cream. Spoon over crumbs. Sprinkle remaining crumbs over top. Freeze 6 hours or overnight. Cut into squares. **Serves 15–20.**

Do Buffington, First Congregational Church, Littleton, New Hampshire

Lemon Bisque

Make this church supper favorite with honey—you'll love it.

1 package (3 ounces) lemon
   gelatin
1¼ cups boiling water
⅓ cup honey or sugar
⅛ teaspoon salt

3 tablespoons lemon juice
   Grated rind of 1 lemon
1 can (13 ounces) evaporated
   milk, chilled overnight
2 cups crushed vanilla wafers

Soak gelatin in a little bit of cold water for 3–5 minutes, then dissolve gelatin in boiling water and add honey or sugar, salt, lemon juice, and lemon rind. Put in freezer for about 15 minutes until partly congealed. Whip evaporated milk until thick, and whip in gelatin mixture. Sprinkle 1 cup vanilla wafer crumbs evenly over bottom of 9" × 13" glass dish. Pour bisque mixture over crumbs and top with remaining 1 cup crumbs. Refrigerate. **Serves 12–15.**

Mildred Dimock, Ellington Congregational Church, Ellington, Connecticut

Lemon Delicacy

Somewhat like a pudding cake, this dessert comes out of the oven a lemon jelly topped with a nicely browned crust.

1 cup sugar
2 tablespoons flour
Pinch of salt
2 egg yolks, beaten
1 cup milk

Grated rind and juice of
1 lemon
2 tablespoons butter, melted
2 egg whites, stiffly beaten

Sift together sugar, flour, and salt. Stir in egg yolks. Beat in milk, lemon rind and juice, and butter. Fold in egg whites. Pour into greased 8" pie plate or 1-quart baking dish. Set pie plate or baking dish in pan of hot water (about halfway up sides of pie plate) and bake at 350°F for 30–40 minutes. Serve cold. **Serves 6.**

Mildred Lakeway, First Congregational Church, Littleton, New Hampshire

Lemon Pie Filling Dessert

Very rich and sweet; disappears fast. Double for 9" × 13" pan.

1 package (3 ounces) lemon pie
    filling (not instant)
¾ cup sugar
2¼ cups water

2 eggs, separated
2 tablespoons lemon juice
16 ladyfingers, split
1½ cups whipped cream

Combine lemon pie filling and ½ cup sugar in saucepan. Gradually blend in water, slightly beaten egg yolks, and lemon juice. Cook, stirring, until mixture thickens. Remove from heat. Beat egg whites until soft peaks form. Add remaining ¼ cup sugar and continue to beat until stiff peaks form. Fold into lemon mixture. Arrange ladyfingers in bowl or serving dish and pour lemon mixture on top. Chill. Just before serving, spread with whipped cream. **Serves 9.**

Evelyn Shaw, Pilgrim Congregational Church, New Haven, Connecticut

Lime-Chocolate Delicious

Really elegant in both taste and appearance. Good make-ahead hot-weather dessert.

1 package (3 ounces) lime gelatin
2 cups chocolate wafer crumbs
½ cup melted butter
1½ cups hot water
1 cup sugar
2 teaspoons lemon juice

¼ cup lime juice
1 can (13 ounces) evaporated
    milk, chilled overnight in
    refrigerator
3 cups whipped cream
    Chocolate syrup

Soak gelatin in a little bit of cold water for 3–5 minutes. Combine crumbs and butter; press into 9" × 13" pan. Chill. Mix gelatin and hot water. Cool in refrigerator until consistency of unbeaten egg white. Whip, adding sugar and lemon and lime juices. Whip evaporated milk into peaks and fold into gelatin. Pour into pan and chill. Cover with whipped cream and drizzle with chocolate syrup. **Serves 24.**

Arlene Foulds, Center Congregational Church, Torrington, Connecticut

Pumpkin Shell Dessert

Put it in a pumpkin shell, and there you'll keep it very well!
Combine leftovers with a package of mincemeat and make pies or tarts.

1 small (7" diameter) pumpkin or hard-skinned squash	1 teaspoon lemon juice
2 cups peeled, chopped apple	1 cup raisins
⅓ cup sugar (dash more if brown is used)	1 cup chopped pecans
	¼ teaspoon cinnamon
	¼ teaspoon nutmeg

Wash and dry pumpkin or squash. Slice off top for lid. Scrape out fibers and seeds. Mix together apple, sugar, lemon juice, raisins, pecans, cinnamon, and nutmeg. Fill pumpkin with mixture. Top with pumpkin or squash lid. Place on large pie dish. Bake at 350°F until apples are tender. Begin checking after 40 minutes—it may take as long as 1 hour and 45 minutes. Serve from shell, spooning some pumpkin with each portion. Top with sour cream or ice cream, if desired. ***Serves 6.***

Evelyn H. Chase, Concord Unitarian Church, Concord, New Hampshire

Strawberry Mousse

Scrumptious substitute for ice cream, this is good without macaroon crumbs, but even better with the slight hint of almond donated by the macaroons (see page 196).

½ tablespoon gelatin	3 tablespoons corn syrup
1 pint fresh strawberries	Pinch of salt
⅓ cup sugar	½ pint heavy cream, whipped
3 tablespoons cold water	½ cup macaroon crumbs (optional)

Soak gelatin in a little bit of cold water for 3–5 minutes. Wash and hull berries and sprinkle with sugar. Let stand for 1 hour, mash, and rub through sieve. In top of double boiler or in metal bowl, dissolve gelatin in cold water. Place over pan of simmering water and stir until gelatin thickens. Pour into berry puree with corn syrup and salt. Chill, and fold in cream and macaroon crumbs, if using. Freeze. ***Serves 6.***

Vacation Pudding

By its very nature, could also be called Holiday Pudding.

Pudding

1 cup chopped walnuts
1 cup chopped dates
3 tablespoons flour
1 teaspoon baking powder

½ cup sugar
2 eggs, separated
1 teaspoon vanilla

Combine walnuts, dates, flour, and baking powder. Mix sugar with egg yolks and vanilla and add to walnut mixture. Beat egg whites until stiff and fold in. Pour into 1-quart casserole dish set in pan of hot water. Bake at 300°F for 1 hour. *Serves 6.*

Sauce

½ cup butter
1 cup confectioners' sugar

¼ cup milk
1 teaspoon vanilla

Cream butter and sugar. Blend with milk and vanilla and warm over pan of boiling water. Serve pudding either hot or cold, with warm sauce.

Katheryn Blood, Harwinton Congregational Church, Harwinton, Connecticut

Recipes to Feed a Big Crowd

Whether it is a wedding, church supper, scout banquet, high school reunion, block party, or teenage invasion, most everyone has to feed a big crowd at least once in a lifetime. It won't be difficult with these recipes, including everything from soup to salad, contributed by experts in the art.

Corn Chowder

With cold sliced ham (or hot dogs), rolls, and salad, an excellent supper.

½ pound salt pork, cut into ¼" dice
1 pound onions, finely chopped
5 pounds potatoes, peeled and
   sliced
4–5 quarts water
2 gallons milk

8 cans (16 ounces each)
   cream-style corn
   Salt
2 teaspoons pepper
¾ cup butter

Fry out salt pork, remove browned bits, and reserve. Add onions to fat, and sauté until transparent. Add potatoes and cover with water. Boil gently until potatoes are tender, and pour off cooking water. Add milk, corn, salt pork bits, salt to taste, and pepper. Heat but do not boil. Add butter at serving time. *Serves 50.*

Mildred A. Dimock, Ellington Congregational Church, Ellington, Connecticut

Gazpacho

Brenda McKay relishes this recipe from her mother-in-law in Louisiana. The refreshing soup, topped with crispy croutons, is particularly welcome at summertime gatherings.

2 bottles (46 ounces each) V-8
   juice
4 cups finely chopped fresh or
   canned tomatoes
2 cups celery, finely chopped
2 cups cucumber, seeded and
   finely chopped
2 cups green bell pepper, finely
   chopped
2 cups green onions, white and
   light green parts, finely chopped

½ cup red wine vinegar
¼ cup olive oil
2 tablespoons fresh parsley, finely
   chopped
2 tablespoons minced garlic
2 teaspoons chili powder
2 teaspoons Worcestershire sauce
1 teaspoon salt
1 teaspoon celery salt
1 teaspoon pepper
1 teaspoon Tabasco sauce (optional)

In large bowl, combine V-8 Juice, tomatoes, celery, cucumber, green bell peppers, onions, vinegar, oil, parsley, garlic, chili powder, Worcestershire sauce, salt, celery salt, pepper, and Tabasco sauce, if using. Cover and refrigerate at least 8 hours. Taste and add more seasonings, if needed. ***Makes 5 quarts. Serves 26 (³⁄₄ cup per serving)***

Brenda McKay, Trinity Presbyterian Church, Claymont, Delaware

Old-Fashioned Biscuits

These freeze well. Put uncooked biscuits on cookie sheet, freeze, then put in bags to store. Bake frozen biscuits about 30 minutes at 400°F.

6 cups flour	2 teaspoons salt
½ cup dry milk	2 teaspoons cream of tartar
¼ cup baking powder	2 cups shortening
¼ cup sugar	1¾ cups water

Mix flour, dry milk, baking powder, sugar, salt, and cream of tartar together with fork. Cut in shortening with pastry blender. Stir in about 1½ cups water. If dry, add ¼ cup more. Turn onto floured surface, and knead 8 to 10 times. Roll dough ¾" thick. Cut with biscuit cutter. Bake at 400°F for 20–25 minutes. ***Makes 45 2" biscuits.***

Rosamond Emerson Leland, Community Church of Durham, Durham, New Hampshire

Sauerbraten

In the bowl used by our test cook, this recipe used a lot of wine vinegar (1½ quarts!), but the tenderness of the end product was well worth it.

5 pounds pot roast	1 large onion, sliced
Enough liquid made up of half wine vinegar and half water to cover meat	2 bay leaves
	¼ teaspoon peppercorns
2 teaspoons salt	3½ tablespoons cornstarch mixed with ½ cup cold water

Place meat in glass (or other nonmetal) bowl, and combine vinegar and water, salt, onion, bay leaves, and peppercorns. Pour over meat to cover. Put bowl in refrigerator and let stand 3–4 days, turning meat daily. At end of this time, take meat from bowl and dry off. Strain and reserve brine, removing and discarding bay leaves. Brown on all sides and cook like pot roast with about 3 cups of reserved brine. Simmer, covered, for about 4 hours, adding more liquid if necessary. Remove meat from pot. Add cornstarch and water to liquid in pot. Add reserved brine if necessary to bring up volume to 3½ cups. Simmer, stirring, until gravy thickens. *Serves 15.*

Edith Moritz, Woodmont United Church of Christ, Milford, Connecticut

Shipwreck

Members of the Mission Committee at Grace United Church of Christ voted unanimously to share this popular casserole.

3 pounds lean ground beef	5½ cups tomato juice
12 cups diced potatoes	¾ cup uncooked rice
6 cups diced onion	1 teaspoon salt
3 cups diced celery	1 teaspoon pepper
1 can (40½ ounces) kidney beans, undrained	2 packages (12 ounces each) shredded Cheddar cheese

Crumble beef evenly into two greased 5-quart rectangular baking dishes. Evenly scatter half the potatoes, onion, celery, beans with liquid, tomato juice, rice, salt, and pepper into each dish. Stir with fork to combine. Cover dishes with aluminum foil. Bake at 350°F for 1 hour. Carefully remove foil and stir. Re-cover and bake about 30 minutes or until potatoes are tender when pierced with knife. Remove foil. Sprinkle with cheese. Bake 10 minutes or until cheese is bubbly and golden. *Serves 24.*

Marilyn Miller, Grace United Church of Christ, Lancaster, Pennsylvania

Quick Beet Relish

A favorite at Pilgrim Church dinners.

2 cups sugar	1 cup water
1 teaspoon salt	1 quart finely chopped cooked beets
⅛ teaspoon pepper	1 quart finely chopped cabbage
1 cup cider vinegar	½ cup horseradish

Combine sugar, salt, pepper, vinegar, and water. Bring to boil and pour over beets, cabbage, and horseradish. Refrigerate at least 24 hours to let season. Serve as a condiment. *Makes 25 half-cup servings.*

Mrs. W. H. Kellogg, Jr., Pilgrim Congregational Church, New Haven, Connecticut

Chicken for 16

This thrifty but elegant dish can be doubled or tripled and frozen ahead for a large party.

4 whole small chickens (2½–3½ pounds each, with necks and gizzards for stock)
12 stalks celery, diced (use leaves for stock)
8 peppercorns
4 quarts water
8 medium carrots, scraped and sliced
8 medium onions, sliced

1 teaspoon Italian seasoning
½ teaspoon salt
2 bay leaves
3 cups dry white wine or vermouth
1 cup butter (2 sticks)
1 cup flour
1½ cups heavy cream
4 ounces Swiss cheese, grated
4 tablespoons butter

Cut up chickens as follows: Remove fat and livers (do not use in this recipe); cut out backs and put in large pot with necks and gizzards,* celery leaves, and peppercorns. Add water and simmer uncovered for about 2½ hours, or until liquid is reduced by one-half (2 quarts). Skim and strain.

Meanwhile, divide chickens into quarters (2 leg and thigh sections, 2 half-breast and wing sections), and slice celery, carrots, and onions. In 2 pots—one for leg sections, one for breast sections—place a layer of chicken, then vegetables, some Italian seasoning, and some salt. Repeat until chicken and vegetables are used up. Poke a bay leaf in each pot. Pour half of wine or vermouth into each pot and then pour in chicken stock—about 1 quart per pot. Cook on top of stove or bake at 375°F until chicken is tender—½ hour or longer. Leg meat takes longer than breast.

When chicken is cooked, strain off liquid and boil over high heat until liquid is reduced to 2 quarts. Remove and discard bay leaves. Meanwhile, melt butter, add flour, stir, and cook, bubbling, for 2 minutes (do not burn). Remove from heat and slowly add reduced stock, continuing to stir. Return to heat, stir, and cook until thickened. Remove from heat, cool slightly, and gradually add cream. Pour some of this mixture into bottom of 2 buttered baking dishes. Place leg sections in one dish, breast sections in other. Stir cooked vegetables into sauce and divide between 2 dishes. Cool uncovered. Sprinkle with grated cheese and bits of butter (2 tablespoons per container). Bake uncovered at 375°F for at least ½ hour until top is browned. Or, store covered in refrigerator or freezer. Allow longer cooking time from cold or frozen state.

R. M. Eldredge, All Saints Church, Peterborough, New Hampshire

*Fat and livers can be made into a nice pâté for a first course. Gizzards and neck meat may be ground up with onion and mixed with mayonnaise and seasoning for sandwiches.

Southwestern Chicken Stew

Like most stews, this one comes together quickly and then slowly simmers itself to perfection. Be sure to make it ahead so the flavors can mellow.

7 pounds bone-in chicken pieces, skin and fat removed
Flour
½ cup olive oil
4 tablespoons minced garlic
2 cans (48 ounces each) chicken broth
1 can (28 ounces) whole tomatoes, with juice
1 can (12 ounces) tomato paste
1 tablespoon seasoned salt
1 tablespoon cumin
2 teaspoons oregano
2 teaspoons thyme
2 bay leaves

1½–2 teaspoons crushed red pepper
1½ pounds smoked kielbasa or other smoked sausage, cut into 1" chunks
2 cups 1" cubed new potatoes
2 cups 1" cubed carrots
2 cups 1" cubed zucchini
2 cups 1" cubed yellow squash
2 cups loose-pack frozen pearl onions or 1 jar (15 ounces) pearl onions, drained
1 can (15¼ ounces) whole kernel corn, drained or 1½ cups frozen whole kernel corn
1 cup chopped fresh cilantro

Coat chicken pieces with flour. Divide oil between two large pots set over high heat. Fry chicken, turning as needed, about 8 minutes, until browned on all sides. Remove and set aside. Drain all but 2 tablespoons oil from each pot. Place pots over medium heat. Into each pot, whisk 3 tablespoons flour and 2 tablespoons garlic. Sauté 30 seconds, until fragrant. To each pot, add 2 cups broth; whisk until thickened. Scrape bottoms of pots to remove browned bits. Divide the following ingredients equally between the pots: tomatoes with juice, tomato paste, seasoned salt, cumin, oregano, thyme, bay leaves, 1½ teaspoons cayenne, and remaining broth. Stir, breaking up tomatoes with back of spoon. Bring almost to boiling then reduce heat and simmer 20 minutes. Add chicken, kielbasa, potatoes, and carrots to both pots. Cover pots with lids slightly askew. Simmer 20 minutes. Skim and discard excess fat. Add zucchini and yellow squash to both pots. Cover partially and simmer 30 minutes or until potatoes are tender. Add onions and corn to both pots. Simmer about 5 minutes. Remove and discard bay leaves. Taste and add ½ teaspoon crushed red pepper, if needed. Sprinkle with cilantro. *Serves 18–20.*

Jo Gannon, St. Daniel the Prophet Catholic Community, Scottsdale, Arizona

Three-Step Sweet and Sour Pork for 24

One-two-three and there's your supper!

Step 1

5 pounds pork
4 teaspoons salt or garlic salt

Several grinds of pepper
1 cup shortening

Cut pork into 1" cubes and season with salt and pepper. Divide between two 9" × 13" pans. Add ½ cup shortening to each pan. Bake in preheated 400°F oven for 1 hour, stirring often. Remove from oven and pour off fat from pans.

Step 2

4 large green peppers

2 cans (20 ounces each) pineapple chunks

While meat is browning, cut peppers into strips. Drain pineapple and reserve juice. Set aside.

Step 3

1 cup cornstarch, mixed with 1 cup reserved pineapple juice (above)
3 cups sugar

8 cups (2 quarts) chicken stock
3 cups cider vinegar
½ cup soy sauce

Combine cornstarch mixture, sugar, stock, vinegar, and soy sauce. Mix in green peppers and pineapple chunks. Divide entire mixture evenly between 2 pans of cooked, drained meat and return to 400°F oven for 45 minutes, stirring often. Serve over rice.

R. M. Eldredge, All Saints Church, Peterborough, New Hampshire

South Texas Pork Shoulder

An American adaptation of pit barbecue from Mexico's Yucatan region,
this spicy pork is so tender you can shred it with a fork. Serve with
steaming corn tortillas to soak up the fragrant gravy.

7 pounds pork shoulder roast	2 teaspoons pepper
2 large red onions, each cut into 8 wedges	1½ teaspoons cumin
	1½ teaspoons cinnamon
6 banana peppers, seeded and cut into thin strips	1½ teaspoons coriander
	1½ teaspoons paprika
½ cup coarsely chopped garlic	⅓ cup red wine vinegar
½ cup flour	¼ cup water
2 teaspoons salt	

Cut roast into 8 chunks, cutting around shoulder blade if necessary. Place pork, onions, peppers, and garlic in 8-quart slow-cooker.

In bowl, combine flour, salt, pepper, cumin, cinnamon, coriander, and paprika. Whisk in vinegar and water. Pour into pot. Toss ingredients to coat thoroughly with seasonings. Set cooker to high. Cook for 30 minutes. Reduce setting to low and cook for 7 hours. Uncover; allow to sit for 30 minutes. Skim off and discard fat that rises to surface. ***Serves 14–16.***

Larry's Spaghetti and Meatballs

By using the different quantities furnished by Mr. Barnes in this unusual recipe,
you can feed 8, 16, 24, or 32 people his zesty and authentically Italian dinner.
The pork cutlets that are in the sauce, by the way, cook down
to nothing but a taste, but an important one.

		To Serve		
Sauce	8	16	24	32
Peeled tomatoes, 28-ounce cans	1	2	3	4
Ground beef, pound(s)	½	1	1½	2
Large onions, chopped	1	2	3	4
Cloves garlic	7	14	21	28
Tomato paste, 6-ounce cans	2	4	6	8
Water (use 28-ounce tomato cans)	1	2	3	4
Water (use 6-ounce tomato paste cans)	2	4	6	8
Boneless pork cutlets, pound(s)	½	1	1½	2
Mushrooms, 4-ounce cans, drained	1	2	3	4
Sugar, tablespoons(s)	1	2	3	4
Oregano, basil, marjoram, rosemary, salt, and pepper, teaspoon(s) of each	½	1	1½	2
Red wine, cup(s)	½	1	1½	2

Heat tomatoes and crush with potato masher. Brown ground beef and add to tomatoes. Sauté onions and garlic and add to sauce. Add tomato paste. Fill tomato and tomato paste cans with water and add water to sauce. Blend well and bring to a boil. Brown pork cutlets and add to sauce, along with mushrooms, sugar, oregano, basil, marjoram, rosemary, salt, pepper, and wine. Add meatballs and simmer 3 hours or longer until thick.

Meatballs	To Serve			
	8	16	24	32
Ground beef, pounds	1½	3	4½	6
Medium onions, chopped	1	2	3	4
Seasoned bread crumbs, cup(s)	½	1	1½	2
Parsley, teaspoon(s)	½	1	1½	2
Grated cheese, teaspoon(s)	1	2	3	4
Eggs	1	2	3	4
Salt and pepper		—to taste—		

Mix ground beef, onions, bread crumbs, parsley, cheese, eggs, salt, and pepper well together (a dough hook is helpful) and roll into balls. Brown meatballs on all sides and add to sauce.

Spaghetti

One 16-ounce package spaghetti will serve 8.

Sloppy Joes

A variation of this recipe is to omit the meatballs, but brown the amount of ground beef you would have used for the meatballs and add to the sauce to make a superb Sloppy Joe to serve on buns.

Larry Barnes, The Unitarian Church, Peterborough, New Hampshire

Chili con Carne for 25–30 People

This recipe can be extended with cooked rice to feed up to 40.

10	medium onions, sliced	1½	teaspoons Tabasco Sauce
⅔	cup cooking oil	½	teaspoon oregano
6	pounds ground beef	4	cans (28 ounces each) tomatoes
6–8	tablespoons chili powder	2	cans (6 ounces each) tomato
2	teaspoons salt		paste
2	teaspoons paprika	6	cans (12 ounces each) red
2	teaspoons ground red pepper		kidney beans

Cook onions in hot oil until tender but not brown. Add meat sprinkled with chili powder, salt, paprika, red pepper, Tabasco Sauce, and oregano. Break up meat with fork and brown. Add tomatoes (with juice) and tomato paste. Cover and simmer 45 minutes or longer, adding water as needed to maintain original level of liquid. Add beans and simmer for another 15–20 minutes. You can make this ahead (with or without beans) and reheat. Freezes well, too. Two aluminum-foil roasting pans will conveniently hold the chili (without beans) for freezing. Total volume of recipe—42 cups.

Marion S. Chaffee, First Congregational Church, Newfane, Vermont

Baked Beans for 25

A baked bean supper is both thrifty and popular.
Serve with hot bread, green salad or cole slaw, and dessert.

8	cups dry beans	2½	tablespoons salt
	Soaking water to cover	1	tablespoon dry mustard
¾	pounds salt pork	¾	teaspoon pepper
1	medium onion, finely chopped	1	cup boiling water + boiling
½	cup sugar		water to cover
1	cup molasses		

Soak beans in water to cover overnight. Next morning, add water as necessary to cover, and simmer in soaking water until bean skins wrinkle and part when blown on. Drain. Cut salt pork into 1" cubes and place about a third of the cubes on bottom of baking dish or dishes (large roasting pan or pans covered with aluminum foil are fine) along with onion. Add beans mixed with rest of salt pork cubes. Combine sugar, molasses, salt, dry mustard, and pepper with boiling water until well-mixed and pour over beans. Add more boiling water to cover. Bake, covered, in 275°F oven for about 12 hours, adding more boiling water as necessary. Remove cover for last hour of baking.

Mrs. E. M. Charlton, Saint Matthew's Church, Bedford, New York

Cheese Strata

Contributor Nancy M. Alward tells us that Christ Church of Exeter, New Hampshire, served this puffy egg-and-cheese dish at a brunch for about 200 people (the recipe is easily multiplied), accompanied by sliced ham, orange juice, rolls, and coffee. "Everyone loved it, and it couldn't be easier."

48 slices day-old bread, trimmed of all crusts	10 cups milk
2 pounds Cheddar cheese, thinly sliced	2 teaspoons prepared mustard
	¼ cup minced onion
16 eggs	4 teaspoons salt
	½ teaspoon pepper

Arrange half the bread slices in greased baking dishes 2" deep. Cover with cheese slices. Top with remaining bread. Beat eggs. Add milk, mustard, onion, salt, and pepper, and blend in. Pour over bread and cheese. Refrigerate 1 hour or overnight. Bake uncovered at 325°F for about 50 minutes, or until puffy and brown. ***Serves 24.***

Nancy M. Alward, Christ Church, Exeter, New Hampshire

Macaroni and Cheese for 20–25

This recipe may be made all at once to be served immediately, refrigerated, or frozen. The sauce may be made ahead and frozen, defrosted, and mixed with freshly cooked macaroni.

¾ cup butter (1½ sticks)
¼ cup minced onion
1 cup flour
1 tablespoon salt
1½ teaspoons dry mustard
2 teaspoons powdered ginger
2 quarts milk

2 teaspoons Worcestershire sauce
2 pounds sharp Cheddar cheese, cut into small pieces, finely sliced, coarsely shredded, or grated
2 pounds elbow macaroni

Melt butter in 3-quart (or larger) kettle. Cook onion in butter until soft. Add flour mixed with salt, mustard, and ginger, and cook, stirring constantly, until bubbly. Turn off heat, and add milk, stirring or whisking continuously. Put back on heat and continue stirring until sauce thickens. Turn off heat, and stir in Worcestershire sauce and cheese. Stir until cheese is melted. Mix with elbow macaroni cooked according to package directions. Bake in 400°F oven in 2 buttered 11" × 15" shallow pans, or 3 buttered 2-quart casseroles, or 2 buttered 3-quart casseroles. Bake uncovered for 20 minutes, then covered for an additional 15–20 minutes. (Use aluminum foil to cover if you don't have lids.) If baked frozen, bake an additional 20 minutes.

R. M. Eldredge, All Saints Church, Peterborough, New Hampshire

Baked Onions

A different way to serve onions for any size group. The number of onions depends on the number of people. Plan on 2 slices per person.

Skin Spanish onions and cut them crosswise into three slices. Place slices side by side in greased pan and season with salt, pepper, and paprika. Dot generously with butter. Add boiling stock of onion soup or canned consommé to depth of ¼" in pan. Bake at 325°F, basting for at least an hour until stock is absorbed and onions are tender and brown.

Moira Burnham, Church of the Epiphany, New York, New York

Amounts to Serve 100

This chart is from the Lempster, New Hampshire, Cookbook, published in 1890.

Soup . . . . 5 gallons
Chowder . . . . 8 gallons
Oysters (to be scalloped) . . . . 12 quarts
Fish . . . . 40–50 pounds
Meat for loaf or stew . . . . 20 pounds
Roast beef . . . . 40 pounds
Roast lamb . . . . 50 pounds
Baked ham . . . . 3 12-pound hams
Chicken . . . . 50 pounds
Chicken salad . . . . 15–20 pounds
Potato salad . . . . 24 quarts
Vegetable salad . . . . 20 quarts
Fruit salad . . . . 30 quarts
Mayonnaise . . . . 2 quarts
Beets . . . . 30 quarts
Cabbage (slaw) . . . . 12 pounds
Celery . . . . 8 bunches
Lettuce . . . . 12 heads
Ice cream . . . . 16–20 quarts
Coffee . . . . 2½ pounds, 5 gallons water
Whipping cream . . . . . 1 quart cream makes 2 quarts whipped
Rolls . . . . 18 dozen
Butter . . . . 4 pounds
Layer cakes 12
Pies 18

Courtesy of Louise T. Mac Veagh

Turkey Salad for 50

Unmold onto a bed of lettuce or fresh spinach, and garnish.

4 quarts cooked turkey meat, diced
4 cups diced celery
1 cup finely chopped scallions
2½ cups blanched almonds, toasted
½ cup red wine vinegar
1 cup olive oil
Juice of 1 lemon

¼ cup finely chopped parsley
Salt and pepper
6 hard-boiled eggs, chopped
3¼ cups mayonnaise
¼ cup capers, drained
Parsley, watercress, olives (black or green), and pimientos for garnishing

Combine turkey, celery, scallions, and almonds with ¼ cup vinegar and chill in refrigerator. Beat together olive oil, remaining ¼ cup vinegar, lemon juice, parsley, and salt and pepper to taste until well-blended. Add to chilled turkey mixture and mix well. Then add eggs, mayonnaise, and capers. Taste and add additional seasonings as required. Pack into 1 oiled 4-quart mold or 2 oiled 2-quart molds and chill for several hours

R. M. Eldredge, All Saints Church, Peterborough, New Hampshire

Manchu Garden Salad for 50

A green salad with attractive touches of color and interesting textures.

Salad

4 heads lettuce, washed and torn
6 apples, cored and diced
3 cans (11 ounces each) mandarin oranges, drained

½ head cabbage, shredded
½–1 cup shredded raw carrot
1 can (5 ounces) sliced water chestnuts, drained, or walnuts

Toss together lettuce, apples, oranges, cabbage, carrot, and water chestnuts or walnuts.

Dressing

1 teaspoon salt
2 tablespoons wine vinegar
1 tablespoon prepared mustard
¾ cup salad oil

⅓ cup honey
1 tablespoon finely chopped onion
1 tablespoon poppy seeds

Combine salt, vinegar, and mustard; gradually add oil and honey until well-blended. Add onion and poppy seeds. Cover and chill. Toss salad with dressing.

Evelyn H. Chase, Concord Unitarian Church, Concord, New Hampshire

Quick Bread

A crunchy slice of this biscuit-y bread can be buttered
within an hour and fifteen minutes of sifting the flour.

12 cups flour
½ cup baking powder
1 tablespoon salt
¾ cup sugar
1 cup melted shortening

2 eggs (optional)
1 quart (approximately) milk
½ cup chopped dates (optional)
2 tablespoons honey (optional)

Sift flour, baking powder, salt, and sugar. Add shortening and eggs, if using. Pour milk, and stir promptly. Add more milk if necessary until batter will pour into greased pans. Mix dates and honey and stir into batter, if using. Fill six 8" × 4" loaf pans about half-full. Bake at 425°F for 40 minutes. ***Makes 6 loaves.***

Walter Clement, United Methodist Church, Plymouth, New Hampshire

The More or Less Tuna
and Macaroni Salad

Designed for a flexible number, 50–75, without unwieldy leftovers.
With tuna, a one-dish meal; without it, an excellent salad for a bean supper.

6 pounds elbow macaroni
¼ cup salad oil
8 heads leaf lettuce
2 whole unblemished lemons
1 quart chopped green peppers
2 quarts sliced celery
2 cups chopped scallions or mild
   onions

2 quarts mayonnaise
1 cup lemon juice
1 cup plain yogurt
10 cups tuna (one 6½-ounce can
   equals 1 cup)
Salt and pepper
Garnish: whatever is handy—such
   as tomatoes, parsley, watercress

DO AHEAD: Cook macaroni as package directs in two 3-pound lots—a canning pot works well. Add 2 tablespoons oil to each pot of cooking water to prevent macaroni from sticking together. Because pot is usually too heavy to drain safely all at once, use a small sieve to remove most of macaroni from pot when done. Cool as quickly as possible and refrigerate.

WASH LETTUCE: Fill 2 sinks or large bowls, one with very warm water and one with very cold water. Dip each whole head upside down in warm water; leaves will open up so dirt will fall out. Quickly dip head into cold water to revive. Shake off excess water, take head apart, and put in spinner if you have one or can borrow one. Store damp lettuce divided between 2 plastic bags with a whole lemon in each one (the lemon acts as a crisping agent). Close bags securely and refrigerate.

VEGETABLES: Cut up green peppers, celery, and scallions or onions and store in separate containers in refrigerator.

TO SERVE: The above ingredients used all at once in amounts specified will make about 75 cups of salad. Mix up only the amount you think you will need. (All leftover ingredients can be used in future dishes.) Thin mayonnaise with lemon juice and yogurt. Combine macaroni, green peppers, celery, scallions or onions, and tuna. The large canning pot works well here, too. Add salt and pepper to taste. Put in serving bowl or platter and garnish. Serve lettuce separately.

LEFTOVER INGREDIENTS: Use macaroni in macaroni and cheese or other favorite casserole. Eat now or freeze for later consumption. Onions and green pepper can be either frozen or stored a few days in refrigerator. Use celery in casseroles, store a few days in refrigerator for salads, or freeze as creamed celery. Keep lettuce stored with the lemon in refrigerator for use in salads—a happy few days ahead with no lettuce to wash!

R. M. Eldredge, All Saints Church, Peterborough, New Hampshire

Refrigerator Rolls

A soft and very light potato roll.

1 package dry yeast	1 cup hot sieved mashed
1 cup lukewarm water	potatoes
½ cup butter	1 cup cold water
½ cup vegetable shortening	1 teaspoon salt
¾ cup sugar	6–6½ cups sifted flour

Dissolve yeast in lukewarm water. Combine butter, shortening, sugar, and potatoes. Stir in yeast and let stand 2 hours in warm room. Add cold water, salt, and flour. Cover tightly and re-frigerate 24 hours. (Dough may be kept in refrigerator as long as 2 weeks.) Punch down. Shape as desired and place on greased baking sheet. Let rise 2 hours and bake at 425°F for 12 min-utes. *Makes 7 dozen rolls.*

Helen T. Dwelley, Portland, Maine

Cole Slaw for 24

As a general rule, use ½ cup dressing for every 2 cups cabbage,
and allow ½ cup cabbage per person.

4 cups mayonnaise	¼ teaspoon pepper
1 cup sugar	8 teaspoons prepared mustard
1 cup vinegar	2 teaspoons celery seed
4 teaspoons salt	12 cups shredded cabbage

With electric mixer or blender, combine mayonnaise, sugar, vinegar, salt, pepper, mustard, and celery seed. Toss with cabbage and chill.

Edith Downing, Killingworth Congregational Church, Killingworth, Connecticut

Blueberry Muffins

A good recipe to use when you need lots—makes 18 muffins as is and can be multiplied.

2 eggs
⅔ cup sugar
½ cup cooking oil
3 cups flour

1 teaspoon salt
4 teaspoons baking powder
1 cup milk
2 cups blueberries

Beat together eggs, sugar, and oil. Sift flour with salt and baking powder. Add to egg mixture with milk and blueberries, stirring just enough to blend. Fill greased muffin tins three-quarters full and bake at 400°F for 20–25 minutes.

Frances Harding, Harwinton Congregational Church, Harwinton, Connecticut

Aunt Lois's Bran Muffins

This batter may be kept in the refrigerator for up to 2 weeks
and used in whatever portions may suit your particular needs.
Do not stir the batter after it has been refrigerated.

5 cups flour (½ cup more if you use molasses)
3 cups sugar, or 1½ cups sugar and 1½ cups molasses
5 teaspoons baking soda
2 teaspoons salt

1 box (15 ounces) raisin-bran cereal
1 quart buttermilk
4 eggs
1 cup oil

Mix together flour, sugar or sugar and molasses, baking soda, salt, and cereal. In a separate bowl, mix together buttermilk, eggs, and oil. Combine with dry ingredients. Bake in greased muffin tins at 375°F for 15 minutes (a little longer if batter is cold). ***Makes 6 dozen.***

Jeananne Farrar, United Church of Christ, Keene, New Hampshire

Double-Chocolate Chip Pecan Cookies

This Southern take on the classic American cookie features pecans
and a double dose of chocolate—chocolate chips *and* milk chocolate. True chocoholics
may want to replace the milk chocolate with dark bittersweet chocolate.

5 cups uncooked rolled oats	2 cups dark brown sugar
4 cups flour	4 eggs, beaten
2 teaspoons baking powder	2 teaspoons vanilla
2 teaspoons baking soda	1 bag (24 ounces) semisweet chocolate chips
1 teaspoon salt	3 cups chopped pecans
2 cups butter, softened	1 bar (8 ounces) milk chocolate, coarsely chopped
2 cups granulated sugar	

In blender or food processor fitted with a steel blade, grind oats into powder (in batches if necessary). Remove to large bowl. Add flour, baking powder, baking soda, and salt. Stir with fork; set aside.

In bowl of a large heavy-duty stand mixer with flat beater on high speed or by hand in large bowl, beat butter until creamy. In two additions, add granulated and brown sugars; beat until creamy. On medium speed, beat in 2 eggs until smooth. Add remaining eggs and vanilla. Beat until smooth. On low speed or stirring slowly, add one quarter of dry ingredients, blending well before adding more. Continue until all dry ingredients are mixed in. Stir in chocolate chips, pecans, and chopped chocolate. Roll dough into 1" balls and place 2" apart on greased cookie sheet. Bake at 375°F for 10 minutes (for chewy cookies) to 12 minutes (for crisp cookies). Continue baking in batches. Remove to cooling rack. ***Makes about 14 dozen.***

D'Idra T. Plain, Second Baptist Church, Baton Rouge, Louisiana

Index

Note: **Boldfaced** page references indicate photographs.

Conversion Chart

These equivalents have been slightly rounded to make measuring easier.

Volume Measurements

U.S.	Imperial	Metric
¼ tsp	–	1 ml
½ tsp	–	2 ml
1 tsp	–	5 ml
1 Tbsp	–	15 ml
2 Tbsp (1 oz)	1 fl oz	30 ml
¼ cup (2 oz)	2 fl oz	60 ml
⅓ cup (3 oz)	3 fl oz	80 ml
½ cup (4 oz)	4 fl oz	120 ml
⅔ cup (5 oz)	5 fl oz	160 ml
¾ cup (6 oz)	6 fl oz	180 ml
1 cup (8 oz)	8 fl oz	240 ml

Weight Measurements

U.S.	Metric
1 oz	30 g
2 oz	60 g
4 oz (¼ lb)	115 g
5 oz (⅓ lb)	145 g
6 oz	170 g
7 oz	200 g
8 oz (½ lb)	230 g
10 oz	285 g
12 oz (¾ lb)	340 g
14 oz	400 g
16 oz (1 lb)	455 g
2.2 lb	1 kg

Length Measurements

U.S.	Metric
¼"	0.6 cm
½"	1.25 cm
1"	2.5 cm
2"	5 cm
4"	11 cm
6"	15 cm
8"	20 cm
10"	25 cm
12" (1')	30 cm

Pan Sizes

U.S.	Metric
8" cake pan	20 × 4 cm sandwich or cake tin
9" cake pan	23 × 3.5 cm sandwich or cake tin
11" × 7" baking pan	28 × 18 cm baking tin
13" × 9" baking pan	32.5 × 23 cm baking tin
15" × 10" baking pan	38 × 25.5 cm baking tin (Swiss roll tin)
1½ qt baking dish	1.5 liter baking dish
2 qt baking dish	2 liter baking dish
2 qt rectangular baking dish	30 × 19 cm baking dish
9" pie plate	22 × 4 or 23 × 4 cm pie plate
7" or 8" springform pan	18 or 20 cm springform or loose-bottom cake tin
9" × 5" loaf pan	23 × 13 cm or 2 lb narrow loaf tin or pâté tin

Temperatures

Fahrenheit	Centigrade	Gas
140°	60°	–
160°	70°	–
180°	80°	–
225°	110°	–
250°	120°	½
300°	150°	2
325°	160°	3
350°	180°	4
375°	190°	5
400°	200°	6
450°	230°	8
500°	260°	–